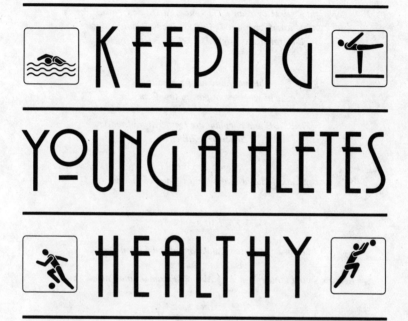

KEEPING YOUNG ATHLETES HEALTHY

**ALAN R. FIGELMAN, M.D.,
AND PATRICK YOUNG**

A FIRESIDE BOOK
Published by Simon & Schuster

New York • London • Toronto • Sydney • Tokyo • Singapore

FIRESIDE

Simon & Schuster Building
Rockefeller Center
1230 Avenue of the Americas
New York, New York 10020

Designed by Liney Li
Manufactured in the United States of America

1 3 5 7 9 10 8 6 4 2 Pbk.

Library of Congress Cataloging-in-Publication Data
Figelman, Alan R.
Keeping young athletes healthy / Alan R. Figelman and Patrick Young.
p. cm.
''A Fireside book.''
Includes index.
1. Sports—Safety measures. 2. Athletes—Health and hygiene.
3. Sports—Accidents and injuries—Prevention. I. Young, Patrick.
II. Title.
GV344.F54 1991
613.7'11—dc20 91-15146 CIP

ISBN 0-671-67578-8 Pbk.

The list of six questions on page 33 is reprinted by
permission of Elsevier Science Publishing Co., Inc.,
from ''Another Look at the Sports Preparticipation Examination
of the Adolescent Athlete,'' by Paul G. Dyment,
Journal of Adolescent Health Care, November 1986 Supplement,
pp. 130S–132S. Copyright 1986 by The Society for Adolescent Medicine.
The table ''Classification of Sports by Risk'' on page 27 is reprinted with permission from Pediatrics, May 1988; 81(5). Copyright © 1988 American Academy of Pediatrics.
The table ''Precautions to Take Based on Wet-Bulb Temperatures'' on page 111 is reprinted by
permission of W. B. Saunders Company from ''Heat Problems in the Tennis Player,'' by Robert J. Murphy, Clinics in Sports Medicine, vol. 7, no. 2, p. 433, 1988.

For Anne and Leah

·CONTENTS·

·INTRODUCTION·

BY JANE E. BRODY

A sound mind in a sound body . . . These words, from the first-century sage Juvenal recounted by John Locke in "Some Thoughts Concerning Education," impressed me more, I'm afraid, than they did the folks who determined the essential ingredients of my education. "Phys Ed" was a sick joke, a boring three-day-a-week period that we girls did our best to get excused from. The boys, who had a chance to play team sports, showed somewhat more enthusiasm, but few left school feeling as proud of their bodies as of their grades and fewer still learned the joy of movement and the types of activities that can be pursued for a lifetime.

As adults, my generation (the teens of the fifties) has had to discover the many benefits of a sound body the hard way—on our own, starting out with flabby arms and legs and unfit hearts and lungs that tired upon climbing one flight of stairs. Many of us—though not nearly enough—have indeed learned. We have taken up activities like running, brisk walking, cycling, skating, aerobic dancing, swimming, and even weight training. While weight and flab control are undoubtedly our primary motivators, we also reap such rewards as reduced stress, happier dispositions, greater work efficiency, improved sleep, and, of course, a diminished risk of developing such crippling disorders as heart disease, hypertension, diabetes, arthritis, and osteoporosis.

But knowing all this, are our kids doing any better than we did four decades ago? It appears not, neither in school nor after school. If anything, studies show that today's youth are less fit and more fat than the children and teens of the sixties, who in turn were less fit and fatter than their counterparts in the forties—before that big two-letter word, TV, infiltrated nearly every American household.

Not only are youngsters today less active at home, they are often also less active at school. For as school budgets shrink, physical education and extracurricular sports are often the first to hit the cutting-room floor. It is increasingly up to parents to see that their children learn to exercise their bodies as well as their minds, but with more and more parents working outside the home, there is often no one around with the authority to unplug the TV, send the kids outside to play after school and on weekends, and organize and supervise team sports.

Those of you smart enough to be reading this book no doubt already believe in the value of physical activities and sports participation for young and old. But perhaps you are worried about the risks your youngsters may be taking in pushing their bodies to the limits of physical tolerance. Even I fretted—and still fret—over my twin sons' bruises and batterings, strains and sprains, falls and collisions as they pursued tennis, basketball, football, roller skating, and bicycling with uncommon vengeance. They routinely carry ice packs and Ace bandages to the basketball court, and return to play as soon as they can hobble about on twisted ankles or with bruised thighs. Will this prolong their pain or compromise their physical abilities in the future? I wonder.

Then there are the many youngsters who start running and weight lifting long before their bones have stopped growing. Will such activities somehow impair their growth? And what about the psychological stresses on youngsters participating in competitive sports, either on teams or as individuals? Does competition strengthen or damage their psyches? There is also the matter of the kind of fuel a young, growing, active body needs to run on. Can fast food, sugary pop, and Twinkies sustain the young athlete? Are supplements necessary or even desirable? Do active kids drink enough to keep their muscles and joints well lubricated? Can those who repeatedly struggle to "make weight" damage their health?

The answers to these and many other questions that properly concern the parents, teachers, and coaches of both presently active and potentially active youths can be found in the immensely valuable volume now in your hands. *Keeping Young Athletes Healthy* is written in terms that are both adequate to foster sensible action and understandable even to those with no particular expertise in or familiarity with medicine or sports. You will come away with an appreciation for not only the physical benefits and stresses but also the mental and emotional aspects of sports participation and the roles that parents and coaches can play in keeping youthful activities fun-filled and health-promoting.

Currently, far too many young sports enthusiasts are pushed by well-meaning adults into highly competitive activities that unduly emphasize winning. Not only can this form of "sports abuse" result in physical and psychological injuries, it has the double misfortune of often turning children away from the very activities they are being urged to excel in.

Everything in life involves some risk. Those who are stay-abeds risk heart disease, osteoporosis, and obesity and its attendant hazards. Those who are active encounter other risks in return for their pleasure and their improved health status. Most active adults and virtually all active youngsters will quickly say the joy of movement and sports participation is well worth the price. But, as Dr. Alan R. Figelman and Patrick Young so ably point out, much can be done to minimize the risk and maximize the joy of sports participation.

Ideally, the time to read this book is while your child is still in the cradle. Proper encouragement of physical activity should start even before your infant is first able to throw food off the high chair. But however old your children are now, you can glean valuable information on how to approach youthful sports sensibly and important advice on preventing injuries and minimizing their extent. I only wish I had had this book to guide me when my own sons first picked up a tennis racquet.

"I've never heard of that injury. Where can I read about it?"

"Are kids' injuries really different from adults'?"

Any physician who treats sports injuries in children and adolescents has heard these two questions—along with a good many others—countless times. In large part, it was to answer these questions that we—a physician specializing in adolescent medicine and a science writer, both interested in fitness—wrote this book. Remarkably, despite the millions of American youngsters playing sports and the explosive growth in the 1980s in sports medicine, few books on the athletic injuries of children and adolescents exist for parents and volunteer coaches. There are plenty of books for adults, but none provide prevention advice that takes into account the unique risks, injuries, and emotional problems in sports confronting youngsters.

Many parents and coaches assume that anatomically, children and adolescents are but small adults—a fallacy that can lead to unnecessary problems. In truth, a child's anatomy differs from an adolescent's, and both differ from an adult's. The growing body is a changing body, an important point emphasized and illustrated in this book. Take, for example, the back. It is not completely mineralized until about age 25, meaning it does not have its full bony support through childhood and adolescence, or even early adulthood. This is important with regard to weight training, so frequently used now in training for other sports. Emerging evidence indicates that, if done properly, strength training by adolescents can improve performance. Yet young people frequently try to lift more than their bone structure can tolerate. As a result, they may suffer lower-back pain, sometimes severe enough to hinder performance or even sideline them.

Two major themes underlie the information and advice provided in this book. First, the prime motivator in organized youth sports is fun. Second, parents and coaches are necessary partners in preventing injuries and preserving kids' sense of fun. The more parents and coaches know, the wiser their actions will be, and the better off their youngsters. Our discussion of injury prevention and treatment is comprehensive, covering physical conditioning and nutrition, as well as the role of parents and coaches in injury treatment and rehabilitation. We stress preparation, protection, and prevention, and tell how to deal with injuries if they occur.

Unlike so many sports medicine books that rely almost exclusively on the physician's point of view, *Keeping Young Athletes Healthy* draws on a vast body of research, including the work of nutritionists, pharmacologists, physical education specialists, physical therapists, physiologists, and podiatrists. As a result, we have been able to provide an unusually broad, deep, and detailed look at the risks facing young athletes—along with an intensive look at the characteristic injuries encountered in 14 specific sports.

Parents and coaches often don't realize how important they are to what children take away from sports—good and bad. We fully believe that sports can provide a wonderful experience for youngsters. But athletics in America has its dark side as well, and whether intending to or not, parents and coaches can contribute to this unsavory aspect of sports. We believe that some parents and coaches need to pay less attention to winning and losing in youth sports, and more to the opportunities these activities provide youngsters for learning and growth. Parents and coaches can make a big difference—in promoting fun, preventing injuries, and influencing the futures of young athletes.

We wish we could promise that a child or adolescent who followed our prevention advice explicitly and faithfully would never suffer a sports injury. Unfortunately, that's not the way the body or the world of sports works. Sprains, strains, and overuse injuries will still occur. What we can do is offer suggestions that will prevent injuries for many youngsters, and may do so for years. We aim to lower the risks of injury, without any hope of preventing them all.

We wish to thank several organizations for their assistance: the

National Youth Sports Coaches Association, the National Athletic Trainers' Association, and the President's Council on Physical Fitness and Sports. Several people graciously read selected chapters and offered their advice: Michael Pfahl, York Onnen, Gary Giffen, Michael Gray, and Robert S. Behnke. While we thank them for their much-welcomed suggestions, and Edward Walters for his able editing, we must take sole responsibility for any errors of omission or commission in this book.

Finally, we wish to thank our wives, to whom we dedicate *Keeping Young Athletes Healthy*, for their support, patience, and forbearance. It's been a long odyssey for us all.

ALAN R. FIGELMAN, M.D.

PATRICK YOUNG

PART ONE

KEEPING SPORTS SAFE FOR YOUNG ATHLETES

1

Are Sports Worth the Risks?

For millions of youngsters and their parents, the answer to this question is a resounding "Yes!" Playing a sport is lots of fun. That alone attracts youngsters to sandlot games, youth leagues, and school athletics. Fun is what they really care about in sports. As children grow into adolescence and body image becomes so important, fitness as well as fun enters their thinking. But the documented benefits of sports go far beyond pleasure and a better-looking body to improved physical and mental health, self-confidence, and leadership skills. Of course, parents want their children to enjoy themselves, but more and more, mothers and fathers have realized the added advantages that participating in sports offers. As many adults have taken up jogging, tennis, swimming, aerobic dance, and other fitness programs in the last two decades, they have encouraged their children to engage in athletic activities as well. The Big Bang in youth sports that is the result of their encouragement still reverberates through the United States.

Still, physical activities are hardly risk-free, for adults or children. Injuries do occur, even in the seemingly safest sports. Swimmers, golfers, and badminton players all suffer their share of muscle, joint, and bone pain. Competition can create psychological stress among competitors, whether the player is a second-stringer in Little League baseball or a professional athlete earning a seven-figure salary. And, yes, death does, on uncommon occasions, visit the playing field or running course. Little wonder, then, that even in sports-minded families there may be conscious and subconscious concerns about athletic safety, and questions about what sport a child should play and at what age. Such conflicts have existed throughout much of this century. Still, the concerns of parents and grandparents today often reflect their own experiences growing up—and the adult attitudes of those times—more than they do the realities of the 1990s.

THE CONTROVERSY OVER YOUTH SPORTS

While it seems perfectly natural now to see children 8, 9, 10, 11, or 12 playing a variety of sports in organized leagues, this is largely a phenomenon of the last two decades. Indeed, until well into the 1960s, physicians, psychologists, physiologists, educators, and assorted athletic groups heatedly debated the wisdom and value of allowing preadolescents to engage in strenuous sports activities. The concern went well beyond the possibility of physical injuries and their potentially adverse effects on growth and development. Some adults worried more about what they considered a destructive emphasis on competition and winning, and the threat of devastating emotional stress and psychological damage this would cause in youngsters. Often, in their learned discussions and exchanges, the experts overlooked the desire of many children—a desire supported by their parents—to play sports from an early age. Their argument emphasized the risks, while the very real benefits such activities provide received inadequate attention.

How has that situation changed?

Today, the issues of youth sports are in better balance. The National Athletic Trainers' Association puts the number of interscholastic sports participants in the United States at nearly 6 million, and the National Youth Sports Coaches Association estimates that some 20 million American youngsters, ages 6 through 16, play organized out-of-school sports. By any count, that's a lot of kids having fun, and learning some valuable lessons for later life. In part, this growth in youth sports reflects years of research that have more precisely defined the physical risks and benefits of athletic activities—and failed to confirm fears that the stress generated by the emphasis on winning caused widespread emotional harm in youngsters. Indeed, studies have revealed the opposite—that the majority of children benefit psychologically as well as physically from athletic participation. The debate over the potential problems associated with playing youth sports continues, but at a more informed level, one that includes a recognition of the potential physical and psychological benefits of athletics, especially for preadolescents, as well as the risks. The dangers of raising a generation of inactive, flabby "couch potatoes" now concern experts as much as the stress of competition.

Does this change in attitude explain the boom in youth sports?

The past quarter century's explosive growth in youth sports—particularly among younger children and girls, and in out-of-school athletic programs—stems largely from the greater leisure time available to children and from the growing recognition of the benefits, both immediate and long-term, that result from exercise and participation in team activities. Athletics build health habits and social skills that children and teens carry on into adulthood. America's playing fields are not simply playgrounds, but in their own ways, training grounds for later life and leadership.

For years, parents and physicians equated "physical fitness" with athletic ability. Today, the President's Council on Physical Fitness and Sports measures five specific physiological features: muscle strength and endurance, flexibility, body composition (including the degree of fatness), and cardiorespiratory endurance. A child with only limited athletic skills can be physically fit, even if he or she rarely shines in any sport.

HOW FIT ARE OUR KIDS?

Despite the growth of youth sports and exercise, experts give poor grades to the nation's youngsters for physical fitness.

In the early 1980s, the U.S. Public Health Service conducted the National Children and Youth Fitness Study, a two-year, nationwide examination of 8,880 students in the fifth through twelfth grades. The results proved discouraging. Only about half the nation's youth engaged in "appropriate physical activity," and body fat measurements showed that children of the 1980s carried significantly more fat on their frames than those measured in a 1960s study by the National Center for Health Statistics. In the fall of 1986, researchers followed up these findings with the National Children and Youth Fitness Study II, in which they surveyed and tested a nationally representative sample of 4,853 students and 4,435 of their parents. Again, the results proved disappointing. Children still carry considerably more fat than they did in the 1960s; the more television children watch, the less likely they will be physically fit.

Can't kids get the exercise they need in physical education classes?

Many parents rely on the schools to keep their children physically fit. Unfortunately, this trust is often misplaced. Experts regard the time devoted to physical education in most U.S. schools as grossly inadequate to maintain a child's fitness—a legacy from the nation's forty years of undervaluing the benefits of sports and physical exercise. A 1987 survey of the American Alliance for Health, Physical Education, Recreation and Dance found that only one state, Illinois, required daily physical education classes for students from kindergarten through high school graduation; and while most states required high school students to take some physical education, only six states required such classes all four years.

NCYFS-II found that just over one-third (36.4 percent) of the nation's elementary and secondary students took physical education daily; 37.2 percent got instruction only one or two days a week; and on average, students spent four times as many hours watching television as they did in physical education classes. Young children generally got more physical education exposure than older children. While 98 percent of fifth graders took at least weekly classes, only about half of all high school seniors enrolled in P.E. This situation appears likely to worsen. Tight budgets and widespread public disenchantment with educational "frills" already have forced some school districts to cut back on physical education instruction.

The nation's schools obviously aren't keeping our youth fit. Far too many children and adolescents are overeating, underexercising softies, who prefer television and junk-food snacks to jogging, swimming, bicycling, dance, or football, baseball, or basketball. In 1980, the U.S. Surgeon General declared the physical fitness of the nation's youth "a national tragedy." More recent data offer no evidence of any significant improvement. The latest nationwide study by the President's Council on Physical Fitness and Sports, the National School Population Fitness Survey, found no significant improvement in the physical condition of the United States' younger generation between 1975 and 1985: "The physical fitness levels of public school children, ages 6 to 17, as measured by the nine tests reported, revealed no significant overall changes when compared with previous years. . . . Extrapolated to the entire population, the study data show there is a low level of performance in important components of physical fitness by millions of our youth."

Since physical education isn't an academic subject,
why inflict it on schoolchildren?

There are four basic reasons for encouraging children and adolescents to exercise: Exercise helps promote optimal physical growth and development for safety and productivity; it aids good psychological and social adjustment; it ingrains an interest and the habits necessary for an active, healthy life-style in the adult years; and aerobic exercise in particular can reduce some of the risk factors associated with coronary heart disease and early heart attacks. In childhood and adolescence, moderate exercise performed regularly each week appears to be equally effective in achieving these goals as intense physical activity, and at less risk of injury. Some evidence even suggests that youngsters can exercise at 50 percent of their maximum heartbeat and still make significant gains in their heart and lung functioning, although achieving this takes longer with a lower intensity level.

COUNTING THE BENEFITS

Why should a child exercise?

Physicians and coaches know that children who exercise regularly will grow up stronger, leaner, more supple, and with better heart and lung capacity and function than their layabout contemporaries. When exercise is begun in childhood, healthy habits become ingrained—often for life—that can cut the risk of serious physical problems in adulthood, most notably coronary heart disease. Surprisingly, evidence now suggests that through prepubescence, a healthy child's cardiorespiratory system operates at maximum efficiency whether the child exercises daily, occasionally, or not at all. But all this changes at puberty, when nature decrees: Use it or lose it. By about age 17, adolescents who don't exercise, boys and girls alike, have only half the heart and lung efficiency of those who follow a rigorous program of aerobic exercise.

Children do need exercise. Researchers find that without a minimum amount of physical activity, children fail to grow and develop normally. Yet too much of this good and necessary thing can prove detrimental. Studies indicate that excessive exercise may *retard* a youngster's growth and development. No one knows (yet) the optimal level of exercise for best promoting growth, but we can say that the range between inadequate and excessive is wide, and that only a relatively few children ever push their exercise levels to the point of actually endangering their development. Inactivity poses a far greater threat to the health of America's youth than overexercise.

Can you be specific about the benefits of athletics?
In the young as well as adults, a fitness program of regular, properly executed physical activity improves muscle strength, endurance, and flexibility; raises personal energy level; increases the ratio of lean body tissue to fat; promotes better lung functioning and cardiovascular efficiency; helps reduce stress; eases the symptoms of anxiety and mild to moderate depression; and improves body image, self-esteem, and self-confidence. A fitter, more flexible body lowers risks of muscle and joint injuries, prevents obesity, and builds stronger bones, which helps delay and reduces the severity of osteoporosis, the development of brittle, more breakable bones in later life.

Increasing evidence shows that the early stages of coronary artery disease often appear in childhood, and numerous studies document the role of aerobic exercise in reducing some conditions that raise the risk of coronary artery disease and heart attacks. These risk factors include high levels of cholesterol in the blood—particularly low-density lipoproteins (LDLs), the so-called bad cholesterol that increases a person's chance of heart attack; high blood pressure; obesity; and the mental anxiety and physical reactions that result from psychological stress. Exercise also reduces the amount of insulin needed to control insulin-dependent diabetes (also known as type I or juvenile diabetes). People engaging in sports are also less likely to increase their chances of early death by smoking cigarettes and less inclined to take needless risks with drug use and alcohol abuse.

THE ADVANTAGES OF SPORTS

1. Increase physical fitness for employment
2. Improve physical appearance and self-image
3. Help release tension and improve emotional well-being
4. Encourage academic improvement
5. Discourage use of cigarettes
6. Help in weight loss
7. Help prevent coronary heart disease

8.   Help prevent lower-back pain
9.   Help prevent hypertension

What mental benefits do sports offer?

Building a sound body helps build a sound mind and a more self-assured individual. Several studies report that physically fit children tend to do better academically, a direct contradiction of the popular stereotype of the "dumb jock." In France, for example, researchers found that children who engaged in physical activity eight hours a week matured faster, showed more independence, and earned better grades than a group of children who got only 40 minutes of physical education a week. A Canadian study compared two groups of children. One group exercised vigorously five hours a week; the second group did so two hours weekly. The children exercising five hours a week did significantly better in increasing the fitness of their heart and lungs, and in school, they did better in French, English, mathematics, and science.

Some school systems now require students to maintain a minimum academic level, typically a 2.0, or C on a 4.0 system, to remain eligible to participate in student activities, including sports. Interestingly, many young athletes with poor grades have responded by improving their school performance to ensure their eligibility. Sports participation and academic success require organizing personal time and adhering to a formal structure of activity, two valuable lessons in life. And together, academics and sports set rules and limits that youngsters learn they must follow if they want to succeed. This helps them develop the set of personal values that will guide them through life.

For the latchkey or single-parent child, sports participation offers adult supervision and instruction, important not only in providing a role model, but in easing some of the loneliness these children may feel. In some families, sports is the major communication channel between child and parents during the difficult years of adolescence.

CALCULATING THE RISKS

As early as the late 1930s, a national survey of 4,620 wrestlers at 126 high schools revealed a 5 percent injury rate, with bad scrapes, cauliflower ears, and rib damage the most frequent injuries. Yet, while coaches, trainers, and physicians are thoroughly familiar with the specific types of injuries that most commonly occur in the various types of sports, surprisingly little is known about how often young athletes are injured or the total number of such injuries that occur annually in the United States. What is known suggests that athletic injuries are quite common, and the potential for reducing them is quite great. At one health maintenance organization, for example, researchers discovered that 3 percent of all visits by children involved recreational injuries. A study of 466 junior high and high school football players in North Carolina found that 17.5 percent of all the injuries they suffered were preventable, and largely resulted from poor equipment, improper playing techniques, or stepping in or on an object. (The importance of having good protective equipment and enforcing its proper use is discussed extensively in later chapters.)

Results from a series of studies done in the mid to late 1980s of high school athletic injuries, carried out by researcher John W. Powell for the National Athletics Trainers' Association, have surprised even professionals concerned about sports safety. For example, projections from Powell's studies indicate that interscholastic football players suffered more than half a million injuries per year in 1986, 1987, and 1988. These did not include every scrape, bruise, and bump, but only those injuries that forced a player to miss at least one game or day of practice. The national injury estimate was based on statistics gathered from a total of 21,233 high school varsity and junior varsity players. Most of the injuries suffered during these three years were not serious. Sprains and muscle strains accounted for 49 percent; another 28 percent were bad cuts and bruises. More than 72 percent of the injuries healed within 7 days. Yet nearly 17 percent took 8 to 21 days to recover, and almost 11 percent—1 injury in 10—took longer than three weeks to heal.

Another study by Powell, of girls' basketball, proved equally disquieting. Based on scientific samplings during three consecutive seasons ending in 1988–89, Powell projected over 110,000 injuries annually to female high school basketball players nationwide. Ankles and feet accounted for 32 percent of those injuries; knees, 18 percent. Both the football and basketball estimates are probably low, because Powell studied players at high schools that employed certified professional trainers to monitor training and equipment usage, and to see that youngsters didn't resume playing before they were fully fit. (Less than 10 percent of the nation's secondary schools have such trainers.) Some researchers, however, have attempted to compare the dangers of various sports in one way or another. Richard B. Chambers recorded the number of orthopedic injuries suffered in one 12-month period by children ages 6 to 17 who played six supervised sports at Fort Leavenworth, Kansas. He devised an injury index that took into account the number of injuries that occurred in each sport, the number of participants, the average number of hours of participation, and the number of weeks in the season of a sport. Using this index, he found football players twice as likely to suffer an orthopedic injury as basketball players and gymnasts. Soccer players had only one-sixth the orthopedic-injury risk of football players, and youngsters who played baseball had only one-twelfth the chance of injury of football. Although none of the swimmers participating in the Chambers study suffered an orthopedic injury, such problems do occur in the sport, as we discuss in Chapter 11.

What is the most dangerous sport kids play?

Parents and sports experts generally regard football as the most dangerous, largely because players do die as the result of injuries or exertion that overtaxes a player with an unknown heart problem. Paralysis and permanently damaged knees are two other serious consequences of football injuries. No fall passes without a few reports of tragic deaths suffered by high school or college players on the playing or practice field. Yet the number of deaths and catastrophic injuries occurring in the sport dropped sharply after a 1976 rule change that prohibited "spearing," the use of the head and helmet in blocking and tackling an opponent. In the 10 years prior to the rule change, 210 sandlot, high school, and college players died directly as the result of football injuries, mostly to the head and neck. Deaths among those age groups due to football injuries totaled 85 in the decade after the ban on spearing, according to statistics compiled by the American Football Coaches Association. This is one example of how recognizing the cause of sports injuries can provide ways to at least reduce them. Another example is that many youth football leagues now use body weight rather than age in assigning players and determining what teams will play each other—a recognition that a player with a heavy body weight, especially among young players, is more likely to injure a lighter player than someone roughly his own poundage.

Is there anything a parent can do to reduce a child's chances of injury?

One way to lower the risk of certain injuries is to choose a less risky sport. The following table groups the various athletic activities popular with children and adolescents by their degree of strenuousness and physical contact. As a general rule, the more strenuous a sport and the more contact it involves, the greater the likelihood of injury. But situations vary, and with them the risk. Some schoolyard basketball games turn just short of full contact action, and more than one young woman has hobbled off after a field hockey game with muscles feeling as if she had just completed a 180-yard running game against a pro football team. Still, physicians find this table helpful in educating parents about the general risks of sports participation for their children.

CLASSIFICATION OF SPORTS BY RISK

| | | Noncontact | | |
Contact collision	Limited Contact/Impact	Noncontact	Moderately Strenuous	Nonstrenuous
Boxing	Baseball	Aerobic	Badminton	Archery
Field	Basketball	dancing	Curling	Golf
hockey	Bicycling	Crew	Table tennis	Riflery
Football	Diving	Fencing		
Ice hockey	Field	Field		
Lacrosse	High Jump	Discus		
Martial arts	Pole vault	Javelin		
Rodeo	Gymnastics	Shot put		
Soccer	Horseback riding	Running		
Wrestling	Skating	Swimming		
	Ice	Tennis		
	Roller	Track		
	Skiing	Weight lifting		
	Cross-country			
	Downhill			
	Water			
	Softball			
	Squash, handball			
	Volleyball			

Source: American Academy of Pediatrics, *Sports Medicine: Health Care for Young Athletes.* (2nd ed.) Evanston, IL, 1991.

THE BOTTOM LINE

***What is the bottom line on the benefits versus
the risks of sports?***
The benefits of physical fitness, in youth and adulthood, are well
documented. And while it is never too late for a healthy male or
female to begin a fitness program, the best time to get in the habit
and rhythm of regular exercise is early in life. But exercise routines
and athletics always carry with them the chance of injury, and although there is no clear evidence that serious injury is any likelier
in organized sports than in free play, the possibility of permanent
harm is a real and legitimate concern of parents. Some are so worried
about the danger of injury that they refuse to allow their children
to play certain sports—or any sport at all.

In truth, athletics, like innumerable other activities in life, are
a matter of risks and benefits. But we firmly believe that the overall
benefits of sports participation, properly practiced and supervised,
far outweigh the risks. Physically and psychologically, a fit child is
better suited to carry on in life and contribute to society. At the same
time, no sport is perfect for everyone, and no sport is perfectly safe.
Some sports are clearly more dangerous than others, and some sports
are clearly less beneficial in maintaining fitness and reducing the
chances of future ill health. Therefore, parents selecting a sport for
their child or trying to influence a teenager's choice of athletic activity
need to know what physical dangers exist, how parent and child
can help reduce the chances of injury, and how the risks and benefits
of various youth sports compare. Parents and coaches also need to
know how to reduce the chances of injury and exactly what to do
when an injury occurs to avoid further harm.

Despite the risks involved, children continue to flock to sports,
and to benefit from them. Clearly, in their minds and the minds of
many parents, the fun and benefits outweigh the risk of injury.

2

The Essentials of Safe Exercise Programs

Physical fitness today is not what it used to be. For decades, physicians and laypersons alike considered as physically fit solely those children who possessed physical attributes that enhanced athletic abilities: speed, agility, power, and muscle strength. Yet, as necessary as these qualities are in competitive sports, using athletic prowess as the measure of physical fitness ignores other, more important aspects of a healthy body. So today, physicians, physiologists, and other professionals also emphasize the condition of the body's physiological systems in assessing physical fitness. Besides speed, agility, power, and muscle strength, they also consider a person's muscle endurance, flexibility, reaction time, body composition in terms of percentage of body fat, and heart and lung strength and endurance.

Although studies show that people benefit from beginning an appropriate exercise program at almost any age, one basic rule remains: The younger, the better—within reason. It takes a youngster until about 4½ or 5 years of age to acquire and develop the neuromuscular skills needed to begin any sport, although running skills may emerge a bit earlier.

EXERCISE AT DIFFERENT AGES

No single exercise regimen is appropriate for all ages. Children are not young adolescents, and adolescents are not young adults. Different phases of growth and development demand different programs. The younger and less physically mature the child, the more care and supervision are needed to ensure that exercise enhances health, rather than poses a threat of injury or even permanent damage. In this section we describe how different age groups respond to exercise and the effects of exercise on their physical development. We present only general guidelines, based on statistical averages of healthy children. Parents should discuss their children's exercise programs with their pediatrician or family physician, and the more vigorous the program, the greater the need to seek a physician's counsel. Pushing a child too hard too early can cause problems.

Should infants exercise?

Pediatricians regard formal exercise programs for infants as unwise. An infant's skeletal structure lacks the strength of later life; some bones of the feet and hands have yet to grow together; muscle strength is inadequate; protective reflexes and other neuromuscular skills—the vital link between brain and body movements—exist only in formative stages. Certainly a stimulating, nurturing, safe play environment that allows an infant's body to strengthen and develop is important. But the boom in structured infant exercise programs—which involve massage techniques, passive exercises using special equipment, and holding a child in various positions—poses dangers beyond any yet recognized benefits. The American Academy of Pediatrics Committee on Sports Medicine warns: "The possibility exists that adults may inadvertently exceed the infant's physical limitations by using structured exercise programs."

What about preadolescents?

Physically, children aren't really ready for sports until around age 5, and relatively few enter into competitive athletics before age 7. Participation, after all, requires a degree of coordination, strength, and endurance that comes only with the process of physical maturation. Even during the prepubescent years of roughly 9 to 12, little difference exists in average weight and height between boys and girls, with boys usually two to five pounds heavier in muscle mass. The two sexes also differ little in muscle strength until about age 13, when boys begin increasing their strength at a much faster rate. The biggest differences in weight, height, and strength occur between children of the same sex but who mature early and late, rather than between members of the two sexes who are at the same stage of physical development. For this reason, matching teams by weight—particularly in contact sport such as football—provides safer and fairer competition than matching them by age.

Younger, smaller children tend to lose more body heat than

older, bigger children. The body converts to heat about 80 percent of the chemical energy it burns to contract muscles. The longer and more intensely a person exercises, the greater his or her heat production. Younger children lose heat faster because their body surfaces are proportionally larger—and therefore dissipate heat more readily—and young children tend to have a thinner layer of fat to insulate them from heat loss. As a rule, younger athletes are more likely than older ones to suffer a drop in performance during sustained activity in cold weather or cold water.

What happens during adolescence?

Adolescent growth patterns follow changes in hormonal secretions controlled by the pituitary gland and the brain. As these hormonal levels in the blood change, the organs associated with sexual development mature and also secrete hormones that affect both sexual maturation and musculoskeletal development. An orderly progression of external changes occurs in the distribution of pubic hair in both sexes, and changes in breast growth in females and in the testes and scrotum in males also follow an orderly pattern of maturation. These secondary (external) sexual changes have been staged by J. H. Tanner: stages 1 through 5 for breast and pubic hair in females, and for pubic hair and genitalia in males. Although the Tanner stages are beyond the focus of this text, they serve as markers that physicians can discuss with their young patients to help them better understand their own growth and development.

Certain facts concerning adolescent growth are well known:

1. Males experience growth throughout adolescence, but they undergo one year of peak growth during which they add at least four inches to their height. This period usually correlates with Tanner stage 4—pubic hair. Following this year of peak growth, a surge of testosterone results in increased muscular strength. Obviously, paying attention to these growth changes is an important part of selecting training programs and sports.

2. Full mineralization of the skeletal spine is not completed until the mid-twenties, again influencing the choice of training programs and mandating bone protection.

3. All organ systems grow during puberty, except the tonsils, which shrink. Thus, the skin and cardiorespiratory system are capable of improved control of heat dissipation. Still, maintaining adequate hydration remains an overlooked and serious problem.

4. Acne may become a more difficult problem in athletes because of additional skin conditions caused by weather effects, sweating, and abrasions.

5. Females also experience a year of peak height increase. During this time—often two years earlier in life than for males—females add at least 3.75 inches in height. This year of most rapid growth often occurs at Tanner stage—breast 2–3. First menstruation (menarche) often follows soon after this peak growth year. This onset of menstrual periods coincides with a rise in blood levels of estrogen, which causes the sealing off of a bone section called the epiphysis. As a result, cessation of growth occurs within one to two years after menarche.

THE IMPORTANCE OF PREPARTICIPATION PHYSICALS

When a young athlete collapses and dies during play or practice, the lament is often heard: "But he had a sports physical!" Few things in sports medicine are as common and yet as misunderstood as the preparticipation physical, the medical examination most young athletes must take before they can compete for their school teams. During such exams, a physician seeks to assess the child's or adolescent's overall health and physical condition, to determine whether he or she can safely play in sports, and to identify any existing conditions that could predispose the youngster to injury. Unfortunately, not all sports physicals are all they should be, and not all serious conditions will be detected by preparticipation exams.

How often are such examinations needed?

The greater intensity of play at all levels of athletics, from grade school through professional, has resulted in more frequent and sometimes more detailed preparticipation physicals. Although the American Academy of Pediatrics advises its members that a preparticipation examination is necessary only every two years after a student successfully undergoes his or her first, many schools still require their players to have one annually. The standards for sports physicals vary greatly from state to state, and sometimes also from school district to school district. Some merely require a signed statement from a physician certifying that a youngster is physically fit for sports. Others list specific things physicians must include in a sports physical.

What should a preparticipation examination include?

Specialists in pediatric and adolescent sports medicine generally agree that the single most important element in this preventive screening is a sports-specific medical history. Examination of the chest, cardiovascular system, abdomen, genitalia, eyes, and lymph glands, as well as a thorough look at the body's muscles and bones to check strength, functioning, alignment, and for any signs of neuromuscular disorders should comprise the physical examination. Roughly 1 percent of students who take preparticipation physicals have problems that exclude them from at least one sport.

A preparticipation examination should differ from the typical medical physical in the kinds of questions asked in the taking of a sports-specific medical history and in the greater attention paid to the musculoskeletal system. Long experience shows that urine and blood tests routinely given during standard physical exams simply aren't cost-effective in young athletes. For them, the most common previously unknown problems turn out to be ones of the lower extremities (hips, hamstrings, knees, ankles, feet), mouth, teeth, cardiovascular system, and genitalia. According to Paul G. Dyment of the Maine Medical Center in Portland, and for years chairman of the American Academy of Pediatrics Committee on Sports Medicine, writing in the November 1986 *Journal of Adolescent Health Care,* six basic questions offer important clues to conditions that may preclude a student from playing a specific sport:

1. Have any members of your family under age 50 had a heart attack or heart problems?
2. Have you ever been told that you have a heart murmur, high blood pressure, extra heartbeat, or a heart abnormality?
3. Do you have to stop while running around a quarter-mile track twice?
4. Are you taking any medications?
5. Have you ever passed out or been knocked out?
6. Have you ever had any illness, condition, or injury that:
   a. required you to go to the hospital either as a patient overnight or in the emergency room or for X rays?
   b. required an operation?
   c. lasted longer than a week?
   d. caused you to miss a game or practice?
   e. is caused by allergies (hay fever, hives, asthma, or medicine)?

Shortness of breath may indicate advanced coronary artery disease, an uncommon but potentially fatal condition in youngsters. A fainting episode may warn of an abnormal left coronary artery or of abnormal heartbeats that can cause a young athlete to die suddenly while participating in some sport. Getting knocked out indicates a concussion, and more than one concussion should raise questions in a physician's mind about the wisdom of allowing a youngster to continue playing contact sports.

What is the purpose of examining a youngster's muscle and bone structure?

This review takes only a few minutes, yet can provide important information about congenital deformities and problems remaining from a previous injury that may predispose a youngster to injury or renewed injury while playing sports. In his or her underwear, the young athlete faces the physician and carries out a series of movements directed by the physician. Some of these movements include shrugging the shoulders, fully rotating the arms, flexing and extending the elbows, spreading the fingers, making a fist, and touching the toes with the knees straight. A child with muscle weakness or limited flexibility is at increased risk of injury, and a program to build strength or increase range of motion may prevent future problems. During this part of the exam, physicians should also check for various conditions—such as misaligned bones and muscle-tendon imbalances—that may increase a young athlete's risk of developing "tennis elbow" or numerous other overuse injuries.

Physicians find many students in poor physical condition, with inadequate muscle tone and flexibility. These alone obviously do not preclude them from participating in sports, and indeed, these young people should be encouraged to pursue athletic efforts. But the physician should recommend a program to improve their muscle tone and flexibility, and their parents should see that they follow it, making sure they do the exercises correctly.

Will preparticipation physicals detect heart problems?

Surely the greatest tragedy to strike a child or adolescent participating in a sporting event is sudden death. Usually, this results from some unknown heart abnormality. Such hidden conditions are uncommon among children (evidence of most congenital defects appears early in life) and a routine preparticipation sports physical is unlikely to detect their existence. Nonetheless, an examination of the heart and lungs can identify a number of potentially serious problems. Heart disease often runs in families, and for the student whose medical history reveals a close family member with an early-in-life heart attack, a serious problem with abnormal heartbeats, or a sudden death before age 50, a physician should provide a more-detailed-than-normal evaluation of his or her heart. The child should be referred to a specialist if the physician suspects some heart abnormality.

A sports physical should always include a blood-pressure measurement. Hypertension, or high blood pressure, eventually can cause serious heart damage and death if left untreated. A single high reading may indicate nothing more than "white coat hypertension"—that the sight of the physician or nurse giving the test made the patient extremely anxious, thus raising his or her blood pressure. So physicians ask people with high readings to come back for a second or even third measurement before diagnosing high blood pressure. Hypertension rarely rules out athletics for youngsters, but it is important to get the student's blood pressure back to the normal range.

Does a congenital heart problem bar a child from all sports?

Congenital heart disease does not automatically rule out some forms of sports participation, but the exact nature of the problem and any potential dangers it may pose must be fully understood. Among the issues a physician needs to evaluate before recommending or forbidding a sport for youngsters with heart defects are the type of malformation and its severity, how seriously it affects the heart's output and volume, the condition of the heart muscle itself, and the presence of any abnormal heartbeats.

THE LIFTS GUIDELINES FOR YOUTH EXERCISE

In the following paragraphs, we offer some general guidelines for an adolescent exercise program. The mnemonic LIFTS offers an easy way to keep in mind the essentials of such a program, with each letter serving as a reminder of a key element: Length, Intensity, Frequency, Type, Stretching. Remember, however, that these suggestions apply only to healthy youngsters who have entered puberty.

Exercise programs can, indeed, help prepubescents and many chronically ill or handicapped children, but parents of such children should consult their child's physician before starting them on an exercise regimen.

How long should a youngster exercise?

For the well-conditioned individual, 15 minutes of intense exercise a day, five days a week, will maintain fitness. For most adolescents, however, a continuous aerobic workout of 30 to 60 minutes produces the best results. Generally, neither adolescents nor adults are in peak physical condition, and so they are incapable of mounting the intensity of effort needed for an effective 15-minute workout. Nor are most of us inclined to exercise five days a week. A longer, gentler exercise period three days a week keeps most people happier—and thus more likely to continue their programs—and less intensity generally means fewer injuries.

What do you mean by intensity?

Intensity involves the speed at which one performs an exercise and the energy expended. It is usually measured in terms of pulse rate. The heartbeat does not endlessly increase to help fulfill the body's needs created by exercise, and the heart's maximum number of beats declines with age. For adolescents, the maximum heart rate runs around 200 beats per minute. When adolescents exercise for aerobic benefit, they should keep their heart rate at 60 to 90 percent of the maximum, or 120 to 180 beats per minute throughout their workout. Teens vary in their ability to maintain a high heartbeat during exercise because of such factors as musculoskeletal development, cardiorespiratory condition, and motivation. Teens should learn to take their own pulse, so they can monitor their heart rate about every 15 minutes during exercise to ensure that their level of intensity is adequate.

How frequently must one exercise to gain full benefit?

The advantages of exercise, particularly the physical benefits, depend on exercising aerobically at least three times a week. The number of youngsters who follow this pattern remains markedly low, compared to those who engage in sports occasionally or seasonally. Indeed, the first National Children and Youth Fitness Study found that exercise in the winter and fall fell to half that of the summer.

Regularity is the key to benefiting from exercise. Running or swimming for an hour once a week, even for considerable distances, provides scant advantage compared to briefer but more regular workouts. An effective program requires exercise three to five times a week. Since this takes commitment and time, youngsters may find they have to give up some television or other leisure activity to meet their exercise schedule.

What are the different types of exercise?
Physiologists divide exercise into two categories, aerobic and anaerobic. *Aerobic* (literally, with oxygen) exercises work the heart and lungs as well as the large muscle groups. They require large amounts of oxygen over a long period and involve rhythmic motions, such as those used in long-distance running and skating, swimming, cross-country skiing, and aerobic dancing. These exercises greatly strengthen the heart and lungs, and help reduce the risk of heart attacks. *Anaerobic* exercises—such as weight lifting, diving, and gymnastics—require much less oxygen intake and do little or nothing to improve cardiorespiratory functioning. They do, however, increase muscle strength and muscle endurance. Few sports are 100 percent aerobic or totally anaerobic. Most mix the two types, with either aerobic or anaerobic the dominant. Soccer, for example, is about 30 percent aerobic and 70 percent anaerobic; a two-mile run is about 80 percent aerobic and 20 percent anaerobic. The more aerobic an exercise, the better in terms of long-term health effects.

Why are warming up and stretching so important?
In one respect, muscles resemble an old auto on a cold morning: they need warming up to function well. Before stepping out on the street to jog, or plunging into the pool, or taking the field, court, or track, an athlete should warm up. This basically means doing stretching exercises, followed by walking, jogging, or jumping jacks. This period of stretching exercises and warm-up activities has become an accepted way of preparing an athlete's mind, heart, lungs, and muscles for athletic activity. Stretching gradually increases blood flow to the muscles and stretches the tendons and ligaments, thus improving the athlete's range of motion and reducing the risk of injury. Daily stretching increases flexibility and the comfort that goes with it.

Various sports differ somewhat in the parts of the musculoskeletal system that require the most flexibility for optimal perfor-

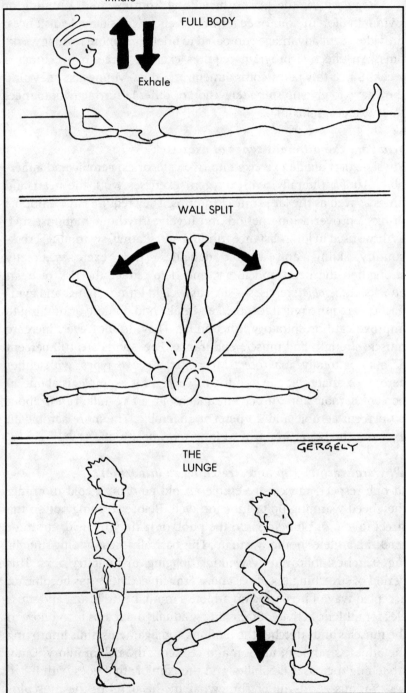

Inhale

FULL BODY

Exhale

WALL SPLIT

GERGELY

THE
LUNGE

mance. The list that follows presents a group of stretching exercises that young athletes can use to improve their range of motion. We will discuss specific warm-up requirements for 14 sports popular with children and adolescents in Chapters 10 through 19, and in those chapters, we will refer back to these directions. Beginners should gradually work their way up to the full number of repetitions, letting their bodies get adjusted without suffering aches and pains.

1. *Full body:* Easy and effective, this is a good way to start any set of stretching exercises. Lie on your back with your knees straight and your shoulders flexed. Then close your eyes and, with all your muscles relaxed, breathe in deeply. Hold your breath for a long one-count and exhale. Repeat 15 or 20 times.

Athletes young and old commonly suffer injuries of the lower extremities. So let's work our way down the lower body with a series of exercises that can help prevent such injuries.

2. *Wall split:* This exercise helps the lower back, hips, and hamstrings. Lying on your back, raise both buttocks up against the base of a wall and extend your legs straight up the wall, with your knees slightly bent. Slowly straighten your legs as if trying to press the backs of your knees against the wall. When your legs are fully extended, hold that position for one minute. Then, keeping your knees straight, open your legs along the wall in a split until you feel stretching in the middle of your thighs. Hold this position for another minute.

3. *The lunge:* Stand with both feet together and put your hands on your hips. Then step well forward with your right foot. Keep your right knee straight and your right foot pointed forward. Keeping your left knee straight and your left foot pointed straight ahead, let your left heel come up off the floor. Holding your shoulders even and back, your eyes looking forward, and your hips straight, flex your right knee and push your pelvis forward, as if trying to touch the floor with it. Stop when you feel stretching at the front of the hip and in the back of the leg. Hold this position for one minute.

4. *Pelvic tilt:* Lie on your back with your legs extended and your hands at your sides. Tighten your abdominal muscles and buttocks, and try to push your lower back and buttocks into the floor. Repeat 5 to 10 times. Hold for 10 seconds each time.

5. *Hamstring stretch I:* Sit on the floor and extend your legs and knees fully in front of you with your ankles together and your toes

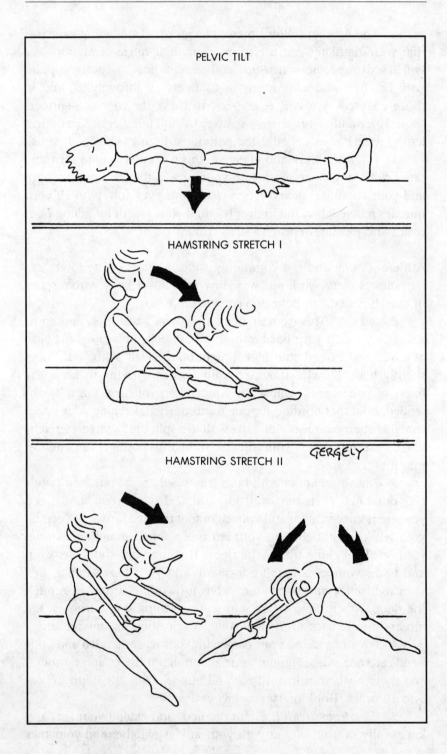

PELVIC TILT

HAMSTRING STRETCH I

HAMSTRING STRETCH II

GERGELY

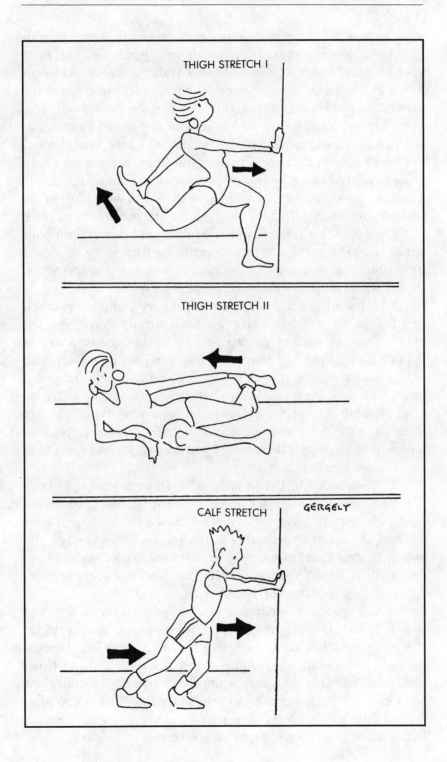

pointing upward. Then put your hands on the floor beside your thighs and, looking ahead, slowly slide your hands forward. Keep your back and knees straight and lower your chest as close to your thighs and knees as possible. Stop when you feel stretching at the back of your knees and thighs. Hold this position for one minute.

6. *Hamstring stretch II:* Sit on the floor and spread your legs as far apart as you comfortably can. Make sure your toes point upward. Put your hands on the floor in front of you. Then, keeping your back straight, your head up, and your eyes focused straight ahead, slowly slide your hands ahead until you feel stretching in the middle of the back of your thighs. Hold this position for one minute. Next, place one hand on either side of your right thigh and slowly push your hands forward until you feel stretching in the back of the thigh and knee. Hold this position for one minute. Repeat this maneuver at the left thigh, again holding your position for 60 seconds.

7. *Thigh stretch I:* Kneel on your right knee and place your left foot flat on the floor with your left knee directly above your left ankle. Steady yourself by placing your right hand against a wall or holding on to a piece of furniture. Now flex your right knee and, reaching back with your left hand, grab your right ankle and pull it away from your buttocks. With your shoulders straight and your head up, push your pelvis and upper body forward. When you feel a stretch in the outer muscles of your right leg, hold your position for one minute. Repeat this exercise with the left leg and again hold the position for 60 seconds.

8. *Thigh stretch II:* Lie on your right side with your right knee and hip flexed at a 90-degree angle. Your left hip and knee should be straight. Reach down with your left hand and slowly pull your left heel toward your buttocks. When you feel stretching on the outside of your leg, slowly lower your left knee to the floor and hold this position for 60 seconds. Reverse legs and repeat the stretch, again holding your position for 60 seconds.

9. *Calf stretch I:* Stand facing a wall or post at arm's length and with your feet shoulders' width apart. Keeping your knees straight, slide your right foot back about two feet. Keep both heels flat on the floor, hips and shoulders squared, and look straight ahead. Now, bend your right knee and move your pelvis forward slowly until you feel a stretch in the lower calf and Achilles tendon. Hold this position for one minute. Switch legs and repeat this exercise with your left leg, again holding your position for 60 seconds.

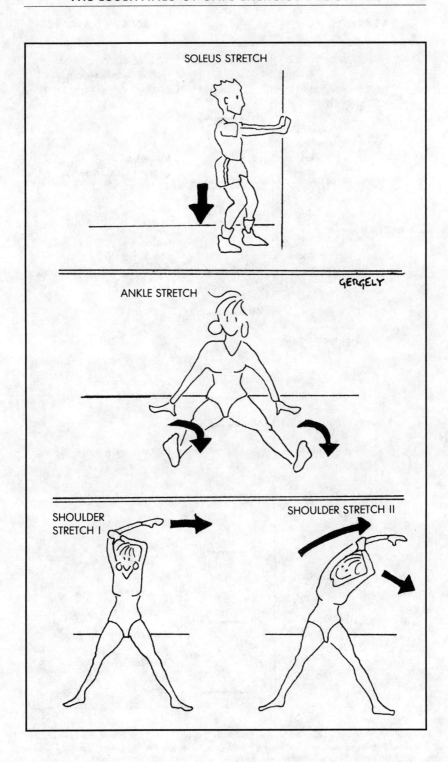

SOLEUS STRETCH

GERGELY

ANKLE STRETCH

SHOULDER
STRETCH I

SHOULDER STRETCH II

AEROBIC %		ANAEROBIC %
Weight lifting	0 —— 100	100-meter dash
Diving		Golf & Tennis swings
Gymnastics		Football
200-meter dash		
	10 —— 90	Basketball
Wrestling		Baseball
Ice hockey		
Fencing		Volleyball
100-meter swim		Skating (500 meters)
	20 —— 80	400-meter dash
Tennis		
		Lacrosse
Field hockey	30 —— 70	Soccer
	40 —— 60	
800-meter dash		
		200-meter swim
Boxing	50 —— 50	Skating (1500 meters)
Rowing (2000 meters)	60 —— 40	
1-mile run		1500-meter run
400-meter swim		
	70 —— 30	
		800-meter swim
2-mile run	80 —— 20	
3-mile run		
Skating (10,000 meters)	90 —— 10	
10,000-meter run		Cross-country running
		Cross-country skiing
Marathon	100 —— 0	Jogging

Reprinted by permission of Elsevier Science Publishing Co., Inc., from "Adolescents and Exercise," by Douglas B. McKeag, *Journal of Adolescent Health Care*, November 1986 Supplement, p. 123S. Copyright 1986 by The Society for Adolescent Medicine.

10. *Calf stretch II:* Stand facing a wall or post with your heels on the ground and your feet shoulders' width apart and your toes pointed slightly inward. Raise your hands straight out at shoulder height and allow yourself to fall forward to touch the wall. With your back and knees straight and bending your elbows, slowly thrust your chest and hips forward until you feel stretching in the upper calf. Hold this position for one minute.

11. *Soleus stretch:* This exercise stretches a key calf muscle which attaches to the ankle. Again, face a wall or post at arm's length and with your feet shoulders' width apart. Move your right foot forward about 18 inches. Then, with heels flat on the floor, bend both knees until you feel a stretching in the lower calf and Achilles tendon. Repeat the exercise with your left leg forward. Both times, hold the position for one minute.

12. *Ankle stretch:* Sitting on the floor, fully extend your legs and knees with your ankles about a foot apart and your toes pointed upward. With all your leg muscles relaxed, rotate both feet at the same time in the biggest circles you can. Do 15 circles in one direction, then reverse direction and do another 15.

The upper torso, while less prone to injury than the lower part of the body, nonetheless requires stretching to protect it. Here are several excellent warm-up exercises that too often are neglected.

13. *Neck stretch:* Each of these stretches should be held for half a minute. Sitting cross-legged, twist your head as far to the right as possible, as if trying to see over your right shoulder. Then try to look over your left shoulder. Next, with face forward, bend your head slowly to the right in an effort to touch your right shoulder with your ear. Repeat this maneuver to the left. Then, with your head upright again and your back straight, bend forward and try to touch your chin to your chest. Finally, tilt your face upward and hold your head so you are looking at the ceiling. Remember, each of these movements should be held for 30 seconds.

14. *Shoulder stretch I:* Standing with your feet shoulders' width apart, raise your right arm with the elbow bent so the elbow is at your right ear and your arm is behind your neck. Take hold of your right elbow with your left hand and gently pull, as if trying to pull your elbow behind your head. Stop when you feel a stretch in your shoulder and right triceps and hold this position for 60 seconds. Repeat this with your left arm and again hold for one minute.

15. *Shoulder stretch II:* Stand, flex your shoulder, and with your left hand, grasp your right elbow and slowly pull your right arm up against your ear. Bend your upper body to the left until you feel stretching in your upper right back and in your trunk. Hold for one minute. Repeat with the opposite side and again maintain your full stretch for 60 seconds.

Should these exercises be performed in any particular order?

Coaches and trainers vary in the exercise routines they assign their players. The important point is to get all the major muscle groups, joints, tendons, and ligaments ready for action. The following head-to-toe regimen will provide excellent stretching for young athletes: full body (1), neck (13), shoulder stretches (14 and 15), the lunge (3), wall split (2), pelvic tilt (4), hamstring stretches (5 and 6), thigh stretches (7 and 8), calf stretches (9 and 10), the soleus stretch (11), and the ankle stretch (12).

Why is cooling down important after vigorous exercise?

Cooling down after exercise—too often overlooked by athletes of all ages—also plays a major role in keeping young athletes healthy. After play or practice, youngsters should walk around and run through the same stretching exercises they used to warm up. The cool-down period should last as long as the original stretching exercises. Cooling down helps prevent stiffness, muscle cramps, and later strains and sprains, and allows the heart and lungs to reach a new equilibrium. This facilitates heat dissipation and replenishes any oxygen debt, thus reducing the risk of heat exhaustion or fainting after exercise. Athletes should remove constricting clothing as soon as possible and shower with warm—not hot—water.

PARENTS' QUESTIONS ABOUT SPORTS PARTICIPATION

How do I know what sport is best for my child?

Actually, most kids do a wonderful job of picking a sport or sports for themselves, even at a young age. In today's urban and suburban communities, youngsters get involved in youth leagues at a younger age than ever before. Children watch their parents, siblings, and the neighborhood kids playing or watching various sports and they develop and pursue their own interests quite well. For example, at age

11, Stephen loved softball and hated baseball. When queried about his strong feelings, he explained his preference quite rationally. He "always" struck out in baseball, but in softball, "you get to hit the ball."

Some parents remain concerned about the dangers of certain sports. We discussed the relative risks of the sports children commonly play in Chapter 1. The evidence indicates that youth sports— even contact sports—generally present a limited risk of serious injury, certainly in comparison to high school and collegiate competitive sports. As a rule, preadolescents don't have the size, strength, or speed that results in significant injury.

Two groups of children—the late maturers and early maturers— do face some potential problems that parents should be aware of. Late maturers are often, but not always, smaller than their peers, have poorer motor skills and coordination, and lag behind in social and emotional development. With such traits and limited athletic abilities, late maturers too frequently wind up as bench warmers and being put down as "losers" by fellow players and sometimes coaches. These children quickly come to hate the team, the sport, and perhaps athletics in general. Typically they quit the team, or sustain or feign an injury to protect themselves from the embarrassment of actively participating. The parents of such children need to counsel them so they avoid competitive sports until they are physically and emotionally ready to compete effectively. As these children grow into adolescence, they frequently find they do best at such sports as tennis and racquetball, track, soccer, diving, wrestling, and the martial arts.

For the early maturer, things often come too fast and too easily. Their advanced size, speed, and strength for their age give them an advantage that often raises them to star status at a young age. But eventually the biology of others in their age group catches up and the player who was a star running back at age 11 may find himself losing his position at age 13. Parents and coaches need to explain to earlier maturers that their successes relate largely to their biology, and that future stardom will take hard work and development of their natural athletic talents.

Aren't a person's athletic abilities inherited?

The answer to the old question of whether athletes are born or made turns out to be, "A bit of both." For example, a person's level of strength and power depends in large part on his or her physical size, muscle mass, and physique. Youngsters can increase their muscle growth and development through exercise (although, as discussed later, the use of weights to build muscle can lead to injury unless done properly). On the other hand, muscle endurance—the ability of muscle to function without tiring—is at least partly inherited. And such important athletic characteristics as speed, agility, and flexibility depend primarily on a person's genetic makeup. So like many things in life, athletic skills depend on both nature and nurture.

How do variations in body structure affect sports preferences?

Not surprisingly, what sport a young person pursues successfully depends in large part on his or her body build. In sports played by both males and females, rowing, basketball, volleyball, and field events attract the taller and heavier athletes of both sexes; the athletes in the middle range of height and weight gravitate to such sports as cycling, swimming, and skiing; and shorter males and females often look to running events or gymnastics. The sport with the most striking sex discrepancy is bodybuilding, where males tend to be tall and heavy and females short and lightweight.

At what age can my child begin competing in sports?

Many children play sports, whether sandlot softball, swimming, or ice skating, long before competing formally. True, the age at which many kids begin playing on organized teams has dropped during the last couple of decades. A Michigan study, for example, found that children on teams in organized leagues in that state first joined at an average age of 8, with some starting as early as age 5. But just as no one expects every child who begins playing in youth leagues before puberty to reach the professional ranks in sports, almost every sport has its stars who began playing in high school and even later. Opinion varies considerably as to the "right" age for children to begin formal sports competition. Certainly a parent doesn't want an 8-year-old getting into power-lifting weights, because of the sport's potential for spinal column injury in children and teenagers. We remain committed to the ideal that fun, skill development, and physical exercise should remain the top priorities in sports, for both children and adolescents. Let your child be your guide: Does he or she want to play? Does the child have the physical and emotional maturity to handle the technical and competitive aspects of the sport?

What about playing on unisex teams?

As children, boys and girls are essentially equal physically, so they can play on the same teams and compete against each other up to age 11 or 12 on equal terms and without concern that girls will suffer graver injuries than if they played only against other girls. After puberty, however, we regard unisex teams as generally unwise, particularly in sports in which collisions occur. Some exceptions include mixed doubles in tennis, golf foursomes, and bowling. However, the rationale of restricting girls from collision sports because of a concern for their smaller bones and body size is only logical if smaller, shorter boys are restricted from competing with taller, larger boys too.

On the psychological side, a young boy who cannot accept defeat by a girl, or whose father or mother thinks it is unmanly for a boy to lose to a girl, should avoid mixed teams. At some point, some girl surely will outplay the boy, perhaps causing his team's loss. If this prospect threatens a boy or his relationship with his parents, we suggest he stick to boys-only play.

At what level should my child compete?

Given the explosive growth of youth sports, it is obvious that many Americans regard competitive athletics for youngsters as valuable. For some children, however, too much competition too soon can damage their self-esteem and sense of competence. Often parents recognize this, and want to protect their children from competition that is too intense. Yet the degree of competition in organized youth leagues is so high that today's parents have little comparable experience to guide them in advising their children. Each sport has its own unique set of potential injuries and negative repercussions. Parents should choose the level of competition for their child on the basis of all the factors previously mentioned in this chapter: (1) the child's age, growth, and physical capabilities; (2) the child's emotional maturity; (3) their own commitment; (4) their child's commitment; and (5) the importance of prepubertal training in the particular sport. In general, we recommend that parents help their children choose a sport at a competitive level that is not only comfortable but also challenging, instructive, and, most of all, fun.

Before my child plunges into an organized league,
what questions should I ask about the sport,
and what questions should I ask myself?

Certainly, you want to know if your child is physically and emotionally ready for that specific sport, an assessment that may require a talk with the child's physician. You can ask other parents involved in the league about the quality of coaching, the level of interest in athletic safety, and whether coaches and league officials believe that "winning is the only thing." On the home front, the questions you should ask include:

- Does your child truly want to play the sport, or is the real push coming from a parent or coach?
- Is your child emotionally mature enough to take instructions, orders, and constructive criticism from a coach? Pouts and temper tantrums can quickly sour an adult's attitude toward a young player.
- How intense is the competition? Within some communities, several leagues exist for the same sport, each requiring a different level of ability and intensity of competition.
- Will the child have fun, learn new skills, and get a chance to play regularly? Perpetual bench warmers have less fun and never really get the full benefits sports can offer.
- Does your child have the emotional maturity to handle both winning and losing? We've all heard of good losers, but accepting victory with grace and consideration for the losing team is equally important.
- Can you acccept it if your child's athletic abilities fail to match those of most other team members? This may be the hardest thing in athletics for a proud parent to handle, particularly one who played well as a youth.
- Are family members willing to accept the inconveniences and devote the time needed for the child's participation? Getting active in a youth league usually involves such things as carpooling to practices, showing up to watch the child play, and arranging meals and vacations around the team's schedule.

Assessing your answers to these questions—so important to the psychological side of sports and to the contentment of a young player—

should help you decide whether you and your child are ready to deal with the stresses of a particular sport and youth league.

How can we decide whether to let our children participate in the riskier sports?

Such issues can create disagreements and tensions beween a child and his or her parents, between two parents, and between parents and grandparents. Frequently, such conflicts reach their zenith in the teen years when the child is in the painful process of finding his or her own identity and separating from parents.

For example, Philip was 13 when he and his parents talked with a physician during a preparticipation sports physical. Philip liked everything—school, athletics, his hobbies, and his family life. There seemed to be nothing that disturbed this rather upbeat young fellow. But as the conversation continued, it became clear that one subject divided the family. Philip played soccer and swam in out-of-school leagues and played tennis for his school team. But what he really wanted was to play football. His mother, however, softly but firmly opposed the sport as too dangerous; his father ventured neither support nor opposition. Philip's mother also expressed her concern about his weight, which she complained was too high.

One year later, Philip returned to the clinic with his mother, complaining of knee pain. He had dropped tennis and swam only sporadically, but was playing soccer and bicycling long distances on weekends. His mother blamed soccer for Philip's condition and again volunteered her opposition to football. The knee condition, however, proved to be the fault of the boy's cycling, not his soccer. Philip had grown, but he had never raised his bicycle seat. This meant that his leg never fully extended on his downstroke when he pedaled; his knee was continually bent. This stress on his knee resulted in pain. Philip raised his bicycle seat to the proper height, which solved his pain problem, and continued playing soccer.

The following year, at age 15, Philip again arrived for a pre-participation sports physical, accompanied for the first time only by his father. Philip announced he would be playing football and talked enthusiastically about it. His father tried hard to contain his own pleasure that his son had chosen football. Philip described his mother as "handling it all right," although he confessed to some tense times in the family during the previous year before his mother acceded to his insistent demands to play football. And his mother, still worried about the danger of injury, focused her pleasure on the fact that Philip had lost his body flab and was doing better than ever academically. If Philip had been denied the football team, would he have improved academically? Links between learning and self-esteem, between task completion and independence are difficult to prove, but not hard to imagine. Philip had made his choice to play football and asserted himself against his mother, winning a degree of independence and the support of his father in the process.

KEEPING SPORTS SAFE FOR KIDS

According to the President's Council on Physical Fitness and Sports, 100 million Americans swim, 75 million bicycle, 60 million walk, and 34 million run or jog. Yet many children and adolescents regard exercise as something for "jocks" and so remain passive and flabby. Parents can help change this unhealthy attitude. Especially parents who exercise themselves have a surprisingly strong ability to influence their children's physical activities and to encourage them to find sports or exercise programs they enjoy. Still, exercise should fit a child's age. Remember: Infant programs may be dangerous if not carefully limited; preadolescent competition is often best organized by weight rather than age; the spine isn't fully mature until the mid-twenties, so heavy weight lifting can cause harm; always warm up and stretch the muscles gradually before playing sports or exercising. One of the authors neglected this simple dictum and suffered a torn calf muscle in a picnic volleyball game that left him hobbling on crutches for a month.

3

Nutrition for Young Athletes

The teen years witness a grand and sometimes painful passage from childhood to adulthood, a time of great growth—intellectually, emotionally, and physically. For the young athlete of any age, but particularly the adolescent, proper nutrition bears directly on his or her performance. Athletes learn about the importance of nutrition to achievement, often from an early age. But what they learn from fellow players at the practice field and in the locker room frequently consists of misinformation and myths that are as likely to affect their play adversely as to enhance it. Some common untruths held dear by many youngsters include the notions that drinking water during practice or a game causes cramps, and that amino acid supplements build better bodies. In fact, cramps result from dehydration due to drinking too little water, and consuming amino acid supplements rarely benefits any athlete. Some myths, such as eating bananas daily for extra potassium, are harmless; others, such as taking salt tablets before a game, contain the potential for injury and pain. So a basic knowledge of human nutrition, both as a performance enhancer and as an injury preventer, is important to young athletes, their parents, and their coaches.

The benefits of good nutrition stretch far beyond the playing field and influence a child's health and intellectual achievements as well as athletic performance. For the young athlete, sound eating habits are vital year-round, not just on game day or while his or her sport is in season. Nutrition affects athletes—be they young stars bound for professional careers or those playing simply for fun and fellowship—at every point in their sporting endeavors. And youngsters who begin a season nutritionally fit begin nearer their peak form.

When does good nutrition play its most important role?

Good nutrition is particularly important among athletes in their adolescence. Youngsters typically grow 15 percent of their ultimate height and add 48 percent of their skeletal mass (bone weight) during their adolescent growth spurts. Boys develop later than girls. On average, they reach their greatest rate of growth in height and weight just after their fourteenth birthday, whereas girls usually attain their biggest rate of height increase about age 12 and their greatest rate of weight gain shortly before turning 13. Although these ages generally represent the periods of most rapid growth, the adolescent's legendary capacity for food lasts far longer. At age 16, the average American male eats about 3,500 calories a day and the average female around 2,500 calories. Boys require about 20 percent more protein than girls, a fact of nature that reflects a fundamental difference in male and female body tissue. A woman's body contains about three times as many fat cells as a man's, and this divergence in cell composition develops largely in adolescence. Both sexes add lean muscle during this period, but a greater percentage of a girl's weight gain comes from adipose tissue (fat cells).

Unfortunately, at their time of greatest nutritional need, many American youngsters go through their most discombobulated eating patterns. The concept of three square meals a day too often gets rounded off to one or two reasonably balanced meals and numerous high-calorie, low-nutrition snacks and forays to fast-food restaurants. Breakfast is the most commonly missed meal. And many weight-conscious and/or rushed students worried about doing it all—from earning good grades to participating in extra school activities and to athletics—skip lunch or simply eat a candy bar or bag of potato chips washed down with a soft drink. Parents of any student, especially a young athlete's, should assess their child's eating patterns and work out a plan for balanced meals and nutritious snacks, at home or away, and monitor how well the child follows it.

THE BIG THREE NUTRIENTS

Young athletes seek "the edge," that little extra advantage that will make the difference between winning and losing. Sometimes, certain nutrients—protein, for example—take on almost mystical properties in a youngster's mind as providing the edge. The nutrient then gets consumed in excessive amounts, sometimes in food but more often as a supplement, with potentially unhealthy results either way.

The three most important nutrient categories in the human diet are proteins, fats, and carbohydrates. Learning their role in fueling the body helps us understand how they can enhance athletic performance, if kept in proper balance, or can detract from it when one is consumed in excess or at the expense of the others.

Does a lot of protein help or hinder an athlete?

Dietary protein helps build lean muscle and strengthen the body's vital organs in the chest and abdomen, including the heart, and it helps maintain the body's proper nitrogen balance. Because of its role in muscle synthesis, some athletes attribute almost magical powers to protein. The reverence is misplaced. Protein is a vital part of any diet, but popular myths aside, muscle size depends on training and genetic inheritance rather than extra protein. Study after study has failed to show that a diet high in protein boosts athletic prowess, and an exorbitant intake can actually hinder an athlete.

Exercise does require more protein than lounging around watching television. No one questions that. Endurance exercise, such as running, decreases protein synthesis and increases the conversion of amino acids—the building blocks of protein—to glucose, which cells use as fuel to provide the energy they need to function. Strength exercises, such as weight lifting, actually increase body protein synthesis. Thus both types of exercise, albeit for different metabolic reasons, require more protein intake than sitting idle. One recent study of a group of 18-year-old males found that bodybuilders required 1.2 grams (0.047 ounces) of protein daily for every kilogram (2.2 pounds) of body weight; runners required 1.36 grams per kilogram body weight. However, athletes in both groups exceeded their requirements in their normal diet, without taking any supplements. A group of sedentary students in the same study, whose protein requirements totaled 0.8 grams per kilogram of weight, consumed about 1.6 grams of protein for each of their 2.2 pounds of weight. Females need slightly less protein per kilogram of body weight than males because their bodies contain a smaller percentage of lean muscle. The average American diet consists of about 15 percent protein, which supplies in excess of 1.5 grams of protein per kilogram of body weight, more than enough to fulfill the needs of any healthy athlete, male or female.

While eating a typical diet supplies more protein than the body needs or can use, this excess consumption generally poses no threat to athletic performance. But a very excessive intake can. The body turns extra protein either into immediate energy or into fat for storage and later use as an energy source. Nitrogen is a by-product of this metabolic action, and this nitrogen must be excreted from the body in urine. Urine requires water, and drawing down the body's water content to flush excessive nitrogen can cause dehydration when athletes exert themselves for long periods.

What role do fats play in an athlete's diet?

For all the evils associated with fat—from corpulence to coronary heart disease and some cancers—dietary fat plays a vital role in fueling muscle activity. Indeed, during aerobic exercise fat serves as the main energy source that drives muscle movement. Yet studies show not only that excessive fat intake raises serious health risks, but that when more than 35 percent of calories consumed come from fat, endurance can also suffer. So the question is not whether to eat fat, but how much. After age 2, the American Heart Association recommends limiting the fat in children's diets to 30 percent, while the American Academy of Pediatrics suggests somewhere between 30 and 40 percent. Slightly more than one American child in five now eats a diet with more than 40 percent of calories in the form of fat.

Fats come in three basic forms: polyunsaturated, monounsaturated, and saturated. The body can effectively use all three for energy, and most fat-containing foods contain a mixture of the three, but in greatly varying proportions. While physicians regard a high-fat diet as a potential health hazard, some fats pose greater dangers than others. *Saturated* fats—found in such foods as red meats, whole milk, butter, cheese, ice cream, lard, and some cooking oils, including coconut, palm, and palm kernel—rate highest in risk. Saturated fats slow down the body's ability to clear the bloodstream of LDL cholesterol, the so-called bad cholesterol that increases the risk of heart attacks. The American Heart Association recommends limiting saturated fats to less than 10 percent of calories. *Polyunsaturated* fats, on the other hand, help clear harmful cholesterol from the blood, before it can infiltrate and narrow the heart artery walls, eventually reducing the flow of blood to the heart. Such foods as safflower, soybean, and corn oils, lean fish, and tuna packed in water are high in polyunsaturated fats, and the American Heart Association suggests that these fats should make up more than one-third of the fat a person consumes daily. *Monounsaturated* fats appear to neither increase nor decrease blood levels of cholesterol. Talk with your pediatrician or family physician about how to reduce fats in your children's diets.

Can carbohydrates produce magic in some sports?

Carbohydrates, also known as sugars and starches, play a key role in muscle contraction. Grains, fruits, and vegetables are rich in carbohydrates, which the body breaks down and stores in the muscles and liver as glycogen. When the body demands more energy than it can obtain from the oxygen available to it, the liver and muscles convert some glycogen to glucose, the form of sugar the body uses best for energy. To function at peak efficiency, the body needs a readily available store of glycogen. Unlike the detrimental effects on athletes of diets high in fats or protein, research shows that a diet rich in carbohydrates can enhance performance in endurance sports and increase the time it takes to reach energy exhaustion.

Still, for young, healthy athletes eating an adequate, balanced diet, the benefits of increasing any nutrient are essentially nonexistent. Exercise increases the need for energy, but not beyond what a good diet provides. In spite of all the myths, advertising promotions, and hype, healthy youngsters don't need—and should avoid—vitamin, mineral, or protein supplements. (The exception, extra iron for young women, is discussed later in this chapter and in Chapter 5.)

When and what should young athletes eat, then?

They should distribute their food intake over a minimum of three meals a day, and snack as well if their energy needs require it. Timing is important. Periodically recharging the body's energy supply helps ensure better performance. When youngsters habitually skip breakfast or eat nutritionally poor lunches, they arrive for practice or competition with diminished energy. Athletes should consume a significant part of their daily food supply a few hours before practice or a game. This ensures a ready supply of nutrients for energy and for repairing damaged cells and replacing damaged and dead ones. Indeed, some research indicates that eating a big meal in the evening, when energy needs are lower, promotes increased deposits of undesired fat.

Sports physicians and nutritionists frequently advise young athletes to eat a varied diet, with selections each day from each of the four basic food groups—milk, meat, fruit-vegetable, and grain. A typical recommendation calls for the following daily allotment: four servings of fruits and vegetables; four servings of grain foods, particularly those made with whole grains (breads, rolls, pastas, high-fiber/low-fat breakfast cereals); two servings of milk foods, preferably low-fat (milk, cheese, yogurt); and two servings from the high-protein meat group, which includes not just beef, pork, lamb, and chicken, but also fish, shellfish, eggs, dry beans, peas, nuts, and soybean extenders. Such a diverse diet provides the more than 60 essential nutrients needed to keep youngsters healthy and growing properly.

EATING TO LOSE OR GAIN WEIGHT

Adolescent sports medicine specialists find dieting to lose weight rather common among certain young participants, particularly wrestlers, dancers, and gymnasts. They often make intense efforts to lose weight or to maintain a low weight, including skipping meals, denying themselves water and other liquids, and forcing themselves to vomit after eating. Such measures can cause chronic fatigue, dehydration, and low blood sugar, all of which will adversely affect performance and health. The long-term effects of such drastic weight-loss measures remain uncertain. But sustained crash diets, which severely limit the intake of calories and needed nutrients, reduce not just fat but muscle mass, and some evidence suggests that such severe dieting may stunt a child's growth. In a study of nearly 750 high school wrestlers, University of Iowa researchers found that those who practiced extreme weight-control measures failed to show normal adolescent growth during the wrestling season. A study of identical twins, who would be expected to reach essentially the same height in adulthood, found that the twin who practiced drastic dieting while wrestling attained an adult height significantly shorter than his twin who ate normally during adolescence.

Should normal-weight youngsters ever diet?
Certainly there are times when a young athlete can legitimately diet to lose weight. The aim is to do so safely, without threat to perfor-

mance and health. And this means losing no more than two pounds—three at most—each week. A physician, dietitian, or other qualified health professional should supervise any such dieting, which should begin early enough so that the desired weight loss is achieved in time for the athlete to begin his or her season at the proper competitive poundage.

What goes into planning an athlete's diet?

Among the things a physician should know in working out a diet plan are the youngster's amount of body fat and the amount of body fat carried by top performers in the young athlete's sport. In wrestling, for example, this optimum body fat is 5 to 7 percent of body weight, and in most sports this percentage provides the best combination of muscle strength, body quickness, and endurance. Children from middle-class and well-to-do families generally carry a good bit more of their body weight in fat. Surveys find that the typical American adolescent male from an affluent home carries about 15 percent of his weight as fat. Such a young man, weighing 150 pounds, could safely drop 7 to 12 pounds with proper dieting.

What is the ideal result of dieting?

The young athlete fares best when a diet sheds fat without loss of lean muscle. Traditionally, physicians have prescribed a diet that provides 500 to 700 fewer calories daily than the youngster requires, with minimum intake set at no lower than 1,700 calories for girls and 2,000 calories for boys. To make up for this shortage in calories, the body taps its fat stores to supplement its energy needs. Any diet requires sound nutrition, with daily selections from the four food groups, to ensure that growth and development remain normal. Frequently, diets for young athletes limit eating to three well-planned meals a day, with high-caloric snacking and desserts forbidden. For years, physicians regarded such diets as perfectly adequate for youngsters not participating in exercise and athletic programs—providing enough energy for their daily activities without adversely affecting their lean-muscle tissues. However, some new evidence suggests that, at least in obese individuals, weight loss without an exercise program can result in loss of lean muscle as well as fat. So a mild amount of exercise appears to be a prudent accompaniment to any diet designed to cut pounds.

How can a young athlete most effectively gain weight?

While some athletes work to shed pounds, others diligently work to add them. Many Americans equate weight-building programs with football, but players in other popular sports, including basketball, baseball, and hockey, also strive to "bulk up" their bodies to improve performance. Surprisingly, this is often more difficult than it sounds, even for active youngsters. Improved performance requires more than simply adding pounds. If a young athlete's extra weight comes only or largely as fat, his or her speed, endurance, and overall performance will suffer. Only if the weight gain occurs as lean muscle will a youngster derive any fitness and athletic benefit. Increasing lean-muscle mass is the key, and accomplishing this effectively requires eating the right foods, in sufficient quantity, and faithfully following a supervised program of weight lifting two or three times a week. Easy as this may sound, following this prescription for weight gain takes high motivation and discipline, certainly as much as that required of people dieting to lose pounds.

The body needs about 3,000 calories in excess of a youngster's energy demands to build a pound of lean muscle. This is best accomplished by eating 750 to 900 extra calories a day, an amount that will supply the additional energy required by the body for the weight-training program and to add 1 to 1.5 pounds of lean muscle a week. For parents of teenagers, adding another 900 calories to a young person's diet hardly seems difficult. But for some, it is. Even with a bodybuilding routine added to their activities, their appetite may remain essentially unchanged, or they may find that they have trouble wedging an extra meal into their busy schedule. In such situations, commercially prepared liquid meals may provide the extra calories needed. And contrary to popular belief, a high-protein diet offers no advantage in a weight-gain program, and may cause so-called weight lifter's gout.

Do nutritional supplements help?

A nutritionally sound diet will supply any extra nutrients the body requires to build lean muscle. Vitamin, mineral, and protein supplements offer the healthy young athlete no advantage, no matter what the testimonials in the bodybuilding magazines proclaim or the guys at the gym say. Moreover, in very high amounts, supplements can cause gastric problems and hypervitaminosis, or vitamin intoxication. For example, James, a 16-year-old wrestler who complained of headaches, was found to suffer from hypervitaminosis A, the result of taking large doses of vitamin A in hopes of improving his performance. When his physician got James to halt his excessive vitamin A intake and adopt a more nutritionally sound diet, the boy's headaches disappeared and his wrestling performance improved. (A month later, however, James's mother reported her son had started taking vitamin C to help him in an upcoming big match.)

Working the muscles and eating an adequate, proper diet adds the kind of weight that enhances athletic performance. No specific food or vitamin will help the young athlete who wants to safely add lean muscle and only lean muscle. In Chapter 9, we discuss the myths and realities of anabolic steroids and the use of other hormones in bodybuilding, and the very real threat these drugs pose to those who abuse them. For now, let us note that their use is dangerous and absolutely *NOT* recommended. Potential harm aside, anabolic steroids actually do little to aid in the athletic development of a child or adolescent.

AN ATHLETE'S SPECIAL NEEDS

Peak performance requires good nutrition daily. But the athlete—whether young, adolescent, or adult—has special nutritional needs before, during, and after competition. A trite but true rule holds that athletes wage Saturday's battle with Thursday's and Friday's food. Equally important, however, is the pregame meal, a ritual verging on the mystical for some school and youth teams. The primary goal of this important repast is to stoke the body with energy and fluid to sustain the athlete during the competition ahead. But it can also provide vital psychological support, a factor increasingly exploited by some coaches and trainers. Players should eat a heavy meal no less than three hours, and preferably four hours, prior to competition; they can consume a lighter meal two to three hours before taking the field or court.

Misconceptions abound about what the pregame menu should include. One particularly enduring myth is "the big steak," erroneously touted as an instant source of protein that will enhance performance. Two other popular mistakes call for sugary foods to provide energy and salty foods to make sure the body has plenty of salt to replace that lost in sweat. In truth, a pregame meal should be high in carbohydrates, moderate to low in protein (which can aggravate dehydration problems), and low in fat, salt, and nonnutritive fiber. Moreover, it should be easily digested, a factor which has led an increasing number of sports nutritionists to suggest that young athletes drink their pregame meals in the form of the liquid meals originally developed for feeding hospital patients.

What should the young athlete eat to win?

Ideally, the calories in a pregame meal should consist of 60 to 70 percent carbohydrates to maintain blood-glucose levels during competition. Chicken, lean beef, bread or rolls, pastas, fruits, gelatin, yogurt (but not other milk products), fruit juices or fruit punches, sherbet, cookies, or angel food cake are examples of the kinds of foods best suited for precompetition consumption. Such a meal can be easily prepared and served, whether the entire team gathers together ceremonially for its pregame meal or the player dines at home.

In an era of two-wage-earner and single-parent families, young athletes sometimes find themselves preparing their pregame meal for themselves. So knowing the right foods to eat, and those to avoid, can help their health and their performance. Foods best avoided include spicy dishes, which increase water excretion and can irritate the digestive system; foods that produce gas, such as Brussels sprouts and cabbage; and bulky or fatty foods that take a long time to clear the gastrointestinal tract. These are sound rules, but not ironclad. Psychology as well as nutrition affects the outcome of any sporting event. And if an athlete believes a certain food helps him or her win, banning the food from the pregame meal will do more harm than good.

Research suggests that athletes should stop ingesting any carbohydrates and fluids containing sugar 30 to 45 minutes before play begins. These foods can trigger an increase in insulin release by the pancreas to regulate the body's blood sugar, and this may mean, at least in some cases, that athletes will take the field with less-than-optimal blood-sugar levels. Once in action, athletes can readily resume their intake of carbohydrates and fluids. About half an hour before beginning competition, athletes should drink 8 to 16 ounces of water to guard against muscle-cramping dehydration. If their sport requires sustained, long-term effort, as many do, additional water must be consumed during time-outs and other breaks.

Is there ever a role for liquid meals?

Some young athletes find nutritionally sound liquid meals, such as Ensure and Sustacal, ideal for their pregame meal. A number of players suffer pregame jitters that affect their gastrointestinal tract, even to the point of vomiting. Liquid meals help many competitors avoid the problem of a nervous stomach; and they can consume these chilled liquids up to two hours before competition starts. Athletes who participate in daylong meets or tournaments, particularly those who compete in more than one event, may find liquid meals particularly advantageous. The body quickly digests and absorbs liquid meals and athletes can drink small quantities several times during the day to help maintain stamina and performance.

THE DANGERS OF VITAMIN AND MINERAL SUPPLEMENTS

No other nutritional component has acquired quite the mystical aura among athletes that surrounds vitamins and minerals. As essential as they are to good health and performance, few nutrients are as poorly understood by the public in general and sports men and women in particular.

Vitamins and minerals perform a variety of functions within the body. For example, certain vitamins help convert fats and carbohydrates into energy, and iron plays a vital role in transporting oxygen through the bloodstream to the cells. The body needs a reserve of both vitamins and minerals that it can tap instantly when it must quickly generate energy. When the body of a well-conditioned athlete, say, a distance runner, goes from essentially resting to a sustained burst of aerobic exercise, it requires 20 times more energy, and very quickly. This well-known fact, coupled with a seemingly national reverence for vitamins and minerals, has led to a "vitamythology," and to a great many athletes' consuming quantities of vitamin and mineral supplements ranging from one tablet daily to potentially dangerous megadoses. Surveys indicate that at least one member in about three-quarters of the nation's households takes vitamin supplements, and a study of athletes participating in one Olympics found that 84 percent took extra vitamins. Yet most sports nutritionists see no advantage, and a potential for harm, in taking vitamin and mineral supplements, when athletes eat a nutritionally sound diet.

What problems can vitamins cause?

Vitamins act as catalysts in the body, helping its chemical reactions without being changed or destroyed in the process. So the body requires only a limited intake of vitamins to fill its needs and replenish its stores. The well-known recommended daily allowances for vitamins are set above the body's minimum requirements to ensure an adequate but safe supply. Consuming large amounts of extra vitamins and minerals can actually do damage; some 4,000 cases of vitamin poisoning occur in the United States each year. Very large doses of niacin can damage the liver. Excessive vitamin D leads to hypercalcemia, whose symptoms include constipation, nausea, vomiting, abdominal pain, and impaired kidney functioning. Megadoses of vitamin A can cause muscle pain, disruption of the menstrual cycle, and central nervous system problems that range from mild headaches to mood swings to optic nerve damage. Megadoses of vitamin C, which some people take in the belief it will prevent the common cold, can produce diarrhea, kidney stones, destruction of vitamin B_{12}, and liver damage, and can even contribute to bone fractures. Excessive vitamin E may result in disorders that include dizziness, skin problems, high blood pressure, and a potentially fatal condition called pulmonary embolism, in which a clot blocks the blood supply to the lungs.

America's love affair with vitamins extends even to false or pseudovitamins. A vitamin, by definition, is a substance the body requires to maintain proper metabolism, and therefore vitamins are essential to good health. But health food stores and other marketeers sell a variety of substances as vitamins that neither aid metabolism nor cause health problems if absent from the body. These include para-amino benzene acid (PABA), which purportedly increases red blood cells, but which in doses over 10 grams a day can cause nausea, vomiting, and blood disorders; and the P group, or bioflavinoids, sometimes said to help boost the activity of vitamin C, and sold as hesperidin, lipoic acid, quercetin, rutin, and ubiquinone. As sports medicine specialist Gabe Mirkin has noted, crickets die without the bioflavinoids; humans remain healthy without them. So the bioflavinoids are a vitamin to crickets, not humans. Megadosing real vitamins poses dangers enough; using pseudovitamins courts problems even more needlessly.

Is there ever a role for nutritional supplements?
Some teens may indeed need vitamin and mineral supplement. Adolescents differ from adults in their daily requirements of vitamins and minerals, including calcium, iron, and zinc, and nutritional sur-

veys typically report inadequate intakes of these vital nutrients among a significant percentage of teenagers—largely because of poor eating habits. Athletes eating low-calorie diets to keep their weight down, such as some wrestlers and gymnasts, may consume insufficient amounts of vitamins and minerals. Even a balanced diet meeting the recommended daily allowance for iron fails to provide enough iron for 20 to 30 percent of females during the years they menstruate, and some adolescent male athletes going through growth spurts while eating irregularly or consuming inadequate diets may suffer from iron deficiency. Low iron levels can reduce energy levels and adversely affect athletic performance. While a daily multivitamin tablet is generally regarded as safe, it is unwise and potentially dangerous for a youngster to consume vitamin and mineral supplements, especially in large doses, unless told to do so by a physician. Diagnosing a vitamin or mineral deficiency, and its cause, requires medical tests and skills, and self-diagnosis and self-treatment could prove harmful.

THE DANGERS OF DEHYDRATION

As we've noted, even the hardest training and most intense competition require no substantial increase in any specific nutrient. Most healthy young athletes eating a well-balanced diet need only consume enough food to meet their peak energy requirements and enough water to keep them properly hydrated. But unfortunately, many parents, coaches, and young athletes too often ignore the need to maintain adequate water within the body. The risk of dehydration runs higher in youngsters than in adult athletes, and higher in girls than in boys.

Why is dehydration a problem for young athletes?
The body requires a water supply to support its energy production and to prevent muscle cramping, heat exhaustion, and potentially fatal heatstroke. As a rule, the higher the heat and humidity, the greater the sweating and the resulting dehydration from the same amount of exercise. If a person loses 2 percent of his or her body weight during exercise, the volume of blood plasma drops and an inadequate supply of oxygen reaches the skin and muscles. A 3 percent weight loss cuts the endurance time for muscle contractions, and a 4 percent loss can significantly compromise performance. A 6

percent loss may result in potentially life-threatening problems. Water can, indeed, be an athlete's lifeline.

Many youngsters believe that taking a drink when thirsty satisfies their fluid requirements. But thirst alone fails to adequately signal the body's water needs. Weighing oneself before and after exercise is a more exact way of gauging one's water loss and intake requirements. Athletes should weigh themselves several times during long-term or repeated exercise, and drink water or very dilute fruit juices every 60 to 90 minutes.

Aren't there better fluids for athletes?

Water alone suffices. Contrary to certain advertising campaigns, all athletes need for proper hydration is an adequate, nutritionally sound diet and water; they gain nothing from the much-touted electrolyte beverages sold commercially or sometimes mixed at home. Studies indicate that in spite of copious sweating and the loss of some electrolytes, athletes' bodies tend to conserve sodium, potassium, and chloride, and eating a proper diet provides enough replacements without the need for liquid supplements. Indeed, these beverages may even unintentionally abet dehydration. They slake thirst because the sweeteners in them cause them to remain in the stomach longer, creating a sensation of satiety and giving the athlete the impression of having drunk enough fluids to meet his or her body's needs.

Salt tablets, once popped like candy by sweating athletes, are another unneeded and potentially dangerous supplement that youngsters and adults alike should shun.

Any final words on nutrition?

Young athletes particularly should avoid the fad diets found in bookstores, drugstores, and supermarkets. Many fail to provide basic, sound nutrition for growing bodies, and even the best must be followed unfailingly to ensure an adequate intake of proteins, carbohydrates, fats, vitamins, and minerals. Young athletes following these diets risk hindering their performances; worse, they may risk their health.

Eating to win is a popular notion, and a surprisingly simple one for those who know the basic rules. Yet with all the nutrition myths that abound, the wise parent, like the physician, always remembers: First, do no harm.

4

The Psychology of Youth Sports

Sports sometimes involve games played in the mind as well as on the field. As we see it, athletic activities at their best help build a healthy mind as well as a strong body. Through wholesome competition, through learning to work with others, through dealing with failure and success, the young athlete gains greater self-esteem and self-confidence, and a greater sensitivity to the feelings and emotional needs of others. Developing these very positive mental attitudes should be the fundamental purpose of youth leagues, along with improving athletic skills and teaching the importance of lifelong physical-fitness activity to personal health.

But as parents, physicians, and coaches know: " 'Tis easier said than done."

For one thing, in structure and motivation youth leagues frequently mimic scholastic, collegiate, and even professional athletics. Children as young as age 6 quickly get introduced to a competitive atmosphere that can prove defeating for some. Teams in such sports as baseball can move from local, to regional, to national or international competition, with the notion of winning gaining increasing importance with each advance. In such situations, the ideals of mental and physical development and "everyone plays part of every game" quickly get subverted. Too often the desires, aspirations, frustrations, and lost dreams of the adults get thrust upon the young athletes. The father trying to live out his own lost or unsuccessful athletic career through his child may see a good or great athlete emerge, but with the heavy penalty of raising a driven man or woman who can never be happy, never be satisfied, no matter how successful.

Some adult awareness of the physical changes that occur during a child's or adolescent's development and the psychological factors at play in youngsters and in youth sports can go a long way to averting or resolving this kind of problem. In this chapter, we aim to provide parents and coaches with some basic facts about the interplay of physiology and a youngster's mental outlook, an understanding of the sports-related emotional pressures young people face, and tips to help them guide young athletes through some of these psychological pitfalls.

GROWTH FACTORS

A number of factors can influence the attitudes and achievements of young athletes. These range from variations in growth and maturity, to family problems such as divorce or parental overinvolvement, to unintentional victimization by coaches. Recognizing these factors—which may seem inconsequential to many adults but often represent matters of utmost urgency and importance to children and adolescents—can help parents and coaches in dealing with young athletes.

What do physicians mean by "normal" growth?
It's the basic pattern of physical growth and development that all healthy children and adolescents experience. Through childhood, we see little difference between the sexes in their growth rates. The two sexes diverge, however, at the beginning of adolescence. Girls enter their growth spurt earlier than boys, at about 12 or 13, and thus many girls at that point tower over boys of the same age. This changes when boys enter their growth spurt, about two years after girls. Because of this delay, boys begin their growth spurt about four inches taller than girls when the girls began their growth spurt, and they quickly surpass girls in height and strength. It is important to remember, however, that while this pattern holds true, the age at which various developmental events occur varies in both sexes. A youngster's maturity level and/or physical development may lag two years or even a little more behind the "typical" growth pattern in both boys and girls, a situation that can cause some problems in sports.

What problems do differences in growth rates cause?
A discrepancy between a child's chronological age and his or her physical or emotional age may go unrecognized by a coach, or even

by some parents. Such a child or adolescent may feel under pressure to perform at a level for which—physically or emotionally—he or she is not ready. And it is not uncommon in such instances for a coach or parent to question the youngster's motivation—or whether something might be amiss physically—thus burdening the child with harmful self-doubts. Whenever a child fails to perform up to expectations, the possibility of unusually slow physical development should rank high among the reasons considered.

But how do you tell if physical development is the reason?

A physician can provide the answer. In children, an evaluation of bone growth plates can reveal whether an individual lags behind the "normal" time line in physical development. At later ages, the development of pubic hair, breasts, and genitalia provides another guide. The so-called Tanner staging system, mentioned in Chapter 2, lists five stages of genitalia and pubic-hair development associated with growth in males. Similar staging systems of breast and pubic-hair development exist for adolescent girls.

Does physical maturity determine athletic prowess?

Very much so in boys; less so in girls. Physical maturity creates strength and size and so correlates quite closely with a young male's ability to perform well in sports. Among girls, the level of physical development makes a real difference in some sports, swimming being a clear example. But in others—including gymnastics, basketball, and volleyball—the premier players often lag behind in their physical maturation.

Does age affect how children view sports?

Different age groups do characteristically bring different attitudes and interests to sports, beginning at a very young age. The desire to win the acceptance of their peers motivates children aged 6 to 12. This is a time when children seek a comfortable identity, and when their sense of self-worth depends heavily on the approval of their friends and fellow players. During these preadolescent years children do best in low-key competition, with each child getting a chance to perform as best he or she can. Adults who ignore or fail to recognize this can create confusion and unhappiness in these very young athletes, some of whom will quit a team—or sports altogether—as a result.

Between 12 and about 15, body image seems always to be on adolescents' minds—both boys' and girls'—and sports provide the opportunity to test their strength and endurance and to improve their physique. In this sense, athletics serve a psychological and physiological purpose for many teenagers. From 15 to 18, adolescent males in particular often find a reinforcement of their sexual identity in sports.

Does sports participation in childhood have beneficial effects on personality development?

You find arguments both ways. Some studies find that, among children and adolescents, athletes are higher achievers, better adjusted socially and emotionally, more outgoing, and more strongly motivated than nonathletes. Other studies, however, have failed to find any significant differences between the personalities of sports participants and nonparticipants. Personal observation (and therefore personal opinion) suggests that athletics may attract youngsters who are already well adjusted and motivated, and may nurture and strengthen these traits in a good number of them. But for now, we must conclude that no one can answer the question of how sports shape the personalities of young participants.

THE ROLES OF PARENTS AND COACHES

Do parental attitudes determine a youngster's interest in athletics?

They certainly do. Particularly among younger children, parents play a larger role even than older siblings in whether a child plays sports. By the beginning of adolescence, the influence of friends, teachers, and coaches increases, but parents still play a significant role. The father usually gets the credit (or blame) as the most influential parent, but a mother may strongly influence a daughter or son to play sports, and a specific sport in particular. As a rule, parents interested in sports who participated in athletics themselves when young and who continue to play a sport or exercise regularly as adults most often encourage and support their children's sports activities.

Do parents in our society overemphasize athletics?

Many do, and often their children pay an unhealthy price. One unfortunate effect of Little League baseball and other organized youth sports on the American athletic scene has been to lower the age at which children first experience intense competition in sports. In terms of competition and the pure fun that goes with playing, a great deal of difference exists between a Little League game and a pickup game of softball in a schoolyard. Formal competition introduces a degree of stress at any age. How well children deal with this stress depends in large part on their parents and their coaches. Sports physicians and psychologists talk of the "victimization" of young athletes by their parents. In simplest terms, this refers to parents who so overemphasize winning and performance that they put enormous pressure and stress on their children, unfairly criticizing their caliber of play, their effort, and their desire. The child's love of playing disappears amid the stress engendered by the need to win to satisfy a nagging, hypercritical parent. The National Youth Sports Coaches Association says that 70 percent of boys and girls 6 years of age and up who participate in organized sports drop out by age 13.

Any physician who deals with adolescents can recount stories of youngsters who, burned out by the insatiable demands of a parent, give up a sport they once loved to play. In one case, at age 16 Bart captained his high school wrestling squad and played second string on the football team. His father felt Bart did pretty well at wrestling, but kept urging Bart to do better and frequently criticized his football play and class grades. Finally, Bart dropped out of school and stopped playing all sports. He eventually returned to school, after intensive counseling, but refused to compete in any sport out of fear his father would resume criticizing his attitude and efforts.

What kinds of parental pressure cause young athletes to burn out?

Some parents—and this holds true for mothers as well as fathers—simply cannot or will not distinguish between their needs and desires and those of their children. They become consumed with a child's athletic endeavors, focusing their attention on this single, narrow part of the child's life. Often without realizing it, they ignore other important needs and concerns in the life of their growing, emotionally developing youngster, leaving the child feeling unappreciated and even exploited. Many such parents cannot detach their own egos from their children's athletic activities; they live out their own dreams, hopes, and fantasies through a child's participation in a child's game. Some see athletics as a passport to economic freedom and higher social status, not just for their children but for themselves as well.

As a result, such parents place enormous, unrealistic demands on their children, pushing them from early childhood to achieve stardom and psychologically punishing them no matter how well they succeed—by always demanding more and never accepting (and rarely praising) the success they obtain. Barbara recalls an office softball game in which she lined a sharp single and won cheers from her teammates. But her son told her, "I've seen you hit better than that. You should've hit that pitch for a home run." Barbara was deeply disappointed until she realized, "I had been doing the same thing to him."

Some parents never seem to realize or accept that their children are not professionals. A 15-year-old boy or girl may stand six feet tall or more and dominate the backboards in basketball. But a child that age has neither the physical development nor the emotional maturity of a collegiate or professional star, and demanding that he or she perform and respond like an adult can lead to psychologically devastating consequences. Too often, such demands are reinforced by parents using guilt as a motivator. Talk of dollars spent, pleasures missed, and sleep lost may push a child to practice and achieve, but in the end, the child and often his or her performance suffer. Mental disturbances, drug or alcohol problems, even suicide attempts among young athletes often stem from parental pressures. Unfortunately, even when told by a physician, psychologist, coach, or other parents of the potentially serious effects their demands pose for their children, many parents will not ease up. They seem unable to accept that they are seeking to live out their own unfulfilled dreams through their children.

What should coaches do about parents who constantly criticize their children's play from the sidelines?

The coach should ignore the criticism and continue doing what works best: positive reinforcement. Such parents usually can't help themselves, but volunteer coaches can serve as an example of enjoyable, effective interaction with children in youth sports. Remember, children may listen to guidance from coaches delivered in a positive manner more readily than they will listen to parental admonitions delivered in a negative manner. More often than not, kids listen to their coaches and ignore a nagging parent. Coaches should also meet

with parents in the pre-season to explain their philosophy and es-
tablish ground rules for everyone.

Do coaches really influence the attitudes and behaviors of their players beyond the playing field?

They certainly can. In one survey of world-class female swimmers,
many still listed their coaches as the most influential person in setting
the direction of their lives—7 to 15 years after these women had
ceased competing in the Olympics and other international events. A
person who coaches a player for one year of sandlot ball probably
won't draw such raves years later. Nonetheless, athletic coaches can
and do play a significant role in the socialization of youngsters.

Studies indicate that youth coaches who stress positive reinforcement and support in working with their players, rather than
gruff criticism and put-downs, make sports more fun and do better
at instilling positive attitudes. For example, such coaches may dem-
onstrate a stroke in swimming and have team members try it. Those
who do it correctly are praised; those who don't are shown again—
without derogatory remarks about their intelligence or athletic ability—and asked to repeat their effort. The coach's emphasis is always
on helping the young person learn new skills, improve existing ones,
and feel good about his or her efforts and progress. Supportive
coaches also encourage their athletes to focus on competing against
themselves rather than others, that is, improving their "personal
best," be that a race time, the number of football tackles or basketball
rebounds, or a fielding percentage in baseball. Such positive techniques reduce the stress players naturally feel in competitive sports.
A critical, negative coach runs a far greater risk of creating "choking"
situations, in which players, burdened by pressures and fears, fail to
perform their best in important situations. Any player may choke;
but a positive coach will reassure the player, while a negative coach
will criticize and increase the chances that the player will choke
again, thus creating a spiral of failure devastating to the player and
harmful to the team.

Can "victimization" be a problem with coaches as well as with the parents of young athletes?

Coaches, too, may allow their own egos and dreams to overwhelm
them in dealing with young athletes, so that they pressure youngsters
to win not for the athlete's or the team's honor, but for their own

ego gratification. Increasingly, studies indicate that the coaches who coach best keep their egos in check, and remember they are working with youngsters of varying degrees of skill and experience—not a team of professional All-Stars. A truly sad situation develops when a youth coach devotes all his time and attention to a single player whom he envisions as a future star. Neither that player nor the other team members benefit. A less obvious, but equally unfortunate, situation involves the coach so dedicated to winning that he has no time for or cuts players he considers lacking in ability. While a supportive coach can build the self-confidence of young players, a coach who belittles children and adolescents who have little athletic experience or lesser skills, who are slow to learn, or who take criticism emotionally can damage their sense of self-worth. And while psychologists can't say exactly how devastating such mental trauma may be—especially to adolescents in the process of establishing their personal sense of identity—studies now strongly suggest that it may leave lasting adverse effects.

CONTROLLING STRESS

Doesn't playing a sport put tremendous stress on a child?

It can. We've talked about a number of sources of psychological stress that can affect young athletes: the too-prevalent notion in our society that winning is the only thing; the problems of late and earlier maturers; the issue of femininity among females who want to participate in sports will be discussed in Chapter 5. Parents and coaches of young athletes need to learn how to recognize the signs of stress and what to do about it, for the child's psychological and physical well-being. Studies indicate that a stressed athlete has an increased chance of suffering an injury.

Still, don't think of sports as necessarily the most stressful event among a child's activities. When a researcher at the University of Illinois studied the stress generated in children by seven different sports, playing a musical instrument in public, and several academic challenges, giving a musical recital proved by far the most anxiety-provoking!

What stress-reduction techniques provide relief for young athletes?

Probably the most commonly used technique involves learning to ease muscle tension, an approach known as *progressive* or *deep-muscle relaxation*. The idea behind relaxation exercises is that psychological stress and its accompanying anxiety impede an athlete's body control and performance. Progressive relaxation involves alternately tensing for a few seconds and then relaxing a group of muscles; then after a series of such exercises, moving on to other muscle groups, exercising all the major muscle groups in turn. Such contracting and relaxing relieves tension within the muscles themselves, and the effort of concentrating on carrying out the exercises distracts a person from his or her stressful thoughts, thus reducing stress and anxiety. The benefits of progressive relaxation go beyond sports to any stressful situation, so learning the technique can pay dividends throughout life.

Biofeedback provides another way for athletes to control their stress. In this technique, sensors attached to the body provide the athlete with a running measurement of muscle tension and skin temperature, indicators of stress. A person learns stress-reduction techniques and can watch muscle tension and skin temperature ease as he or she practices them. In time, the sensors and monitoring machinery are discarded, having served their purpose of reinforcing in the athlete's mind the effectiveness of the stress-reduction techniques. Thereafter, the athlete relies solely on the techniques themselves to reduce stress.

Where does "imagery" fit into this?

Imagery training harnesses the mind, not only to provide stress relief but also to psych up an athlete to perform better. Through this technique, people learn to imagine particularly vivid and real scenes in their mind. Mentally visualizing a quiet, beautiful scene—such as a sunset at a deserted beach or the reflection of snowcapped peaks in an alpine lake—can reduce stress. And learning to practice in the mind, step by step, the perfect way to play a golf shot, or shoot a three-point basket, or lead a receiver in football appears to actually help athletes improve their skills. If something goes wrong in the mental practice, the player can stop and start over again without ending in a sand trap, or missing the winning basket or touchdown.

Is "arousal control" aimed at stress management?

Arousal control often uses stress-reduction techniques, but the goal is somewhat different. "Arousal" here refers to the level of excitement an athlete brings to competition, and arousal control aims at fine-tuning the athlete's level of excitement so that it helps rather than hinders her performance. A state of excitement can improve concentration and sharpen an athlete's reaction time. Yet too high a level (overarousal) can impair concentration, timing, and fine muscle coordination. Different sports demand different arousal levels for maximum performance. Divers and gymnasts do better at lower arousal states than do football or soccer players. Through arousal control, the athlete learns to reduce her excitement level to the optimum point for her sport.

THE PSYCHOLOGY OF INJURIES

Psychologists have also documented the importance of an athlete's mental and emotional state in recovering from injury, an often-ignored factor as important for young athletes as for seasoned pros.

Psychologically, what happens when a player suffers a serious injury?

Researchers have identified a general reaction pattern among athletes, which interestingly resembles that experienced by people after the death of a loved one. First comes denial—a refusal to accept the reality that a disabling injury has struck—which often leaves the athlete feeling alone and isolated. Mentally, the athlete insists that the injury isn't serious, or as bad as it first appeared, or that it will feel much better in a day. Anger follows next. The athlete gets irked with himself and others and often lets his irritation show quite forcefully. The third reaction consists of a sense of loss. The physical pain; perhaps the need to wear a bandage, sling, or cast; the realization that he can't compete and must watch from the sidelines, all combine to create a sense of inner grief. This can lead to a fourth phase, depression, which usually gives way to the fifth and final reaction, an acceptance of the injury along with a renewed hope that the damage will heal and that eventually the athlete will return to competition.

***What can parents do to help their children through this
psychological sequence after an injury?***

Recognizing the mood stages injured athletes go through and providing some encouragement and guidance as the child struggles to
cope with her injury can help enormously. The child needs assurance
that it is quite acceptable to regard the injury as an inconvenient bit
of lousy luck, and that anger, frustration, and a sense of loss are
perfectly normal feelings. What needs countering are negative feelings about herself or any sense of hopelessness she may express.
Youngsters usually heal well and quickly from athletic injuries. Much
of the anxiety young athletes suffer after an injury stems from simple
ignorance and misinformation about the nature of their injury, how
long they must remain sidelined, and the best way, laid out in detail,
to effectively rehabilitate themselves. Youngsters, particularly adolescents, often hear things differently than a physician thinks he or
she has explained them. It's always wise to make sure as a parent
that you understand the doctor's explanations and instructions so
you know your child's prognosis and directions for rehabilitation.
That may mean close questioning of your child, and a telephone call
to the physician to clarify any questions.

***What happens if, after recovering from an injury, the athlete
cannot play as well as before getting hurt?***

That always poses a problem, and sometimes serious psychological
difficulties, depending upon how much of the youngster's self-image
depends on his involvement in athletics. Anyone who seriously en-
joys athletics will feel disheartened and discouraged by an injury that
permanently impairs his play. For people whose only interest in life
is athletics, or whose sense of self is defined almost entirely by athletic
ability, such an injury can strip them of status, the major source of
satisfaction in their life, and self-esteem. An understanding physician
and parents who can help a youngster cope with his very real sense
of loss and point out alternative activities he might pursue can help
enormously in guiding a child through this crisis. But sometimes
injured young athletes need professional counseling to come to grips
with their impaired ability.

Do certain injuries need psychiatric help?

Researchers at Harvard Medical School and The Children's Hospital
in Boston report that two quite different groups of injured young

athletes may require psychiatric as well as medical treatment. The first consists of a small number of youngsters who suffer depression following a serious, first-time injury. Their depression usually indicates an inability to cope with a severe sense of loss or major change resulting from their injury. The second group involves children and adolescents who have suffered relatively minor injuries such as sprains or tendinitis, but who continue to complain about pain, fail to progress well in their rehabilitation, and say they cannot participate in their normal activities. The researchers, Francine G. Pillemer and Lyle J. Micheli, found that these children tended to have parents who were either too much or too little involved in their lives; suffered stress from some personal loss or change; failed to draw pleasure from their athletic participation; showed evidence of sexual inhibition; depended on athletics for their self-esteem; and had a narrow range of interests outside athletics. Such children and adolescents often benefit from psychological counseling, when they get it. But the researchers also found in their study that up to 40 percent of those referred for counseling never sought it.

What advantages do youngsters gain subconsciously from playing "the injured athlete"?

Pillemer and Micheli found a variety of "secondary gains" for such behavior. Being "injured" provides a socially acceptable way to avoid athletic activities, which give such youngsters scant pleasure; offers a retreat from the concerns of adolescence; enables youngsters to avoid competing with siblings; gives them an acceptable way of remaining dependent on their parents, especially those youngsters with separation problems; provides a way of winning their parents' approval without playing; and may represent an attempt to bring a troubled family together around the youngster's continuing medical problems.

Does mental outlook contribute to injuries?

A number of things increase a player's risk of injury. Physically, these include a poor state of physical fitness, overly loose or tight joints, poor strength, and malalignment of bones, particularly in the legs. But a player's mental state also can increase his or her chances of injury. When young athletes feel stressed or depressed, or preoccupied with troubling thoughts of school, home, or social life, their concentration suffers. Bad concentration can result in injury because the player wasn't paying proper attention to the game.

Are there people who fail to "listen" to their bodies?

In part; but more often the term describes someone who insists on pursuing a goal in sport in spite of pain. Some athletes truly believe in the motto "No pain, no gain" and thus plunge ahead with a physical activity even though the wise course would be to lay off for a time to let their bodies heal and recover. Such people only lay themselves open to more damaging injuries. Interestingly, they bring the same attitude into rehabilitation, telling themselves they will heal faster if only they push their rehabilitation exercises to the limit. Of course, most plunge beyond the limit and injure themselves, thus delaying their recovery and return to competition.

What mental attitude should an injured athlete bring to rehabilitation?

Certainly it should be a realistic and positive one committed to working and cooperating with the physician, physical therapist, and other members of the rehabilitation team. The player must recognize that no injury heals instantly, and accept the fact that recovery will require a certain amount of time and effort. A detailed talk with a physician will provide the athlete a recovery timetable. Nonetheless, the youngster must realize that such rehabilitation plans are approximate and that pushing herself beyond the physician's instructions for exercise can only cause harm. Patience in therapy is more than a virtue—it is a necessity.

MOTIVATING YOUNG ATHLETES

The psychological side of preparing for athletic competition, particularly in youth sports, has attracted great attention only in the past several decades. Responding to the realization by players and coaches that even the most skilled athletes can lose badly when their mental outlook fails to match their physical strengths, psychologists have explored ways to psych up athletes and put them in a winning state of mind. The key lies in improving athletes' self-esteem, self-confidence, self-discipline, and concentration, and in teaching them to recognize what creates personal stress within them and how to counter it. This, in turn, requires understanding the individual athletes—their degree of dedication to their sport, the benefits they derive from putting in long, sometimes grueling and lonely hours of practice, how they view competition (stressful or exhilarating) and winning (a personal triumph or avoiding failure). Overall, the various psychological approaches used in sports seek to control stress and self-doubts, improve skills, prepare the athlete mentally for competition, and help the athlete deal well with the outcome, whether as winner or loser.

THE RELATIVE IMPORTANCE OF WINNING

The quote attributed to the much-acclaimed football coach Vince Lombardi—"Winning is not the most important thing; it's everything"—in our opinion has done considerable harm to youth sports. Unfortunately, far too many coaches and parents instill this damaging notion in youngsters from a very early age. It equates a loss in sports, something the individual player often cannot control, with personal failure. For youngsters, the message comes across brutally clear: "Lose a schoolyard basketball game, kid, and you're a loser." A "winning-is-everything" philosophy is totally inappropriate and actually counterproductive among players in youth sports, where many play primarily for fun. Fear of failure creates more psychological stress in young athletes than any other factor in sports. This stress can create burnout, a condition where stress becomes so great the young person drops out of sports.

Okay, if winning isn't everything, what is?
Ideally, youth teams provide youngsters the pleasure of participation and companionship, the opportunity to improve their athletic skills, and a positive climate in which to grow as people. Certainly winning has its place, so long as it never becomes the coach's sole focus. The desire to win is a necessary and desirable goal, but a coach should measure a youngster's success by his or her willingness to work hard consistently and give his or her very best. Explaining mistakes and helping a child to overcome them, offering praise and encouragement rather than punishing errors with extra push-ups or laps, impressing upon youngsters that they are never "losers" no matter what the final score—this is the sort of coaching that should dominate youth sports and mark a volunteer coach as a "winner."

Interestingly, studies find that youth coaches who learn to create a positive attitude among their players actually improve their records in the win-loss column. The bottom line for coaches: Encouragement and praise work better as motivators than punishment.

What good is there for children in losing?
Every person's life includes a series of victories and defeats. Sometimes we win big; sometimes the loss seems devastating. Children need to learn how to react appropriately to defeat, and sports participation can help them learn this valuable lesson. Losses in sports usually last but a short time; we play again and eventually triumph. With guidance from their parents and coaches, children can learn to accept a lost game as a temporary setback that, while disappointing, won't ruin their lives. A positive approach to participation and performance by both coaches and parents will always help to smooth over a bad day. This positive attitude facilitates teaching, performance, and improvement.

Fine, but what must a coach do to create this positive attitude?
James E. Counsilman, a professor of physical education and swimming coach at Indiana University, once answered this succinctly: Bring enthusiasm to your coaching, create team unity, and provide good athletic training and guidance. Coaches who seem bored, who don't get excited when a player excels, or who don't yell encouragement and advice when someone errs will rarely motivate. Showing that you like coaching, that you enjoy your team and the time you spend with the players, and that you take pride in them is infectious.

What techniques can create team unity?
Unity, of course, requires a strong team spirit. No team can do its best without a sense of togetherness and cohesiveness. We see this in the pros, in college, in high school, and in youth leagues. A coach's own enthusiasm helps build team spirit. Beyond that, coaches should encourage their players' families and friends to attend games and meets whenever possible. The presence of cheering spectators encourages youngsters and builds a sense of pride and confidence. Uniforms help, even if they're nothing more than T-shirts emblazoned with the team's name. An occasional party, perhaps to start the season or to serve as a pep rally before a big game, gives players a boost. So does publicity. Many community newspapers carry short

articles on youth leagues, often relying on the coach or a team parent to provide information about a game. The idea is to provide a positive, enthusiastic environment in which each player feels he or she has an enhanced status by being part of the team.

Often, studies indicate, children with low self-esteem benefit enormously from a coach who sets guidelines they must follow, takes the time to work with them, and encourages them with praise for their success and sound suggestions to correct their mistakes.

Skilled coaches not only keep their own comments constructive, but see that their players don't get down on a fellow player. A mediocre player or even a skilled one who misses a shot, drops a pass, or falters on defense may draw harsh, biting criticism from his or her teammates. Cutting remarks can wound, and enough of this conduct can savage a team's spirit and unity. Sometimes cliques or rival groups develop within a team, generating animosity and jealousies that can damage or destroy team spirit. A coach needs to keep a keen eye out for such groups and must intervene gently, if possible, to restore harmony. Some particularly severe situations may require dismissing one or two players from the team, although this in itself risks creating further unhappiness and disunity.

5

The Young Female Athlete

The nation's youth sports movement began late in the nineteenth century as a means of keeping young boys out of trouble by occupying their time with athletic activities. The movement remained almost exclusively male for decades. Society deemed sports to be masculine activities and quite inappropriate for women of any age—with a few exceptions, such as tennis, horseback riding, and golf. Only in the past three decades have parents and youth organizations vigorously encouraged wide participation by girls in sports, particularly team sports.

Yet some of the social stigma that branded sports as "unfeminine" remains to this day. A 1967 study found that American men and women either approved or disapproved of females playing a sport depending on how well the sport fit society's traditional view of appropriate feminine behavior. Sports considered inappropriate—including football, basketball, wrestling, and field events—involved throwing a heavy object, using physical force to subdue an opponent, and face-to-face competition in which body contact was likely. In contrast, sports considered appropriate for girls and women—including tennis, golf, gymnastics, and volleyball—involved use of a light object, the body moving gracefully through space, and a barrier that prevented body contact with an opponent. Despite some changes in attitudes, stereotyping of sports as feminine or masculine continues, by adults and adolescents. A 1988 study reported that high school girls who participated in "ladylike" sports received higher status ratings from both male and female classmates than those playing "masculine" sports.

Certainly, girls cannot play on an equal footing with boys in a number of sports because of males' greater weight and muscle mass;

and full-contact sports, such as football and rugby, pose risks to the female reproductive system that make them completely unacceptable to most parents, physicians, and young women. Still, sexual sports stereotyping can prove detrimental, both socially and psychologically, to girls who want to play sports their peers and parents regard as unladylike.

PSYCHOLOGICAL DIFFERENCES

While athletes of both sexes have much in common psychologically, they also diverge on some significant points. Many of these differences appear to be the result of social conditioning rather than biological factors.

What are some examples of the psychological differences?
Scholars have probed the psyches of women athletes, and most of their findings go well beyond the scope of this book. Nonetheless, we can highlight a few of the more prominent psychological differences between young male and female athletes. For example, some studies have found that female athletes are less oriented to winning than males, but still more eager to become the best at what they do than nonathletes of either sex. Another study suggests that women—more often than men—blame their own lack of ability for athletic failure, and more often credit luck rather than their own hard work or athletic talent for victory. Yet, according to other research, adolescent girls tend to take a healthier view of sports competition, regarding winning as a positive event, whereas boys their age often take a negative approach, tending to equate winning with avoiding failure.

How do females compare to males in confidence?
Females are less likely than males to feel confident about their abilities to play sports or perform physical exercise. Psychologists find that girls lack self-confidence most often when they play sports that society, their friends, and their families regard as unladylike or in which they get no or unclear feedback on their performance. Athletes need self-confidence to excel. Counseling can help eliminate poor self-confidence—the pattern of repeatedly questioning one's performance and doubting one's ability—but preventing its occurrence is far better. This is easier said than done, since the undermining of

self-confidence usually begins early in a girl's athletic career and occurs without any evil intent. Girls need the same encouragement, opportunities, quality of equipment and coaching, rewards, and chances for success as boys. That, as Charles B. Corbin of Arizona State University points out, is what "equal opportunity" in sports is really all about. Parents can help by urging schools and youth leagues to provide equal support to young athletes of both sexes.

The woman athlete is very much an emerging social phenomenon. No one can predict whether the psychological stresses on women in sports will remain the same as they achieve greater status and as society changes its views of what constitutes proper athletic activities for females.

Are female athletes somehow less "feminine" than other young women?

This question strikes at a fundamental problem confronting girls and young women who want to play sports. Unfortunately, the long-held view of the "feminine" woman as passive, dependent, and weak still prevails throughout much of American society. Females who fail to fit this stereotype—and those who play sports usually do fail, miserably—get labeled "unfeminine." This can be a serious threat to a young female athlete's self-esteem. Some quit sports; those who remain, and particularly those who show talent and have high expectations for a future in sports, may suffer considerable anxiety, at least through their adolescence. It is up to their parents to recognize the benefits of sports and help their daughters manage these pressures.

PHYSICAL DIFFERENCES

Social acceptance aside, there remains the question of the performance differences between males and females. Although we know a good deal about the physiological differences between the two sexes and how they relate to athletic performance, the broad-based participation of girls and women in sports spans only a few decades. For example, the women's marathon only became an official Olympic event in 1984. Experience in recent years suggests that at the world-champion level, women perform beyond what many expected they could physically achieve, although their times in such events as middle- and long-distance running and swimming remain 6 to

14 percent below the men's best. Researchers won't know exactly what constitutes biological differences in athletic ability until they can study a large number of women who began their athletic training at a young age. Nonetheless, what is known about physiological differences between the two sexes provides insight into the differences in their sports performance, and helps explain why females will probably always be at a disadvantage in certain male-dominated sports.

How do males and females differ in body composition?

They differ considerably in body composition (fat, muscle, bone, etc.), particularly after puberty, and this difference affects the athletic performance of the two sexes. One key difference is the ratio of fat tissue to lean muscle. Typically, American males in their late teens and twenties carry about 15 percent of their body weight in fat, while the bodies of females consist of about 25 percent fat. And a greater percentage of male body weight consists of muscle—about 45 percent for males versus 36 or 37 percent for females. Well-conditioned athletes of both sexes generally pack less fat and more muscle than the average, but the fat differences between the sexes remain at about 9 percent—although the degree of difference does vary from sport to sport. About 3 percent of the fat in the average male and 4 percent in the average female consists of "essential fat"—such things as lecithin and the phospholipids—required for normal physiological functioning and good health. Another 12 percent in males and 15 percent in females is "storage fat"—fat beneath the skin and surrounding vital organs that the body can tap as a ready source of energy. Finally, females also carry "sex-specific fat"—fats in the breasts and those related to a woman's synthesis of reproductive hormones.

How does this extra body fat affect the female athlete's performance?

While a fat profile of an "average" American provides some indication of the differences in fat composition between males and females, considerable differences exist within the sexes as well as between them. Even among young women athletes, fat levels and body composition as a whole vary considerably, depending on their sport and the amount of energy they expend in practice and play. In some sports, carrying the fat of an average young female makes little difference in a female's performance. Indeed, in swimming, it may help. Fat increases buoyancy and this reduces drag and the amount of energy needed to complete a race. This helps explain why in world-class competition, women swimmmers come closer to the records set by male swimmers than, say, female runners do in comparison with male runners.

Some people have suggested that women's increased fat levels mean they also burn fat for energy more effectively than men. According to this argument, females therefore have an advantage in certain sports, most notably marathon running, because they are less likely to draw on glycogen stored in their muscles and liver, whose glycogen depletion seriously reduces performance. Running magazines and books pushed this idea, and as a theory, it seemed fine. But when researchers actually studied female marathoners, the fat theory proved more fancy than fact. Their greater body fat gives female distance runners no extra advantage.

What makes males stronger than females?
The superior strength of males has nothing to do with any superiority in male muscles. Rather, their advantage lies in their greater amount of muscle. Each person has a maximum level of potential strength he or she can reach and cannot exceed. Although the human male's absolute strength surpasses the female's, adolescent girls and young women can reach their potential as readily as teenage boys and young men; they just do not show it as dramatically in their body development.

In spite of the male's clear advantage in lean-muscle mass, muscle quality—the ability of a person's muscle to function—appears to be identical in the two sexes. And the muscles of females seem equally as adept as those of males at handling endurance events. Success in such events as marathons and triathlons depends heavily on the ratio of "slow-twitch" to "fast-twitch" muscles in the legs. The more slow-twitch muscle, the greater the likelihood of success in endurance events. About 80 percent of the leg muscles in world-class cyclists and distance runners are slow-twitch muscles, and the chances are equal that a male and female will have this percentage.

What effect does strength training have on a female's body?
Females can go from softie to Superwoman without a notable increase in muscle size. Strength training will certainly change the look

of a young woman's body and it will slightly increase her muscle girth, particularly in the arms and shoulders, but her biology simply doesn't allow her to "bulk up" the way iron-pumping males do. Muscle growth, but not strength, depends on testosterone, one of the "male" sex hormones. Actually, both sexes produce the hormone, but in most females testosterone levels are quite low and therefore they cannot build great masses of muscle. Weight lifting does reduce body fat, which compensates for the slight increase in muscle mass, so that women do not gain weight from strength training and may actually lose some. The end result is often an improved appearance, as well as improved athletic performance. But weight lifting also carries the potential for injury, particularly in teenagers. So safe bodybuilding requires care and restraint (see Chapter 13).

Is there a difference in cardiorespiratory response between the sexes?

Among males and females of equal fitness levels, the males have greater aerobic power, or heart and lung endurance during continuous exercise. This sex difference is barely noticeable among preadolescents, but by about age 16, and through early adulthood, boys generally have 15 to 25 percent more aerobic power than girls, as measured by their maximum oxygen intake. Differences in body composition (more total body mass and muscle, less fat in males) primarily account for this difference, but two other factors involve the blood's oxygen transport and oxygen-carrying capacity.

Studies indicate that the hearts of females generally are 10 to 15 percent smaller than the hearts of males with the same body weight, and they pump less oxygen-carrying blood with each heartbeat. After puberty, depending on their degree of physical fitness, females also have 12 to 25 percent less total hemoglobin—the iron-containing protein in red blood cells that binds oxygen so it can be carried to where it is needed—than males. Less hemoglobin and a smaller volume of blood to carry oxygen with each beat again decrease females' aerobic power.

Are these differences true throughout life?

Girls and boys most resemble each other in body composition, physiological activity, and athletic performance prior to puberty. Differences exist, but they are small until adolescence, when the differences in muscle and fat that influence athletic performance begin to appear.

Curiously, a prepubescent girl's maximum potential for aerobic power actually surpasses that of female adolescents and young adults. Yet, at the same time, these young girls burn more energy than older females. As a result, their levels of performance in such aerobic events as distance running and cross-country skiing remain below those of older girls and young women. Anaerobically, prepubescent girls also fall behind; their muscles simply fail to produce the mechanical power of women and adolescent girls, which puts them at a disadvantage in downhill skiing and sprint races on land and in the pool.

Muscle strength develops differently in boys and girls, with girls briefly getting a slight edge. Their strength spurt comes at an earlier age, either during or a few months before their growth spurt. In boys, on the other hand, strength begins increasing about a year after their growth spurt. For this reason, girls in their early teens can often compete effectively against and sometimes surpass boys their age in sports where strength is the key to success. A number of soccer and other youth leagues field mixed teams of boys and girls in the age range of 8 to 12. As long as team members are roughly matched in weight and the sport is noncontact, the American Academy of Pediatrics regards such play as essentially safe for prepubescent girls.

GYNECOLOGICAL CONSIDERATIONS

Many adolescent girls regard exercise, whether done solo or in team sports, as an important part of their life. Many also realize that an active sports life may affect their menstrual cycle or cause other gynecological problems. Too often, however, they or their physicians assume that their problems result from athletic activities. In such cases, the girls simply, and unwisely, fail to seek medical counsel, or a physician may recommend needlessly that a girl curtail or give up her exercise. Every gynecological problem deserves a thorough evaluation, no matter how "obvious" its link to athletic endeavors may appear, to accurately determine the cause and best treatment approach.

Why do female athletes suffer increased menstrual problems?
Exercise can definitely affect the complex cyclic ebb and flow of hormones within the body that produces menstruation. Both physical and psychological factors influence this monthly event, and ex-

ercise can accentuate the roles of both. Exercise can relieve mental stress and anxiety, but it can also cause stress for young women worried about their progress or about finding time to carry out their weekly exercise regimen. Both emotional stress and the physical stress of exercise can affect the brain's signals that control the delicate timing of hormone production in a woman's body. Some of these hormonal changes last but an hour or so after exercise; others are long-term and last as long as a female continues to pursue a vigorous exercise program. Physical changes that accompany exercise also play a role in menstrual problems. The exact mechanism by which strenuous exercise interferes with the reproductive cycle remains unknown, but diet changes, nutritional deficiencies, weight loss, reduced body fat, and low weight unfortunately often go hand in hand with physical activity, and with some gynecological problems in women athletes.

What are the more common problems in female athletes?
They include delayed puberty, delayed onset of menstruation, and decreased frequency of menstruation, called *oligomenorrhea,* which appears to affect about 20 percent of women who maintain vigorous training programs. Physicians regard puberty as delayed if a girl has failed to develop secondary sexual characteristics by age 13, or failed to menstruate by age 16 or within five years after breast budding. Girls or their parents have nothing to fear from delayed puberty; no physical problems result from it, although late menstruators may need some encouraging words to ease the psychological effects of being different from other girls their age. However, if a girl fails to menstruate by age 16, she should see a physician to find out the cause.

Typically, many studies show, athletic girls tend to begin their periods roughly a year later than nonathletic girls, although swimmers tend to reach the age of menarche earlier than nonathletes. Girls who menstruate late tend to have less body fat and narrow hips, to be taller and have longer extremities—clear advantages in a number of sports ranging from track to basketball. Those who menstruate early tend to shorter legs, broader hips, and more body fat—a disadvantage in most sports but an advantage in swimming.

In what sports do menstrual irregularities often occur?
Most often they occur among female runners, swimmers, gymnasts, dancers, and fencers. Some studies suggest that these problems tend

to rise with the intensity of training and loss of body weight; other studies have failed to find a relationship between training intensity and menstrual problems.

Stress on a woman's body can trigger a series of disorders ranging from minor to severe. The most subtle problem, a symptomless condition, shortens the luteal phase of the menstrual cycle and reduces the body's production of progesterone. Physicians commonly fail to spot this deficiency unless they are evaluating a woman for infertility problems. A more serious problem involves *anovulation*, a condition where a woman fails to release eggs even though her body produces the hormone estrogen. Her failure to ovulate cuts progesterone production, which allows a buildup of blood and nutrients on the lining of the uterus, which can result in severe bleeding. Heavy or prolonged bleeding can lead to anemia, and girls who experience such bleeding should seek a medical evaluation. Finally, a young woman may suffer a reduced production of estrogen, a condition that results in fewer or no periods and can create symptoms similar to those of menopause and can result in thinning bones and damage to her vagina.

Never dismiss menstrual problems in young athletes as simply sports-related. Athletes are as susceptible as nonathletes to ailments such as pituitary tumors and low thyroid activity that also can cause these disorders. When menstrual irregularities arise, a young woman should see a physician.

Dysmenorrhea, or menstrual cramps, results from an inadequate blood flow in the uterus during uterine muscle contractions that are triggered during menstruation by body chemicals called prostaglandins. Though painful, sometimes disablingly so, they usually signal no more than a normal body function. Still, young women with severe cramps should consult a physician for evaluation and therapy to ease their pain.

Must a young woman cut back her athletic activities during her period?

There is no reason for a woman to stop exercising during her period; indeed, exercise often reduces the pain, although no amount of exercise will eliminate it entirely. No one knows the mechanism for this pain relief. One leading theory suggests that exercise stimulates the production of natural painkillers in the body called endorphins; another theory suggests the pain relief comes from an increase in chemicals that dilate blood vessels and increase the blood flow in the uterus.

Studies indicate that most female athletes suffer no adverse effects in performance if they compete when menstruating. However, the performance level of a large percentage of endurance athletes, such as distance runners, does drop during their period. With this stated, it is best to let an athlete decide for herself whether she wants to compete during menstruation.

What is amenorrhea?

This disorder, cessation of menstruation, occurs more often among athletes than nonathletes, and more commonly in some sports than others. Researchers have found a high frequency of amenorrhea in gymnasts, ballet dancers, and long-distance runners—up to 34 percent in one study of women running 30 or more miles a week. Amenorrhea results from low levels of the hormone estrogen, which is associated not only with the reproductive system but strongly with the growth of bone in women. A number of studies now indicate that women who experience amenorrhea and oligomenorrhea have less bone density, which increases their risk of injury, including stress fractures. Bone density reaches it peak in women in their late teens or early twenties, and then density begins to slowly decline. The estrogen levels circulating in an adolescent's body play a fundamental role in determining her peak bone density: the less estrogen, the less dense her bones. Since women lose about 1 to 2 percent of their bone density per year until menopause and typically 5 percent or more a year after that, researchers suspect that young athletes who experience long periods of oligomenorrhea and amenorrhea are at increased risk of osteoporosis, sometimes even before menopause. Osteoporosis, a severe thinning of bone that affects a large percentage of elderly women, results in brittle, easily broken bones, including spinal fractures.

Some sports physicians favor treating athletes with decreased estrogen levels with low doses of the hormone in pill form. When Anita, a 17-year-old cross-country runner, complained to her physician about a decrease in the frequency of her periods, he recommended oral contraceptives to increase her estrogen levels, but only after a physical exam, a pelvic exam, and laboratory tests proved normal. Her estrogen levels and menstrual cycle soon returned to normal.

Is infertility a common problem among female athletes?
Although surveys find no increased incidence of infertility among female athletes, this may be more a matter of definition than an indication of the physical condition of the athletes. Fertility, by definition, includes the desire to become pregnant, and many women athletes have no such desire while pursuing their sport. Physicians know that a shortened luteal phase, anovulation, oligomenorrhea, and amenorrhea can all create infertility. Menstruation and fertility almost always return when a young woman curtails or stops her athletic activity. A number of studies indicate that these menstrual irregularities do not permanently harm a young woman's childbearing capabilities, and simply knowing this fact can ease a young athlete's fears.

Will exercise increase breast size?
Since the breast consists mostly of fat and contains no muscle, exercise does nothing to increase breast size. However, exercise will slightly enlarge the pectoral muscles beneath the breasts, giving the bosom a more ample appearance. Exercise alone will not reduce breast size either, although a general loss of body fat will result in somewhat smaller breasts. Finally, exercise never improves breast tone, which declines with age and appears largely determined by genetic predisposition.

NUTRITIONAL NEEDS

Young females differ markedly from young males in one nutritional aspect: their need for iron. Iron deficiency ranks as the most common nutritional problem in either sex, but it occurs in females more often and with greater severity. The daily iron requirements of boys and girls run about the same well into adolescence. But while the iron needs of teenage males eventually decrease, those of adolescent girls continue strong.

Why this need for extra iron?
Largely because of the monthly loss of iron-rich blood that comes with menstruation. By age 19, a young woman typically needs about twice the daily dietary iron of a 19-year-old male. But the amount of blood lost during menstruation varies considerably among females, and some women in their late teens require three or four times as

much iron as men their age. Studies show that 20 to 30 percent of young women athletes in the United States have depleted iron stores. This places them at risk of iron-deficiency anemia, a chronic blood disorder brought on by the progressive loss of the body's iron stores. It typically causes weakness, fatigue, irritability, and such gastrointestinal problems as heartburn, flatulence, and abdominal pain. Athletic participation can increase a young woman's iron loss because the essential mineral is also excreted in sweat. Substantial amounts may disappear over months of rigorous training, unless replaced by extra iron in the diet. Fortunately, iron-deficiency anemia normally responds well to treatment with ferrous sulfate.

What happens before iron-deficiency anemia occurs?
A young woman need not suffer anemia for her athletic performance to slump. A drop in the body's iron stores alone can result in lower exercise capacity. The symptoms of iron deficiency without anemia—fatigue, staleness, and a drop in performance—strikingly resemble those brought on by overtraining. A physician can readily tell if the problem relates to iron deficiency by blood tests that measure the body's store of iron. If it has been depleted, the physician can initiate treatment that will both restore performance and avoid iron-deficiency anemia. We must note, however, that the evidence to date suggests that iron deficiency is common among menstruating women, and athletic women stand no greater risk of it than non-athletes.

Should all young women athletes take iron supplements routinely?
Some researchers have suggested that female athletes should do just that to guard against iron deficiency and improve their performance. Yet an evaluation of studies on iron-supplement use shows no signs that taking extra iron benefits women who are not iron-deficient. For example, studies of healthy female basketball players and bicycle racers who took extra iron failed to find any improvement in their aerobic power. Also remember that in rare cases, prolonged use of iron supplements can result in iron overloading, a serious disorder that causes liver disease, diabetes, and even heart failure.

ANOREXIA NERVOSA AND BULIMIA

Both of these eating disorders appear more common among certain female athletes than among girls and women in general. Dancers and gymnasts are perhaps the most prone to *anorexia nervosa*, literally a form of self-starvation in which a person diets relentlessly out of fear of being fat. The cause of anorexia nervosa, which usually starts in the teens, continues to elude researchers. It also remains unclear if the need to keep a slender body to perform well in ballet and gymnastics pressures young women into becoming anorexic, or whether people with the disorder tend to gravitate to activities where thinness and dieting are not only accepted, but expected.

What are the consequences of anorexia nervosa?

This disorder can cause serious physical problems, even death, and parents and coaches should be alert for its signs. Anorexics may live on as little as 600 calories a day, and some literally come to look like survivors of World War II concentration camps. Behaviors typical of the disorder include excessive exercise, withdrawal from family and friends, lowered self-confidence, obsessive calorie-counting, weighing oneself many times daily, and an exaggerated view of how heavy one looks. Anorexics consistently deny anything is wrong with them, but quick treatment is essential for this disorder. The sooner therapy is initiated, the better the hope for cure.

What is bulimia?

This disorder is marked by an irresistible craving for food and re-peated episodes of binge eating, usually followed by self-induced vomiting. Bulimics will eat thousands of calories at a sitting, and then lose most of them through purging. Such behavior can damage most of the body's organs, particularly the heart and kidney, and occasionally can cause sudden death. Physicians have better luck treating bulimia than anorexia nervosa, but again, prompt treatment means a better chance of successful treatment.

INJURY POTENTIAL

For a time, the fact that women frequently suffer more sports injuries than men led to suggestions that nature had ill equipped the female body for the rigors of athletic competition. Later work, however,

showed that this difference in injury rates resulted far more from
inadequate conditioning by women than from some inherent weakness or defect in their bodies. Indeed, the evidence clearly shows
that injuries relate more to the sport than to an athlete's sex. In sport
after sport, the injury rate is essentially the same when researchers
compare well-conditioned athletes of both sexes.

What can a woman do to reduce her risk of athletic injury?

One major key to injury prevention and better athletic performance
remains strength training to condition the muscles and increase body
strength, a point unrecognized or ignored by too many girls and
young women interested in sports. Some fitness authorities regard
the lack of resistance training by young women as a major flaw in
the nation's sports programs, and a major reason why U.S. women
athletes often fare poorly against those of other nations in events
that require superior strength. There seems little question that young
women can readily adapt to and tolerate intensive resistance-training
regimens. And studies find no evidence that such strengthening programs, when properly designed and followed (see Chapter 13), pose
a great risk of injury to girls and young women, or reduce their
coordination, flexibility, or speed. The last refuge for those opposing
"lifting" by girls and women now appears to be the old saw that
strength training is "unfeminine."

In summary, differences in physical characteristics clearly exist between males and females, some of which do influence a young woman's athletic performance. Nothing about these differences, however,
suggests that females should shun exercise and the pleasures of noncontact sports. Quite the opposite. Girls and young women benefit—
physically, psychologically, and socially—from athletic participation.
And the continuing fall of records in women's sports show they can
perform at a high level.

PART TWO

INJURY, ILLNESS,

AND

OTHER RISKS

6

The Coach's Role in Sports Safety

Volunteer coaches provide the heart and the backbone of the nation's youth sports programs. They serve not only as athletic instructors, but often as role models and counselors to children, who listen to these adults and seek guidance from them as they might not from their own parents.

Most coaches consider their job to be developing athletic skills, teaching game and training techniques, inspiring hard work and dedication, driving home the benefits of team play, and finally, guiding their team to victory. Often, they don't think about preventing or treating injuries until they find themselves dealing with a youngster in pain.

Even physicians aren't immune to this kind of oversight. One physician's first day as an assistant coach with his son's youth soccer team illustrates the avoidable misadventures that may befall the best-intentioned volunteer:

A swift kick sent a ball crashing into the face of a young boy, causing his nose to bleed profusely. The boy needed a clean cloth or tissues to help stop the bleeding. But neither the physician nor the team's head coach nor any parent present had either. Finally, after asking parents watching a nearby practice, the physician got a few tissues and treated the injured boy. Later, he recalled, "All the time I was running around, I was saying to myself, 'I know better than this.' I should have had a just-in-case bag with me for minor injuries so we didn't have to disrupt the whole practice trying to stop one nosebleed." That assistant coach hasn't missed bringing his "just-in-case" bag to a practice or game since.

· Responding to Injuries

Coaches frequently find themselves playing doctor, trainer, and nurse to their young charges. Serving as a volunteer coach means preparing for the worst when it comes to injuries. Thinking ahead can make handling these injuries easier for the child, the parent, and the coach.

BE PREPARED

Injuries happen in sports, no matter how hard we try to prevent them. A ball takes a bad hop and leaves the shortstop with a bloody mouth. A forward falls beneath the basket and twists her knee. A running back lies unconscious after a jarring tackle. Such mishaps happen more often than we'd like, and the best time to start thinking about the proper way to react is *before* they happen.

When an injury occurs, the volunteer coach must assess it and decide what fieldside treatment to give, if any; whether the player can resume action; or if not, whether the player should seek medical attention later or be rushed to an emergency room. The majority of athletic injuries either require only simple, on-site treatment, or their seriousness and the need for medical attention become obvious quickly. Nonetheless, treating or dismissing an injury with more zeal than knowledge can worsen the damage, increase the player's pain, and prolong the time needed for recovery. In our view, all adults supervising young athletes should take a basic first aid course and know cardiopulmonary resuscitation (CPR).

Even before a team takes the practice field for the first time, the coach and assistant coaches, if any, should work out plans to care for acute injuries and to get an injured player to immediate medical attention if necessary.

There's a saying, "If you can't stand a little pain, get out of the game." Aren't injuries an expected part of sports?
Injuries happen and will continue to happen in athletics, but no one seriously interested in youth sports should ever accept the notion that injuries are inevitable. By thinking ahead, knowing the risks of injury and how to lower them, and enforcing team rules on such things as stretching exercises and using protective equipment, a coach can make an important contribution toward reducing injury, pain, and lost playing time among his or her young athletes.

What sort of things should an evacuation plan include?
The coach should know, for each site where the team competes:

- The location of the nearest telephone that can be used to call for assistance (one inside a locked school can't help)
- The telephone numbers of the local police department and the nearest ambulance service or emergency medical team
- The quickest route to the nearest hospital that will treat sports injuries
- Whether a stretcher and crutches are available at the site
- Who will drive an injured player to the hospital, if the coach doesn't call an ambulance
- Who will accompany the player to medical treatment
- Who will accompany the player home

What information should coaches get from their players in advance?
The coach should obtain each player's home telephone number and parents' work numbers; the name and number of each player's personal physician; a medical release form for each player; a list of any prescription medications the player may be taking, and a list of any known allergies or adverse drug reactions he or she might suffer. A power of attorney may be necessary for teams that travel to make sure that serious injuries like broken bones can be treated promptly.

What first aid equipment should a youth coach carry to practice and competition?
A good "just-in-case" bag includes:

- An assortment of adhesive-strip bandages, at least six of each
- Two rolls each of 1½-inch and ½-inch adhesive tape
- Gauze pads, sizes 4×4 and 2×2, six each
- Ice, cold packs, ice bags (In a pinch, a plastic bag of frozen corn or peas does nicely; the soft bag contours well around a leg or ankle.)
- A paper bag to counter hyperventilation (A hyperventilating athlete exhales too much carbon dioxide. Exhaling into the bag and then breathing from it helps return carbon dioxide to the lungs.)
- One box of tongue depressors to use as small splints

- Six cotton swabs
- A dozen alcohol swabs
- One 3-inch, one 4-inch, and one 6-inch elastic-wrap bandage
- Several small sponges
- Cleansing soap
- Two towels
- A penlight
- Sunscreen
- Scissors
- Safety pins
- A pack of facial tissues
- One bottle of hydrogen peroxide
- Ambulance telephone numbers
- Coins for pay phones

This list does not contain—nor should it—any aspirin or other pain-killers. For one thing, some people react adversely to aspirin. But that aside, unless the coach is a physician, he or she is better off letting trained medical personnel or the child's parents provide any analgesics or other medications for the child to swallow.

Finally, if the coach wears a hat and brings and uses a sunscreen, players will get the message and most will willingly follow these important precautions against severe sunburn and the risk of eventually developing skin cancer.

RESPONDING TO SPECIFIC INJURIES

How should coaches respond to head and neck injuries?
The first rule is to regard every head and neck injury as potentially very serious. Indeed, knowing what *not* to do in such injuries may save an injured player from death or permanent paralysis. A coach should assume that any player who falls unconscious during competition has suffered a head or neck injury. And the coach should suspect a head or neck injury if the player seems unalert or disoriented. Can he report the time and the day? His name? Some of his play assignments? Does he know where he is at the moment? Can the player squeeze the coach's hand with a strong grip? Can he blink, stick out his tongue, and move his fingers and toes on command? Does the player report tingling or numbness in any part of

his body, especially the arms or legs? Failing any of these tests indicates a potentially serious problem.

What are the dos and don'ts of responding to severe head and neck injuries?

DO: Call for the paramedics or other emergency medical assistance; make sure that the fallen athlete can breathe, but do not move his head or neck; see that the athlete's parents are notified at once; ask the athlete—or other witnesses—exactly what happened; provide this information to any emergency personnel who respond to give aid.

DON'T: Remove a helmet or other headgear; move the injured player; leave the athlete unattended; give any aid unless you are properly trained.

Rarely will a coach ever confront a situation fraught with more risk to an athlete than a serious head or neck injury. To help ensure a good outcome, the coach must see that emergency medical help is called immediately.

Does all this apply to so-called head dings?

Never underestimate the possible danger of a "ding," or to use another sports term, "getting your bell rung." The terms may sound benign, but in fact they mean the athlete has possibly suffered a mild concussion as the result of a blow that shook the brain inside the skull. The player typically feels no pain, walks about and often wants to continue playing, but suffers a wobbly gait, momentary confusion or disorientation, and memory problems, including an inability to remember plays; this state lasts 5 to 15 minutes. Professional, college, and even high school players frequently return to the field after their heads clear. But in our view, volunteer coaches should never permit a young athlete to return to competition the day he or she suffers a mild concussion, for everyone's sake. These players and their parents should be alerted to watch for any disorientation, headache, dizziness, or sensitivity to light, which are warnings of a more serious head injury, and to see their personal physician.

For additional information on head and neck injuries, see Chapters 11 and 12.

Aren't some bleeding situations potentially life-threatening?

Bleeding injuries commonly occur in sports, but usually pose no serious threat. Nonetheless, coaches should never dismiss any bleeding as unimportant. Even a small scrape may become infected unless properly cleaned and bandaged. Bleeding calls for ICE, an acronym that stands for Ice, Compression, and Elevation. This treatment includes applying a clean towel or cloth to the bleeding area, pressing down on it with ice, and elevating the injured area above the heart. Once the bleeding stops, the wound or cut should be cleaned before a bandage is put over it.

If a player suffers a nosebleed, it should be treated with ICE, keeping the head up and tilted forward a little to prevent the player from swallowing blood. If bleeding continues longer than five minutes, her nose should be packed with sterile gauze, leaving a short tail for the gauze's easy removal, and her nostrils squeezed gently together. The player should not blow her nose for several hours. A bloody nose may signal a broken nose, particularly in contact sports. If swelling and pain follow a nosebleed, the player should see a physician.

An athlete who suffers heavy bleeding should never return home alone, and should see a physician. Anyone who suffers a puncture wound—from a nail or a rusty fence wire—should see a physician because of the risk of tetanus (lockjaw).

Can having the wind knocked out of you cause serious problems?

It may seem so to the gasping player unable to catch a breath after a heavy blow to the abdomen or chest. But by itself, having the wind knocked out of you poses no serious threat.

Recovery takes only a minute or two, although it seems like hours to the fallen player. The player should not be allowed to get up right away or try to walk around. Any mouthpiece should be removed and the player's belt and any pad straps loosened. The athlete should rest where he lies and take rapid, shallow breaths. This panting technique aids a quick recovery; then the player should attempt slow, deep breaths. The player should be questioned to make certain no other injuries have occurred. He should rest a few minutes after recovery—followed by the coach's determination that no other problems exist—before returning to play.

RESPONDING TO ACUTE MINOR INJURIES

Ligament sprains, muscle strains, and bruises—what physicians refer to as soft-tissue injuries—account for most athletic injuries. In themselves, they pose no threat to life or limb. But people working with young athletes must remember that the bodies of youngsters differ from those of adults in ways that can mean more severe injuries from the same kind of blow or twist. One woman's sprain may be a young girl's fracture.

What makes youngsters more prone to serious injury than adults?

Human growth and development involves more than adding height. Many internal parts of the body take years to develop. The spinal column does not fully mineralize, and thus reach full strength, until sometime in the third decade of life, a fact that increases the injury risk to teenagers who lift weights. Likewise, the joints of children and adolescents differ from adults' joints in ways that give them greater protection from some injuries and greater vulnerability to others. Basically, the ligaments around the major joints of children and adolescents are stronger and more resistant to tensile, or stretching, forces than the adjacent growth plates. This has two results: First, it tends to reduce ligament and muscle injuries in youngsters. Second, it increases their chances of suffering fractures of growth plates, the areas at the ends of bones where bone growth occurs. Swelling and pain in a joint may signal a fracture of the growth plate in a child or adolescent.

What exactly are sprains, strains, and bruises?

A *sprain* involves stretching or tearing a ligament surrounding a joint. Physicians classify sprains as first-degree (minimal stretching, local soreness, but no loss of joint stability); second-degree (some tearing resulting in inflammation, some loss of function, but no instability); and third-degree (complete disruption of the ligament, pain, and instability of the joint). A *strain* causes muscle pain resulting from marked stretching or overuse. Strains, too, are classified by degrees: first-degree (mild tenderness and minimal damage to the muscle); second-degree (partial tearing of the muscle, some bleeding, spasm, and increased pain); and third-degree (complete tearing of the muscle or tendon, heavy bleeding at the site, spasm, and considerable pain and movement difficulties). A *bruise*, or *contusion*, is muscle damage caused by a blow that results in a hemorrhage of blood into nearby tissue. Bruises range from mild (localized tenderness with normal motion and no change in gait), to moderate (swelling and tenderness, some reduction of motion in the injured area, perhaps a limp in lower-extremity injuries), to severe (marked swelling and soreness, considerable loss of motion—if the bruised area lies in the legs, the athlete may need crutches).

What kind of immediate treatment should be given to a player who suffers a sprain, strain, or severe bruise?

Remember the four-letter acronym RICE, which stands for Rest, Ice, Compression, and Elevation. Nothing works better. Obviously, an athlete with any of these injuries needs rest and should play no more that day, thus avoiding the risk of further tissue damage. If pain disappears within one to three days, the player can resume his or her activity. But if pain persists after 72 hours, rehabilitative exercises prescribed by a qualified health professional become important.

But why use ice instead of heat in these sorts of injuries?

Ice simply works more effectively. The sooner it is applied, the better it works. Cold slows the firing of nerves. This deadens the pain of the injury itself and reduces the chance of muscle spasm, which causes additional pain. Cold also reduces the release of certain chemicals by injured cells, which, in turn, reduces inflammation. And cold constricts small blood vessels and reduces blood flow in the immediate area, thus limiting further hemorrhage and reducing swelling. Heat, on the other hand, increases blood flow and swelling. Studies show that rapid and continued cold treatments, or *cryotherapy*, shorten the healing time for sprains, strains, and bruises.

Ice works best in cryotherapy, and it costs the least. Cold packs sold in pharmacies also work. Cracked, chipped ice can be packed in a disposable plastic sandwich bag and held, or better yet, molded around the painful area. A cold treatment should last 15 minutes, and care must be taken not to overexpose the skin. After half an hour, the body adjusts to the cold, and the blood vessels reopen. This can increase swelling more than removing the ice. Applying a thin, wet bandage between the ice and the skin helps conduct the cold, maintains compression, and prevents frostnip or frostbite. If pain and swelling persist, it's time to consult a physician.

Why compression and elevation?

Compression proves very effective in treating the swelling that accompanies sprains, strains, and bad bruises. Typically, physicians, athletic trainers, and athletes provide compression by wrapping an elastic bandage snugly, but not tightly, around the injury. The injured athlete should wear the bandage for several days, removing it only for treatment and at bedtime.

Elevation helps reduce swelling from the buildup of fluids in injuries to the arms and legs, and particularly ankle injuries. Raise the injured part of the body to or above the level of the heart and keep it there as long as possible during the day of the injury.

What about giving an injured player some aspirin?
Don't! Aspirin can indeed kill pain, but this commonly used drug also "thins" the blood and increases bleeding, a bad thing for sprains, strains, and bruises. Acetaminophen doesn't increase hemorrhage, but it offers no anti-inflammatory action either. Evidence suggests that ibuprofen may adversely affect recovery of bone strength in some injuries, while it speeds healing in other injuries. If you are a coach, leave medicating injured athletes, even with nonprescription drugs, to their parents and physicians.

What causes delayed muscle soreness, the kind that comes on a day or two after you stress muscles you usually don't exercise much?
Experts still debate this, but many now link it to two things. First, excessive tension damages the contracting and, even more so, the noncontracting parts of the muscle. Second, increased muscle metabolism apparently creates waste products that further damage the muscle. Little can be done to prevent this soreness, except easing slowly into any new exercise, be it soccer, swimming, or softball. Stretching exercises, done gently after the pain appears, can reduce muscle soreness. Drugstores carry a variety of liniments and ointments advertised to relieve aching muscles. These medications neither prevent the problem nor speed recovery, but their active ingredients may ease the surface symptoms of delayed muscle soreness.

RESPONDING TO HEAT- AND COLD-RELATED PROBLEMS

Heat and cold weather pose problems for athletes, and can cause some of the more easily prevented sports injuries a coach will encounter. Temperatures don't have to be extraordinarily high for injuries to occur. Indeed, young athletes experience temperature-related problems, particularly those associated with dehydration, far more often than parents and coaches realize. The crying of a 9-year-old baseball player who breaks down after striking out with the bases loaded may stem more from dehydration-related behavior changes than from embarrassment.

How serious a health threat does heat really pose?

Heat can kill. Heatstroke stands second only to spinal cord injuries as the leading cause of sports-related deaths among athletes. Fortunately, such deaths are uncommon. Nonetheless, heat can cause a variety of physical ailments and pain. One particularly dramatic example of heat's harmful power occurred one hot and humid day at Ohio State University in the late 1950s. Five OSU football players collapsed following a two-hour practice. Four recovered, after athletic trainers cooled them rapidly and gave them fluids. A fifth player failed to respond, and when he was rushed to a hospital emergency room, his rectal temperature stood at 106.2 degrees Fahrenheit. He remained unconscious for 42 hours, suffered serious liver and kidney damage, and remained hospitalized for three weeks. Although he eventually recovered completely, his condition prevented him from playing any football that fall.

Aside from death, what problems can heat cause?

Physicians generally divide heat-related problems into four categories, ranging from heat cramps (the least serious) through heat syncope, heat exhaustion, and finally, potentially fatal heatstroke.

Heat cramps most often strike the calf (60 percent) and thigh (30 percent), with other muscle groups accounting for the remaining spasms. Once blamed on a loss of salt, heat cramps actually occur because the athlete fails to drink enough water during play or practice.

Heat syncope—often mistaken for simple fatigue—produces a weak, rapid heartbeat, lowered blood pressure, weakness, tiredness, dizziness, and faintness.

Heat exhaustion may occur quite gradually. Its symptoms include a slightly elevated temperature, extreme weakness, exhaustion, a strong thirst, profuse sweating, euphoric or giddy behavior, vomiting, delirium, and sometimes unconsciousness.

Finally, *heatstroke* can cause faintness, dizziness, staggering, headache, nausea, hot, dry skin, a strong and rapid pulse, a high body temperature, confusion and/or unconsciousness, and death. Sudden behavioral changes often provide the first obvious clue that a child is verging on heat exhaustion or heatstroke.

What happens within the body to produce these heat disorders?
Exercising a muscle produces heat within each of its cells, which the body must expel. This heat diffuses from the cells to blood passing through the muscle in tiny vessels called capillaries, and makes its way to the lungs. The lungs get rid of some heat, but most remains in the blood as it leaves the lungs, returns to the heart, and is pumped out into the network of arteries. When blood reaches the skin, it loses its heat in four ways—through conduction, convection, radiation, and the evaporative cooling of sweat. During strenuous exercise, sweating provides the major means of clearing excessive heat. Heavy sweating causes the body to lose great amounts of water, resulting in a decrease in the amount of blood flowing throughout the body. If the sweating athlete fails to replace the lost water, two things can happen. First, a decrease in blood volume leads to a decrease in sweating, a decline in evaporative cooling, and a buildup of heat in the body leading to the symptoms associated with heat disorders. Second, a fall in blood volume can trigger a tragic collapse of the blood circulation system. If a person's total body fluids drop drastically, by about 10 percent, then the brain orders a halt to sweating. When sweating stops, the body's temperature may soar to 106 degrees Fahrenheit or above in 20 minutes. Heatstroke may produce severe low blood pressure, irregular heartbeats, acute kidney failure, irreversible brain damage, and death.

A number of things can increase sweating, including hot and/ or humid weather, an athlete's emotional response to competition, and heavy, bulky equipment and uniforms such as those worn in football. A number of drugs increase sweating, including alcohol, diuretics (which some athletes use to keep their weight down), the anticholinergics (used to treat a variety of medical problems, including abdominal cramps, severe hay fever, and diarrhea), and the sympathomimetics (whose uses include asthma control). Certain conditions and illnesses also increase a person's risk of suffering from a heat disorder, including obesity, poor physical conditioning, anorexia nervosa, cystic fibrosis, and diabetes mellitus. Infants and young children are particularly vulnerable to heat-related problems because, compared to older children and adults, they produce more heat per pound of body weight during exercise and their bodies are less efficient in carrying blood to the skin for heat removal.

What's the best way to prevent heat disorders?

In the words of the poet Samuel Taylor Coleridge: "Water, water everywhere." As we've noted, exercise causes sweating; sweating robs the body of its vital water supply. It is imperative that coaches have plenty of water available for their young athletes, encourage them to drink water, and let them drink as much as they want to replenish their fluids. A male high school athlete working out strenuously on a hot day can lose as much as a quart of water an hour, which must be replaced for safety's sake. An athlete who remains well hydrated performs more efficiently and more effectively, and significantly reduces his or her risk of heat-related problems.

Youngsters usually find cold water the most palatable, and the body actually absorbs water at refrigerator temperature better than tepid water. Cold water does not cause abdominal cramps. Many sports physicians now recommend that athletes drink considerable water—"camel-up," as one puts it—prior to practice and competition. Coaches must make certain that their young charges drink enough of the water provided. Unfortunately, thirst alone does not tell a person when the body needs more water, and the youngster who drinks only when thirsty risks dehydration and harm. Coaches must "push the water."

Should children take salt tablets to replace the salt they lose in sweat?

No; absolutely and positively no! Contrary to a persistent myth, taking salt tablets can actually harm athletes rather than help them. Salt supplements can cause a decrease in the body's total potassium, which adds to the risk of heatstroke. Americans in general eat too much salt, and certainly enough to supply a healthy youngster's needs.

What about the beverages advertised to help athletes quench their thirst and restore important body electrolytes lost in sweat?

It's best to avoid them. They are costly, provide no added benefit over water, and can trigger nausea and vomiting, which itself causes fluid loss and further increases the danger of heat-related injury. The American College of Sports Medicine has noted that electrolyte beverages may help athletes who lose 5 percent or more of their body weight day after day in workouts. But this level of exercise intensity is totally inappropriate for children and adolescents. If team members insist on drinking electrolyte beverages, save them for after the game or practice.

What besides adequate hydration can reduce the chances of heat-related physical problems?
Heat conditioning, or acclimatization, helps. This simply means youngsters should start exercising one to three weeks before regular practice begins, starting with a 30-minute workout and building up to the typical length of their practices. Each workout should start with a series of warm-up exercises (see Chapter 2 and the chapter related to the child's specific sport). Good conditioning can prove particularly helpful in avoiding heat cramps early in the season.

Another important rule: Watch the temperature and the humidity. It truly is best to cancel practices or competitions when heat and humidity soar. Admittedly, strict adherence to this advice would all but eliminate some sports activities for four or five months a year in parts of the country. Certainly, practices and games should be held in the coolest part of the day in such areas. If youngsters must play or practice in high heat and humidity, they should start slowly and gradually build up their intensity to get accustomed to the conditions. Remember, the more heat, the more sweating; the more humidity, the more problems the body has cooling itself by evaporating sweat. Several high school football players have died from heatstroke during practices held when the temperature hovered well below 75 degrees Fahrenheit, but the humidity stood above 95 percent.

Young players should wear proper clothing during extreme weather conditions. In hot, humid weather their clothing should expose as much skin to the air as possible, because evaporative cooling is proportional to the amount of skin exposed. That means no rubber suits or sweat suits; shorts and fishnet shirts should be worn whenever feasible. Lightweight, light-colored, absorbent materials are preferable, and youngsters should change out of sweat-soaked clothes into dry ones, and remove headgear when appropriate.

Finally, coaches should try to identify players who have an

PRECAUTIONS TO TAKE BASED ON WET-BULB TEMPERATURES*

Temperature	Precautions
Under 68°F	No precautions necessary except close observation of those athletes most susceptible to heat illness (those who lose over 3% of their body weight as determined from weight charts).
69° to 79°F	Insist that unlimited amounts of drinking water be given. Ice water is preferable.
Over 80°F	Lighten the practice routine. Withhold susceptible players from participation.

*Whenever the humidity is over 95%, alter practice as described for "Over 80°F."

Source: Robert J. Murphy, "Heat Problems in the Tennis Player," in *Clinics in Sports Medicine,* April 1988, pp. 429–34.

increased risk of heat disorders and make extra certain they maintain good hydration. We've noted certain things that predispose individuals to heatstroke. Coaches should also watch for weight loss. An athlete who loses 3 percent of her total body weight during a game or practice is at an increased risk; losing 5 percent puts her at a substantial risk; and losing 7 percent signals a high danger of heat-related problems. A player who loses 5 percent of her weight should gain at least 80 percent of that loss back before returning to play or practice.

What if a player develops a heat cramp or other heat-related problems?

Heat cramps, those painful spasms that develop in major muscle groups dehydrated and stressed by exercise, obviously require the player's removal from competition. Treatment should begin immediately: apply ice packs to the muscle, stretch (don't massage) it, and see that the youngster drinks plenty of water. Occasionally, a heat cramp fails to respond to this therapy. In such cases, a health professional may have to administer intravenous fluids and a muscle relaxant.

If a coach notices the signs of heat syncope—weakness, tiredness, dizziness, faintness—he or she should sit the player down, out of direct sunshine; provide plenty of water; loosen or remove clothing; and apply iced towels to the skin to promote cooling. The coach should continue to observe the player, and if recovery fails to occur, seek medical attention.

What if a player suffers heat exhaustion or heatstroke?

Both conditions are serious, and heatstroke is potentially fatal. Both require prompt fieldside aid and medical attention.

A player who shows the symptoms of heat exhaustion should be moved immediately out of the sunlight and given plenty of water, if he is conscious and able to swallow. Next, all of his clothing should be removed, his body fanned to help cool it down, and his feet elevated. If vomiting, unconsciousness, or a very rapid pulse rate occurs, the youngster should be rushed to a hospital emergency room. Otherwise, the child should consult a physician following treatment at the playing field, to ensure that no serious heat-related problems develop.

Heatstroke may strike without warning and without prior symptoms to indicate problems from the heat. The first sign of trouble may come when a player collapses, unconscious. Heatstroke must always be treated as a life-threatening medical emergency. It is absolutely a life-or-death situation and requires reducing the player's temperature quickly. A temperature over 106 degrees Fahrenheit can cause irreversible liver, kidney, and brain damage in only a brief time. Preventing serious injury or death requires getting the body temperature, which can rise as high as 108 degrees, to drop within minutes. The victim should be stripped and his body rapidly cooled with ice packs and ice water–soaked towels. Medical assistance should be sought immediately. The player should not be transported to the hospital until his temperature is reduced. Cold therapy can be continued as the child is rushed to the hospital by ambulance or private vehicle. Such fast action can save a life. One 17-year-old football player who suffered heatstroke and a rectal temperature of 108 degrees was rushed to a hospital literally packed in ice. He returned to his team three weeks later to play the rest of the season.

We cannot stress too strongly the importance of seeing that young athletes have plenty of water readily available to drink, and that they are constantly encouraged to drink enough to keep themselves well hydrated.

For additional information on heat disorders, see Chapters 10 and 12.

What cold-related injuries threaten athletes?

Primarily, frostnip and frostbite—isolated, local tissue damage that results when skin gets exposed to freezing temperatures. Both involve injury to the skin, underlying tissue, and the blood vessels running through them. *Frostnip*, marked by a sudden whitening of the skin, occurs when ice crystals form on the skin surface. No skin freezing occurs and the condition causes no permanent damage. With *frostbite*, the skin and the cells beneath do freeze. Frostnip and frostbite most often strike the nose, earlobes, cheeks and chin, but any exposed skin surface can prove vulnerable. The two can also damage unexposed skin; fingers in tight gloves and toes in constricting shoes and boots are the most commonly affected body parts. One man suffered frostnip of his genitalia after jogging in tight-fitting pants one winter morning.

What increases the risk of frostnip and frostbite?

Risk factors include exposing bare skin to the wind and cold; being very young or very old; restricted blood flow to the body's surface areas, either because of disease or tight-fitting clothing; fatigue and poor nutrition; drinking alcohol; and smoking. Even snorting cocaine apparently increases the risk of freezing inside the nostrils.

What's the best way to counter frostnip and frostbite once they occur?

Forget the old-fashioned notion of rubbing snow on the damaged skin; it will only compound the damage. Treating frostnip is rather simple. Blow warm breath on the whitened skin; or place a warm hand on it and press firmly; or, in the case of a hand or finger, place it in an armpit. The frostnipped area will tingle and turn red as the warmth begins its cure. Frostbite, which usually occurs in very cold temperatures and/or severe winds, requires care not to further damage the frozen area. The young athlete should go indoors, if possible, or seek as sheltered and as warm a place as possible. The injured area should be warmed, but never rubbed, massaged, or soaked in hot water. Dipping the frostbitten area in water heated to 104 to 108 degrees helps. Circulating water, such as in a whirlpool bath, decreases thawing time. It is vital to ensure that once thawed, the injured area is not refrozen again by immediate re-exposure. Pain, sometimes severe, accompanies thawing and the return of blood flow to the area. A physician should examine any frostbitten flesh as soon as possible.

⊡   *The Coach as Athletic Trainer*

In an ideal world, a certified athletic trainer would assist the coaches of every youth sports team. Unfortunately, less than 10 percent of the nation's high schools employ even a single athletic trainer in their athletic programs. So the chances that a volunteer coach will ever have a professional athletic trainer working with him or her range from slim to zero. That means the nation's volunteer coaches must fulfill, as best they can, the role of athletic trainer for their teams.

What do athletic trainers do?
Their responsibilities include a wide range of injury-prevention efforts, providing first aid and emergency care, treating minor injuries, and supervising athletes as they rehabilitate their injuries.

A coach should always be aware of preventing injuries. This includes making sure that team members warm up properly and adequately prior to practice or competition. Properly stretching muscles can reduce muscle soreness and the risk of strains and sprains (see Chapter 2 and chapters on specific sports). Beyond that comes the protective taping, wrapping, and padding of athletes. The coach should see that these are done properly, when and if they are done.

What else should the coach anticipate?
Many sports require or benefit from protective equipment, ranging from helmets to mouthpieces to goggles. (The appropriate equipment is discussed in the chapters on specific sports.) The coach-trainer should check the condition of such equipment and require players to wear it, and to wear it properly. For example, a broken air cell inside a football helmet reduces the helmet's protection and increases the danger of a concussion. Helmets should be checked before a game and at halftime. Even something as seemingly unimportant as a worn-down running shoe can cause blisters or sore legs.

Finally, the coach should inspect practice and competition sites for possible hazards to players—holes, rocks, or broken glass on fields or tracks; unpadded goals; broken or loose boards on courts; improperly placed mats in wrestling or gymnastics; bleachers or other obstacles too close to the playing area; and slippery floors in locker rooms and showers.

What role does the volunteer coach have in rehabilitating an injured athlete?

Proper care when an injury first occurs can prevent or reduce hemorrhage, swelling, inflammation, and spasms, and thus reduce the time required for recuperation. In a sense, quick, proper care is the first step in rehabilitating an injury. Beyond that, the coach can supervise and encourage the player to follow, and perform correctly, the rehabilitation-exercise regimen recommended by a physician or physical therapist. Finally, a coach should never pressure players back onto the field or let players argue their way back into competition before they have recovered. A premature return may well end in another, more serious, even athletic career–ending injury.

How much taping do players actually need before practice and competition?

Taping prevents excessive movement of joints, and can help prevent injury or reinjury. Adhesive tape also can "splint" damaged soft tissue, which eases pain and promotes healing. So in certain situations taping plays an important role in athletics. Some authorities, however, feel that it has no place in youth sports, and that any youngster needing taping should not play or practice. Taping takes time, can cost a considerable amount of money, and is an art not easily learned. A great many taping methods exist (far too many to cover in this book). Properly done, these techniques provide support, stability, or tissue compression, depending on the athlete's needs. But a bad job of taping can do more damage than good. And interestingly, some players develop a psychological dependency on tape to the point that not having tape adversely affects their. play. For these reasons, volunteer coaches probably should avoid getting involved in extensive taping of their players, but they should become familiar enough with the process to recognize problems and inform players and their parents about them. Inevitably, a coach will find some team member who needs to wear tape for some reason, whether medical, psychological, or simply because the pros do it.

What are the basics of taping?

Proper taping must do the job intended effectively, and it must be comfortable. This means properly preparing the skin before applying any tape. The skin must be clean and dry, without dirt, sweat, or oily compounds. Many athletes shave hair from the tape area to allow the tape to hold better and to come off more easily. Tape should go on skin at room temperature; placing tape on skin too hot (for example, right out of a hot tub) or too cool (from ice, for example) can damage the skin.

When applying tape, make certain to overlap each strip by half its width. Apply tape with an even tension, and avoid making twists or wrinkles in the tape. These can cause blisters to form beneath the tape. Using a narrower-width tape helps prevent twists and wrinkles, and allows the tape to conform to the skin contour much more easily.

Finally, don't underestimate the importance of removing the tape correctly. An enduring sports adage holds that "If you don't want it to hurt, rip it off." Don't believe it. Ripping tape off does hurt, and it can irritate the skin and leave an annoying discomfort. Tape comes off least painfully when pulled gently along the long axis of the tape. Pushing the skin away from the tape actually produces less pain than ripping the tape off the skin. If the tape lies atop some hair, go with the grain; remove the tape in the direction the hair lies.

What problems can arise from improper taping?
Poor taping often mimics a tourniquet by compressing blood vessels and reducing the flow of blood through the taped area. Cold, numb, or blue toes, for example, indicate an improper taping of an ankle. Tape can also irritate the skin by damaging cells, or can occasionally cause allergic reactions, both of which manifest themselves as skin rashes. Consider any taping that causes pain or aggravates existing pain a bad job and remove it.

7

Overuse Injuries

The boom in youth sports has brought a puzzling array of injuries called overuse syndromes to pediatricians' offices and sports medicine clinics—puzzling because physicians previously had seen such injuries in adults but rarely in children. Physicians and physiologists long had regarded the breakdown of aging tissues as the cause of these ailments, which can range from a number of tendinitis problems to stress fractures. The increasing appearance of these ailments among children and adolescents required the experts to rethink and research the cause further. Today, the term "overuse injury" refers to a variety of problems that result when the body's ability to heal itself fails to keep pace with the microscopic injuries, or microtraumas, that occur with some repetitive action such as running or throwing a baseball. These chronic, unhealed microtraumas eventually produce changes in the body's soft tissue and bones that build into a noticeable injury.

The tendency of many youngsters to specialize at an early age in only one or two sports, and to play or train for them throughout the year, accounts in part for the great increase in overuse injuries in children and adolescents. These problems often prove difficult to diagnose and manage in young athletes. Unlike such acute injuries as a sprained ankle or a broken finger, overuse syndromes are characterized by a gradual onset and vague, often subtle symptoms that many players think they can "work out" or "play through." Some overuse injuries are associated largely with one sport, and we will discuss them in the chapters on specific sports. In this chapter we describe overuse problems that strike in a number of different athletic endeavors.

RISK FACTORS

Much remains unknown and in dispute about the precise mechanisms that cause overuse syndromes and the factors that predispose people to them. At present, we can only provide the best information available, and offer the prevention recommendations that flow logically from it.

The risks associated with overuse injuries fall into two basic categories: intrinsic (or inherent) and extrinsic (or outside) factors. *Intrinsic* factors include bone malalignments and other structural defects within the body. *Extrinsic* factors include improper technique, training errors, and using poor or improper equipment. Overuse usually results from some change in an activity, such as an increase in time devoted to training, number of practice sessions, or intensity of practice. Or the change may come in the form of new equipment—such as new shoes or a new tennis racquet—or a new playing or running surface. It is important to determine what caused an overuse injury, or the youngster will continue as before and suffer a recurrence. Overall, we can list the risks associated with overuse syndromes as anatomic malalignments; changes that occur in a growing body; poor flexibility; muscle-tendon imbalances; certain diseases; and problems caused by training methods, playing surfaces, and equipment.

Exactly what parts of the body can be out of alignment?
Malalignments of the spine, hips, or legs can affect the performance of young athletes and predispose them to injury. Because of a malalignment, the body carries out an activity, such as running, improperly or less efficiently. This can lead to overuse of a joint or a group of joints.

How do growth and poor flexibility contribute to overuse injuries?
Growth affects both the body's bones and its soft tissues. During growth spurts, the muscles and tendons around the joints tend to tighten, resulting in a loss of flexibility. Unless the young athlete makes a conscientious effort to maintain flexibility during periods of accelerated growth, the risk of injury, both acute and from repetitive motions, increases. Then, too, many young athletes enter their greatest growth period at about the same time their interest in a particular

sport intensifies. If their efforts to improve their skills through frequent and repetitive practice become overzealous, they increase their
risk of overuse problems. Finally, growing evidence indicates that
the cartilage of a still-growing youngster is more prone to microtrauma and overuse injuries than the cartilage of an adult.

What do you mean by a muscle-tendon imbalance?

With growth comes increased strength. But for the young athlete,
this increased strength and the overdevelopment of certain muscle
groups can create an imbalance between the strength of the muscles
and tendons of specific joints, which appears to play a role in some
overuse syndromes. Baseball pitchers, for example, may experience
a pattern of muscle development that may predispose them to partial
dislocations and "impingement" problems in their throwing shoulder (see Chapter 17). Muscle-tendon imbalance ranks high among
the risk factors for overuse syndromes.

What diseases can increase the risk of overuse injuries?

While an uncommon factor in young athletes, a variety of health
problems can pose a threat. These include infections, arthritis, circulatory problems, previous fractures, and nutritional deficiencies.
Young women with continued menstrual irregularities resulting from
running (see Chapter 5) risk losing some bone-mineral density,
which increases their risk of suffering overuse injuries in general and
stress fractures in particular.

Everyone emphasizes training. How can this harm a young athlete?

In a few words: Too much too soon. Overuse syndromes really do
result from overexercising the body to the point that it can't repair
the microscopic damage inflicted upon it. Sports medicine specialists
say that by far the largest percentage of overuse injuries they see
occur in people who have just recently taken up a sport, or have
markedly increased the intensity of their training. Prudence in practice makes for a healthier, stronger body. The idea is to build strength,
endurance, flexibility, and speed at a pace that doesn't push the body
beyond its powers to heal itself. Too often, youngsters plunge into
training too quickly, running too long and too often, say, or training
on an inappropriate surface, such as concrete. Training errors probably account for more overuse injuries than any other risk factor.

Do training errors include a player's choice of equipment?
Definitely. And as we indicated above, playing and practicing surfaces can also cause overuse syndromes.

Shoes can literally break a player. Whatever the sports, the shoes should be well made, properly fitted, and designed for that sport. Not all shoes suit all sports, no matter how high their quality. Runners need shoes with a different construction than, say, basketball or aerobic dancing shoes. Some tennis racquets appear more likely to cause overuse injuries than others. Runners increase their risk of injury when they run on very hard surfaces or banked tracks. Dancers need some give in the floor on which they practice or perform.

MECHANISMS OF INJURY

Inflammation is the common symptom of the overuse syndromes. Studies indicate that repetitive motions create repeated microtraumas which over time result in the local destruction of tissue. That initiates the inflammation process, which plays a vital role in the healing process. Inflammation demands respect, and treatment. If a young athlete ignores this clear warning of tissue damage and continues to play, the inflammation grows worse and can become chronic, increasing the destruction of surrounding tissue. Typically, the athlete who fails to get treatment or to change the cause of the repetitive microtrauma goes from mild pain that lasts a few minutes after a workout, to moderate pain and some tenderness, to pain during workouts severe enough to throw the athlete off motion, and eventually to disabling pain and stiffness.

What is the most common overuse problem?
In terms of the type of tissue affected, the tendons clearly suffer most often. Tendons connect muscle to bone and they stretch when muscles contract. For the most part, tendons are quite resistant to injury from this natural process. However, the recurrent stretching associated with frequent, long, intense practices can fatigue the tendons and result in tiny tears and *tendinitis*, or inflammation of the tendon. Moreover, as noted earlier, growth makes adolescents more susceptible to tendon problems than adults. The type of tendinitis most likely to strike young athletes depends upon their sport. The knee is a prime target in a number of sports, including distance running,

basketball, and volleyball. Baseball and tennis players more often suffer tendinitis in the shoulder and/or elbow.

What is bursitis, and how does it affect young athletes?

It's a real problem for some, and the cause often appears to be overuse. Bursas are sacs that act as cushions between tendon and bone, or skin and bone, in joints and other parts of the body. *Bursitis* means an inflamed bursa. The repeated friction of tendon or bone rubbing against a bursa during a recurrent motion can lead to this inflammation. Much less often, the degeneration and calcification of a nearby tendon releases chemicals that trigger bursitis.

Is there a particular risk of overuse injury to youngsters' cartilage?

Yes. The presence of "growth cartilage" in their bodies makes young-sters susceptible to several overuse injuries not seen in adults. Growth cartilage exists at three sites: the growth plate of bones; the articular, or joint, surfaces; and the apophyses, or points where tendons insert into bones. Growth-plate cartilage rarely suffers damage from re-petitive motions, but joint-surface cartilage—particularly in the knee, ankle, and elbow—is highly susceptible to overuse injury.

Can overuse affect the nervous system?

Yes, but rarely and largely indirectly. The body's peripheral nerves may suffer as the result of overuse injuries and create sensory and motor problems for a young athlete. Such a problem may occur when swelling associated with an overuse inflammation compresses a nerve. Excessive muscle growth also may press on a nerve. A few athletic endeavors themselves create direct pressure on a nerve. For example, bicyclists sometimes grip so hard and put such pressure on the hand's ulnar nerve that they develop a condition called "han-dlebar palsy."

Where do stress fractures fit into the overuse picture?

An *acute* fracture results from a severe injury—for example, a sudden blow or fall that breaks bone. A stress fracture, on the other hand, evolves from an overuse, or overstressing, of normal bone that causes microtrauma and eventually bone failure. Tight muscles and tendons and certain anatomic malalignments appear to increase the risk of stress fractures. The problem was recognized in military recruits in the mid-1800s and called "march fatigue." But with the growth of organized youth sports, the problem became apparent among young athletes in the early 1950s. Stress fractures are sometimes called "the great masquerader" because their symptoms mimic those of a number of other problems.

Don't X rays reveal stress fractures?

Frequently not, at least not for six or eight weeks after a youngster begins complaining of pain. Although costly "bone scans" that use radioactive isotopes may reveal stress fractures missed by X rays, physicians usually rely on symptoms and a medical history to diagnose stress fractures. Typically, symptoms—pain and localized tenderness—come on gradually and worsen over two or three weeks. Players usually notice the pain initially after practice or play. Sometimes swelling arises at the fracture site, or the youngster will feel pain at the site when another place on the bone is struck. Any time a young athlete complains of persistent, bone-related pain occurring during and after play or practice, a parent should consider a stress fracture as a possible explanation.

Do girls get stress fractures more often than boys?

Apparently, and for two reasons. First, some girls tend to be less physically fit when they plunge intensely into a sport. Second, female runners, gymnasts, and dancers suffer a higher rate of stress fractures than males, and this appears related to a reduction in their estrogen levels (see Chapter 5). Women in these sports suffer an increased rate of amenorrhea, or a failure to menstruate, resulting from lowered estrogen, which also adversely affects the body's ability to metabolize calcium. If amenorrhea lasts longer than one year, the body's ability to build new bone will suffer, increasing the danger of stress fractures. Calcium metabolism may also suffer as the result of the excessively low-fat, low-calorie diets consumed by many dancers and gymnasts.

In what bones and what sports do stress fractures most often occur?

Both the incidence and the location of stress fractures vary from sport to sport. No national figures exist, but the evidence available suggests that in general, the more running a sport requires, the greater the risk of stress fracture. One recent study of 320 athletes with stress fractures found that 69 percent suffered their injury from running,

8 percent in fitness classes, 5 percent in racquet sports, and 4 percent playing basketball. The rest of the injuries occurred across a spectrum of other sports, including soccer, gymnastics, football, and hockey.

The tibia, the larger of the two lower leg bones, ranks as the bone most often damaged by stress fractures. About half these injuries occur in the tibia, with the metatarsals (the long bones of the foot) and the fibula (the thinner lower leg bone) coming in a distant second and third. In recent years, sports medicine specialists have noted an upswing in stress fractures of the kneecap among adolescents engaged in running and jumping sports. However, stress fractures have struck just about every bone in the lower extremities, and in any number of non-weight-bearing bones as well. Baseball pitchers, for example, most often suffer stress fractures of the scapula (shoulder blade) and humerus (upper arm bone), while too much batting practice can cause a stress fracture in a rib.

How do you treat stress fractures?
Most stress fractures respond very well to brief treatments with an anti-inflammatory medication and a painkiller, and prolonged rest—which means cessation of whatever activity caused the injury. Without rest, the player runs a high risk of further damage. Usually a physician will recommend alternative exercises to maintain the young athlete's conditioning.

A stress fracture develops slowly, and painfully, and pain constitutes a warning sign that young athletes all too often ignore. If a stress fracture occurs, it is time to look into the player's training techniques, intensity, duration, and equipment to see what might be altered to prevent further injury. Unless these things are assessed and problems are corrected, the youngster stands a high risk of suffering a recurrence.

SPECIFIC OVERUSE INJURIES

Overuse injuries essentially signal overtraining. Some overuse syndromes occur almost exclusively in one sport; others strike players in several sports. In the following pages we will explain the more common of these multiple-sports problems.

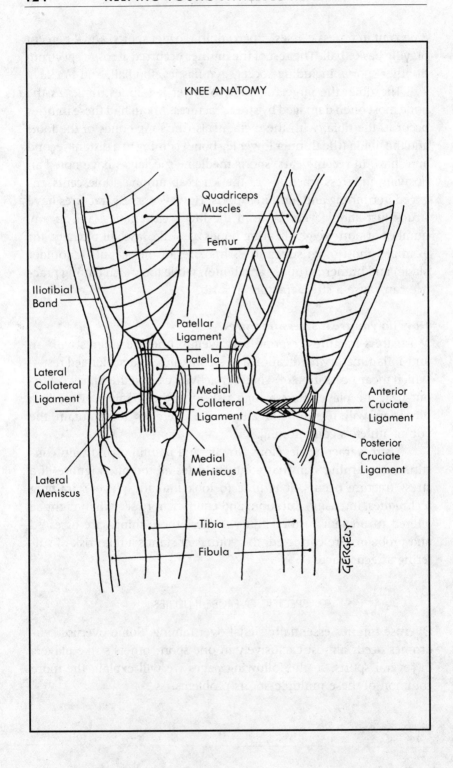

KNEE ANATOMY

Quadriceps Muscles

Femur

Iliotibial Band

Patellar Ligament

Patella

Lateral Collateral Ligament

Medial Collateral Ligament

Anterior Cruciate Ligament

Posterior Cruciate Ligament

Medial Meniscus

Lateral Meniscus

Tibia

Fibula

GERGELY

What is the most common type of overuse syndrome in young athletes?

A group of injuries known medically as *traction apophysitises* are among the more common. The most prominent of this group is Osgood-Schlatter disease.

Traction apophyses are the active growth sites in children and adolescents where growth cartilage joins tendon and a bone. Overuse can result in microtrauma that produces pain and swelling, and sometimes an overgrowth of bone and cartilage. This condition is known as a traction apophysitis. While Osgood-Schlatter disease at the knee, Sever's disease in the heel, and medial epicondylitis in the elbow are the most common types, all the apophyses have the potential for injury from overuse.

What exactly is Osgood-Schlatter disease?

This traction apophysitis, named for the two physicians who first described it in 1903, occurs at the base of the knee where the tendon attaches to the tibia. Pain, tenderness, and sometimes swelling or a bony prominence gradually develop directly over the injury, about an inch below the kneecap. The pain grows worse when the area is pressed or the young athlete forces the leg to full extension.

Osgood-Schlatter disease appears soon after a growth spurt begins, and historically it has generally occurred more frequently in boys than in girls. However, this pattern appears to be changing rapidly. As more and more girls play sports requiring jumping, such as gymnastics and basketball, the incidence of Osgood-Schlatter disease in females has risen.

What treatments work for Osgood-Schlatter disease?

In some cases, Osgood-Schlatter disease appears to be as much a symptom of growth as it does of injury. For this reason, an increasing number of physicians allow youngsters with mild Osgood-Schlatter symptoms to continue playing their sport. If pain necessitates treatment, it may be alleviated with RICE (see Chapter 6) and a nonprescription anti-inflammatory drug such as ibuprofen.

This overuse problem may persist for a year or more without progressing to any risk of damage to tissue in the knee. However, if swelling occurs, both the patient and his or her training techniques need to be carefully examined to identify the cause of this more serious symptom. A physician who can identify no specific cause may recommend what are called relative rest and strengthening exercises. If this is the recommendation, the young athlete stops the activity associated with his or her injury, but substitutes another activity to keep physically fit. In addition, rehabilitation should include straight-leg-raise strengthening exercises and exercises to stretch the quadriceps. In those rare cases where a tiny piece of bone has also torn away, wearing a leg brace for a brief time when returning to training may prove beneficial to the young athlete. For more common cases, an "Osgood-Schlatter pad" protects the injury site from direct pressure and thus eases pain. These felt pads can be fitted easily, worn comfortably, and work quite effectively.

What is Sever's disease?
Sever's occurs at the heel bone, and again, the ailment is characterized by localized pain and tenderness. It occurs most frequently in children and young adolescents who participate in running sports, and usually follows an increase in the amount of running.

How do physicians treat this ailment?
In Sever's disease, once a physician has ruled out other sources of heel pain, therapy includes stretching and strengthening exercises for the lower extremities and sometimes orthotics, or special shoe inserts. Some physicians allow many of these youngsters to continue sports while treating them with RICE and a nonprescription anti-inflammatory medication.

What is medial epicondylitis?
Medial epicondylitis is another traction-apophysitis disorder, which develops in the last of the elbow's growth sites to close, the medial epicondylar apophysis. It can strike as late as age 19, and usually occurs in youngsters who play racquet or throwing sports. A gradual onset of pain and tenderness provides a warning signal.

What is the treatment for medial epicondylitis?
Youngsters who develop this disorder must cease the sports activity that led to their injury, but they may substitute another that won't aggravate their sore elbow. Once cleared to resume their sport, they must ease themselves back into play. A baseball pitcher, for example, must begin by throwing slowly and only for short distances, say, 10 or 12 yards, and progressively increase the speed and distance daily.

Aside from Osgood-Schlatter disease, what overuse injuries affect the knee?

In young athletes, the knee and kneecap suffer more microtraumas than any other part of the body. Most knee overuse injuries develop in the muscles and tendons responsible for straightening the leg, rather than in the knee's bones, ligaments, or meniscus cartilage. These muscles, which support the knee joint, must accommodate the rapidly growing bones of adolescents. Failure to do so can create damage that grows greater with repetitious motion. Sometimes the pain develops gradually, sometimes it occurs suddenly during or after some particularly stressful activity, such as running up and down stairs at a stadium.

Sometimes youngsters develop *chondromalacia* ("runner's knee"), a painful condition in which cartilage in the knee softens and even erodes.

Isn't kneecap pain a significant problem in youth sports?

A number of problems can cause pain at the kneecap. Medically, we call these problems *patellofemoral syndromes,* and together they constitute the most common causes of chronic knee pain among young athletes. Typically, they occur in sports that involve running. In most cases, a youngster will complain of pain at the knee, although some talk more about a "weak knee" or a sensation that something isn't right in the knee. Players usually first notice the problem after running or when they force their leg from flexed to completely extended. Some even feel pain with the leg fully bent, or report a grinding sensation when they extend the leg. Occasionally, swelling occurs. The pain most commonly occurs on the outside of the knee. Unfortunately, the pain also can occur anywhere in the knee, often making an accurate diagnosis of patellofemoral syndromes difficult.

Sometimes these knee problems follow an acute injury to the knee, such as a blow from a football helmet or shoulder pad. But far more often, patellofemoral pain results from a combination of problems such as anatomic malalignment of the legs, tight hamstrings, and overtraining—usually running too far too often.

Do children and adolescents with these lower-extremity problems risk more than pain?

The kneecap may have a tendency to slip out of alignment, usually toward the inside of the knee. This *subluxation* (partial dislocation) of the kneecap may cause irritation of the underlying knee cartilage, thus causing pain and perhaps leading to eventual softening of and damage to the cartilage (chondromalacia). A physician often can spot the potential for these problems with a quick anatomic evaluation given as part of a preparticipation physical examination.

Many subluxations can be treated or prevented with exercises that strengthen the quadriceps and stretch the hamstrings. Indeed, tight hamstrings so often play a role in so many patellofemoral syndromes that "hamstrung knee" is another name for patellofemoral pain. For a number of reasons, including their knees, young athletes should keep their hamstring flexible and strengthen their quadriceps.

What can you tell me about "jumper's knee"?

As the name implies, this inflammation of the knee's patellar, or quadriceps, tendon (also sometimes called the patellofemoral ligament) occurs among participants in jumping sports, but it can afflict runners as well. Its cause is more often a problem of overuse of normal knees than anatomic defects. The player complains of pain all around the knee, but particularly under it. Usually, examination reveals tenderness with minimal swelling. However, depending on the severity, symptoms may run from tenderness alone to a combination of tenderness, swelling, redness, and heat. Stretching the hamstrings and quadriceps and strengthening the quadriceps help to prevent jumper's knee. So, apparently, do wearing well-fitted shoes in good condition and training on the proper surfaces.

A player who suspects he or she has developed jumper's knee needs a physician's evaluation. For mild forms of this tendinitis, a physician usually reemphasizes the need for stretching and strengthening exercises and adequate warm-ups, and recommends icing after participation and perhaps anti-inflammatory drugs. If pain occurs during play, the physician may order a rest or add heat treatments before the player warms up. If pain becomes chronic, the player must take a prolonged break to let the tendon heal.

What is "iliotibial tendinitis"?

It's another name for *iliotibial band friction syndrome,* or *IBFS,* an overuse ailment that in sports primarily afflicts athletes who run a lot. The iliotibial band consists of a wide swath of connective tissue that runs down the outside of the thigh from the top of the hip to the lower leg just below the knee. The symptoms of IBFS consist of pain, tenderness, and inflammation that develops gradually at the outside of the knee. The injury apparently results from the continued friction of the iliotibial band moving back and forth over a protrusion of bone, called an epicondyle, at the base of the femur (thighbone). This causes inflammation of the iliotibial band itself and the bursa that lies beneath the band at the knee.

Long-distance running or overstriding, particularly downhill or on banked tracks, aggravates the knee injury and the pain. Several things can predispose young athletes to IBFS. These include training on uneven ground, running in badly worn shoes, having an especially tight iliotibial band, and having anatomic abnormalities, including an especially large epicondyle on the femur.

Prevention provides the best treatment for IBFS. Athletes should stretch their hip flexor muscles and the iliotibial tract, and avoid running on terrains that increase the risk of the ailment.

One simple stretching exercise for the iliotibial band is to stand with the feet about shoulders' width apart and lock the knees. Alternately raise one leg and then the other across the body as far up as possible so the foot ends on a line with and well above the opposite knee. Do 10 sets. Rest briefly and then do a second set of 10 raises for each leg.

If IBFS develops, the young athlete should reduce the amount and frequency of training, and ice the knee after running (see Chapter 6). A physician may suggest the use of anti-inflammatory drugs. Even with mild cases, resolving IBFS can take six weeks or more. If pain persists, the youngster should again consult a physician to determine if there is some other cause.

Can you explain "shin splints"?

Pain at the front of the lower leg, often called shin splints, ranks high among the more common and more confusing overuse syndromes afflicting young athletes. The term "shin splints" tells us little about the specific injury, because people have applied the term to any number of problems, including strained muscles, tendinitis, stress fractures, injuries at the point where muscle attaches to bone, and the so-called compartment syndromes. Today, most physicians and athletic trainers—but certainly not all athletes or the public at large—use the American Medical Association's characterization of shin splints as "pain and discomfort in the leg from repetitive running on hard surfaces or forcible excessive use of the foot flexors'' resulting in injuries that cause inflammation of the muscles or tendons.

Within this definition, the symptoms of shin splints usually consist initially of diffuse pain and tenderness at the front of the lower leg, the shin, at the beginning of a workout that subsequently disappear but return in a few hours. Later the pain begins with the warm-up and continues throughout the workout and for several hours after. In the chronic form of this disorder, even ordinary daily activities can trigger pain. Shin splints most often occur in unconditioned persons, or in athletes who switch to another sport without conditioning the tibialis muscles in their lower legs—say, a swimmer who takes up aerobic dancing. When shin splints strike, they almost always follow an increase in the intensity of training.

Recommendations for preventing shin splints consist of some familiar advice: Wear well-fitted shoes in good condition designed for the specific sport; warm up and stretch the leg muscles well before play or practice; play only on proper surfaces—don't train on cement, for example; and increase training intensity and duration slowly.

Actually, prevention is the best treatment for shin splints. If they develop, nothing works well but rest—stopping or greatly reducing the activity causing the muscle or tendon inflammation—sometimes aided by the use of an anti-inflammatory drug. Athletes with weak tibialis muscles should strengthen them to help avoid a recurrence of shin splints. Some people also benefit from the use of orthotics in their shoes, and some trainers tape an athlete's shins, although taping's effectiveness remains in dispute.

Physicians can usually distinguish muscle and tendon injuries in the lower leg from stress fractures in the shin. It is equally important to distinguish shin splints from the compartment syndromes. A young athlete with shin pain should consult a physician for proper diagnosis, since quick intervention may mean a faster return to sports activities.

What overuse injuries most commonly affect the foot and ankle?
Achilles tendinitis—an inflammation of the tendon that runs down the lower portion of the calf and attaches to the heel—and plantar fasciitis, an inflammation of the thick tissue beneath the bones of the foot that extends from the heel out to the toes.

What kind of problems does Achilles tendinitis pose?

This inflammation frequently recurs in those young athletes who suffer it, leaving them limping and costing them dearly in training and playing time. Its cause is a combination of a short Achilles tendon and stress inflicted by running and jumping, which produces microscopic tears and occasionally even a partial rupture. Runners suffer from Achilles tendinitis more often than other athletes, but players in other sports—including basketball, tennis, and soccer—also develop it.

While pain around the Achilles tendon generally constitutes the chief symptom, discomfort may come in one of several patterns. Some athletes feel pain and stiffness when they get up in the morning or when they begin a workout, but this disappears as the body warms up. Others experience pain that continues throughout any energetic activity, but that eases with rest. Still others suffer constant and disabling pain from their inflamed tendon that leaves them unable to participate in their sport. A medical examination reveals tenderness at the Achilles tendon and sometimes a palpable or even visible thickening of the fibrous cord.

Young athletes can take several steps to prevent Achilles tendinitis. These include doing daily exercises to strengthen the lower-leg muscles and maintain their flexibility; wearing well-designed, properly fitted athlete shoes and replacing them when they become excessively worn; using an orthotic device if prescribed by a physician or podiatrist; and avoiding training on excessively rigid and uneven surfaces. When Achilles tendinitis does develop, a young athlete should reduce his or her training time considerably—even stop, in severe cases—and apply ice to the inflamed tendon after a workout. A physician may prescribe an oral anti-inflammatory drug, a heel lift to ease strain on the Achilles tendon, and heat treatments before a workout.

Two ailments closely related to Achilles tendinitis are *peritendinitis*, a general tenderness due to an inflammation of the sheath covering the tendon, and *retrocalcaneal bursitis*, an inflammation of the bursa where the tendon attaches to the heel.

What is plantar fasciitis?

It is one of the more difficult and incapacitating overuse injuries, often prolonged in duration. Commonly called a "stone bruise" or a "heel spur," this injury occurs when the plantar fascia—the tissue between the long bones of the foot and the sole—comes repeatedly under tension, as it does when someone runs a lot. This causes microtears in the fascia, resulting in a painful inflammation toward the back of the foot where the fascia attaches to the heel bone. Typically, young athletes complain of severe pain when they try to take their first steps in the morning, with the pain then decreasing with normal walking, but increasing with athletic endeavors, especially any running or jumping. Sometimes a bone spur does occur at the heel, but this is a result of the overuse injury and not a direct cause.

A tight Achilles tendon, flat feet, a high, rigid arch in the foot, running uphill or on very soft terrain such as sand, and a sudden increase in weight or training intensity all increase the risk of plantar fasciitis. Efforts to counter these risk factors can help prevent the injury. These include exercises to stretch the Achilles tendon and the feet's fascia; wearing athletic shoes with an energy-absorbing heel cushion; and gradually building up the amount of running, rather than increasing it sharply.

Treating plantar fasciitis calls for reducing or stopping running, icing the sore foot, and if prescribed, taking oral anti-inflammatory and/or antipain medications. Severe cases may require a cortisone injection. Once pain subsides, the young athlete can begin stretching and strengthening exercises and the physician may recommend taping the foot to ease tension on the plantar fascia. Recovery usually takes about six weeks, and often pain persists for three to six months. In some cases, the injury leaves people with mild pain whenever they run or jump.

Do overuse syndromes afflict the hip?

They do, but rarely in children and adolescents. However, three that may occur are trochanteric bursitis, iliopsoas tendinitis, and stress fractures. The bursitis appears to occur particularly in people with one leg shorter than the other, or in youngsters with tight hamstrings and connective tissue in the thigh called fascia lata. The tendinitis, sometimes called "snapping hip," usually develops in young gymnasts and dancers. A snapping sound accompanies pain that strikes the inner hip when they lift their leg, move it outward, or rotate it to the side. Treatment calls for relative rest and strengthening exercises and sometimes ultrasound or deep heat therapy. We have discussed stress fractures earlier in this chapter.

Where does the back fit into the overuse syndrome picture?
Low-back pain occurs commonly among athletes. In general, this can result from three basic "overuse" mechanisms. Some athletes with properly shaped spines develop problems because they subject their backs to excessive amounts of routine forms of stress, which cause microscopic damage that never gets the time needed to fully heal. Others have abnormal spinal structures that produce micro-trauma and pain with even minor amounts of stress. Finally, some athletes have abnormal spines, inherited or otherwise, and risk severe pain when they put their backs under extreme stresses, such as those seen in dance and gymnastics.

Among the overuse injuries of the back that strike athletes are stress fractures of the spine's pars interarticularis (see Chapter 14); pain that occurs with an abnormal inward curve of the spine called *hyperlordosis;* and herniated (ruptured/slipped) discs. Finally, in young athletes only, we see pain that results from microscopic injuries to an apophysis (growth area) of a vertebra. Any of these injuries requires the attention of a physician.

Are the shoulder and elbow subject to overuse injuries, too?
Any joint is at risk of some overuse syndrome. The shoulder is particularly prone in all throwing and overhead sports, such as baseball and tennis. We discuss such overuse injuries as "Little League shoulder" and shoulder impingement syndromes in Chapter 17, and overuse injuries to the elbow in Chapters 15 and 17.

PREVENTION, TREATMENT, AND REHABILITATION

Sports medicine specialists, physiologists, physical education professionals, athletic trainers, and others who research physical activity and its effects on the human body have yet to determine precisely the minimum amount of athletic training that will prove beneficial to children and adolescents and the maximum levels to which they can safely drive themselves. But drive themselves many do, and the result is often an overuse syndrome. Prevention, the emphasis throughout this book, is always easier and less painful than treatment and rehabilitation. But if an injury develops, early recognition and prompt treatment will reduce the time needed to heal it and the amount of time the young athlete will lose from his or her sport.

Once healing has occurred, however, proper rehabilitation must follow, or chances of an injury's recurring remain high.

What general recommendations do you make to help prevent overuse injuries?

The preparticipation sports physical (see Chapter 2) should always include an assessment of the young athlete's specific body type. Since malalignments of various parts of the body contribute to a variety of overuse syndromes, spotting anatomic problems in advance allows athletes to take preventive measures and learn the warning signs of injury. Preparticipation physicals also can detect growth spurts, which can greatly increase a youngster's vulnerability to some injuries, and allow athletes and their coaches to take countermeasures.

Also, we cannot stress enough the importance of flexibility. Warming up and stretching the muscles and tendons can pay huge dividends in preventing injury, and help improve performance. Stretching should always follow a brief warm-up—usually just enough to create a light sweat—because stretching "cold" muscles isn't as effective and can itself lead to injury. Strength training (see Chapter 13) also offers increased protection, but this may best be left until adolescence. And even then young athletes need the guidance and supervision of a knowledgeable coach or athletic trainer in selecting and carrying out a training regimen suited for their sport and their stage of development. Otherwise, a youngster risks potential injury or improper body development, which may reduce flexibility and hamper performance.

Finally, young athletes must not use an improper technique for their sport, and must avoid excessive intensity or duration in their training. These errors, as much as anything, will lead to overuse injuries.

Are there general treatment rules for the overuse syndromes?

Prevention remains the best treatment, because the athlete will continue to repeat the mistake causing the problem unless better educated about the risks of improper technique and overtraining.

Pain and inflammation occur in all overuse injuries. So the first goal is to reduce these symptoms and allow the injury to heal. Treatments vary somewhat from one type of overuse syndrome to another, but typically include abstaining from or participating less in the sport that caused the injury, using some over-the-counter or prescription anti-inflammatory drug, applying ice and/or heat, and sometimes having ultrasound and/or electrical-stimulation treatments. Often physicians or physical therapists will recommend an alternative form of exercise—such as running in deep water, swimming, bicycling, or rowing—to help a youngster maintain strength, flexibility, and cardiorespiratory conditioning.

When can a young athlete compete while injured?

A safe rule is never, and if playing poses any threat of a more serious injury, as with a stress fracture, no one in good conscience can violate that rule. However, athletes by their nature are competitive and many are quite willing to endure some pain and discomfort in exchange for participating in a major athletic event. If participation does not threaten to seriously aggravate the injury, some physicians feel a young athlete can compete. The decision to "play hurt," however, should never be made without consulting a physician and thoroughly assessing any risks.

Do parents have any role in rehabilitation?

They have a very important role. Young athletes' eagerness to get back to their sport is often shared by their parents. Indeed, sometimes pressures from parents are responsible for overtraining or a too-rapid return to play after injury. But going back too early, or too intently, or without evaluating the cause of the overuse injury frequently results in a reinjury that proves even more debilitating. Parents need to understand the course of rehabilitation outlined for their youngster—the specific stretching and strengthening exercises, how they are done, and how often they should be done, for example—and what improvements must occur before their child can return to action. Children and adolescents often don't fully understand or comprehend the importance of rehabilitation. They frequently hear what they want to hear and exclude qualifiers, such as anything following the word "if," in sentences such as: "You can resume playing in two weeks if . . ." Parents need to know the details of a rehabilitation plan to properly ensure that their injured youngsters have made the progress that will allow them to safely return to their sport.

8

Playing with Chronic Illness

Debbi suffered from insulin-dependent diabetes, and at age 15 turned fiercely rebellious against the chronic illness that dominated her life and her relationship with her parents. She frequently refused to administer her daily insulin injections, she skipped school, and her emotional state vacillated between happy and depressed, with the downside of her outlook increasingly evident. Finally, she ran away from home. Psychological counseling helped her mental state, but only slightly improved her willingness to take her insulin as prescribed. Then, at the urging of her physician, and over the initial objections of her mother, Debbi began swimming competitively on her high school team. Almost immediately, her diabetes control and school attendance improved dramatically. She later successfully terminated her counseling sessions and went on to earn a college degree. Today Debbi credits her swimming, which she has continued as an adult, with turning her mental outlook and life around.

Debbi's experience is far from unique. Participating in sports is possible for many children suffering from such chronic ailments as diabetes, epilepsy, asthma, cystic fibrosis, and mental retardation, and for some, is extremely beneficial.

For an adolescent in particular, a chronic illness threatens the ego and prolongs a youngster's sense of dependency at a time when the often conflict-ridden process of separation from parents normally takes place. Parental overprotectiveness and the need for drugs, regular medical checkups, and special diets make many chronically ill adolescents feel weak and inferior to their peers. As a result, such youngsters may deny their illness and neglect their medications and dietary restrictions until their rebellion brings on a serious episode, be it an asthma attack, an epileptic seizure, or the serious consequences of too little insulin. Fortunately, sports participation frequently can help chronically ill children and adolescents shake their feelings of inferiority. Youngsters with chronic illnesses can excel in sports, just as they can in academics, if they have the natural talent and are given the opportunity to develop it.

In this chapter, we hope to alert parents and youngsters to the value of sports for children with serious health problems. But please remember: We cannot list all the risks or assess all the potential benefits for any specific child or adolescent. Before beginning a sports or exercise program, a chronically ill youngster should consult a physician with his or her parents to learn what he or she can and cannot do, and what safety precautions to take.

ASTHMA

Many myths surround asthma, including the enduring and erroneous idea that asthmatics cannot exercise or play sports. Most can, many do, and some have won Olympic medals. In the 1988 Summer Olympics, 52 of the 611 U.S. team members suffered from asthma. These asthmatics accounted for 15 of the 201 Olympic medals won by U.S. athletes, including 5 gold, 9 silver, and 1 bronze. Athletes with asthma captured medals in sports as diverse as fencing, wrestling, rowing, synchronized swimming, volleyball, water polo, track and field, and women's basketball.

Asthma involves a reduced flow of air to the lungs that reverses spontaneously or with medications. During an asthma attack, three things occur that result in a narrowing of the airways leading to the lungs: The muscles of the air tubes known as the bronchi and bronchioles constrict; they become inflamed; and the output of mucus in these air passages increases. When an attack strikes, breathing becomes difficult. A cough or the signature wheezing or whistling sound of asthma follows as the asthmatic fights desperately to draw air down the narrowed airways. A number of things can bring on an asthma attack in susceptible people, including viral infections; certain drugs, including aspirin; chemical fumes, including those from paint; and most often, the same sort of things that cause "allergies"—tree and grass pollens, mold spores, and animal dander, for example.

Doesn't vigorous exercise trigger asthma attacks?
It certainly can. This form of the ailment, known as exercise-induced asthma, affects between 60 and 90 percent of asthmatics. It usually

strikes a few minutes after exercise, not during; more often in cold weather than warm; most often after six to eight minutes of intense activity; less often with shorter or longer periods of exertion. Complete recovery almost always comes in 30 to 90 minutes, faster with the use of antiasthma medications.

Do physicians know why exercise induces an asthma attack?
Yes, finally. Researchers in a series of studies have found that exercise itself is not the true culprit. Rather, the attacks relate to the temperature and humidity of the air inhaled during exercise. Normally, people breathe through their noses, which warms the air bound for the lungs and makes it more humid. But during vigorous exercise, a lot of air enters the lungs via the open mouth, a route that neither warms nor humidifies the air adequately. In asthma-prone individuals, this relatively cold and low-humidity air can send their "twitchy" airways into spasm and trigger an asthma attack.

Another issue now largely set to rest focused on the question of whether exercise led to a second or delayed asthmatic response that followed hours after an attack of exercise-induced asthma. Such delayed attacks occur in some people whose asthma bouts are triggered by dust or pollen. And some evidence in the early 1980s suggested that delayed attacks might pose a problem for those with exercise-induced asthma. But most experts now agree that secondary asthma attacks following exercise are uncommon.

Do physicians feel that asthmatic children and adolescents can play sports safely?
Vigorous exercise clearly represents a double-edged sword for asthma sufferers. It offers definite benefits, yet exercise can precipitate or exacerbate constriction of the airways, and thus trigger an asthma attack. Nonetheless, a number of studies show that most asthmatics can participate in sports safely, although the degree of safety differs from sport to sport. Not every asthmatic child can expect to win Olympic gold, but most can expect to pursue the dream. The key to safe sports for asthmatics lies in properly warming up and taking their asthma medications before exercising.

What benefits do asthmatics derive from exercise that make it worth the risk?
At the least, they gain the same benefits, physically and psychologically, as people who don't suffer from the problem. Some physicians

feel that asthmatic youngsters gain even more in self-confidence and self-assurance than nonasthmatics by successfully competing. Physical training increases the efficiency of an asthma sufferer's breathing, improves cardiovascular strength, tones muscles, improves appearance and attitude, and teaches leadership skills. Too often, a parent's exaggerated fears, rather than any serious risk of harm, hold a child back from sports participation, or even physical education classes.

Specifically, what do asthmatic youngsters need to do to exercise safely?

Asthmatics should never engage in sports without first consulting a physician about what sports are best for them and about the severity of their disease. During this discussion, the patient and doctor should work up a plan that covers what the asthmatic should do before exercising—especially with regard to warm-ups and pre-exercise medication—and exactly what to do and what drug to use should an exercise-induced asthma attack occur. The young athlete should also be aware of any restrictions on medications imposed by sanctioning bodies. For example, the International Olympics Committee accepts the use by asthmatics of some drugs from a group known as beta-adrenergic agonists, but not all. If at all possible, the physician should examine his or her asthmatic patient shortly after exercise, to check for signs of problems short of a full-blown attack.

Asthmatic athletes must also stay in tune with their bodies, avoiding exercise on days when their disorder is not fully under control. Even a mild wheezing should signal to the asthmatic to cut back on exertion until his or her airways recover. Coaches and parents must also remember that in an asthmatic, a cough can signal airway constriction. Ignoring such a cough or episodes when an asthmatic becomes abnormally short of breath can set up a cycle in which exercise induces more asthma. Unfortunately, coaches may unwittingly provoke such a cycle because they tend to interpret any shortness of breath as a sign that the youngster needs to get in better shape. They may then order the asthmatic to run extra laps.

With all this said, perhaps the best way to prevent an exercise-induced attack in an asthmatic who wants to engage in vigorous exercise is to select an appropriate sport.

What sports work best for asthmatics?

By almost universal agreement, swimming poses the least threat of inducing an asthma attack. The reason is the swimming environment. The air a few inches directly above the water—the air swimmers breathe—usually has high humidity and a warm temperature. Thus swimming, whether sport sprints or distance events, is most strongly supported as the sport for asthmatics. For those who prefer not to swim, asthma specialists generally advise sports that do not require sustained exertion, such as baseball, diving, golf, weight lifting, sprint races in track (as opposed to distance races or cross-country), and field events (such as the shot put or hammer throw).

Because of the ill effects of cold air on an asthmatic's airways, most physicians strongly urge asthma sufferers to avoid outdoor sports in winter. If an asthmatic insists on skiing or ice skating, he or she should wear a face mask or scarf over the mouth and nose to warm the air pulled into the lungs.

I've heard some asthmatics can jog and run in long-distance races.
That's a controversial matter, and one best discussed thoroughly with a physician. Considering the existing knowledge about exercise-induced asthma, physicians have good reason to worry that distance running can cause acute or chronic adverse effects in a young asthmatic. However, at least two studies in the 1980s concluded that asthmatic youngsters given appropriate bronchodilator drugs before exercising could safely and successfully engage in the extended, vigorous exertion required of long-distance runners. But both studies involved small numbers of asthmatics—15 in one and 20 in another—and in one of the studies, about half the youngsters repeatedly developed attacks of exercise-induced asthma, although these were readily reversed with prompt administration of an asthma medication. Until further research firmly establishes the safety of distance running for asthmatics, the wise choice seems to be warm-weather sports that require only bursts of exertion.

DIABETES

Diabetes specialists often refer to exercise as "the other insulin," an indication of how important many regard physical activity in treating this serious disorder. Actually, two basic types of diabetes exist. In *type I*, also called *insulin-dependent diabetes mellitus* or *juvenile diabetes*, the body fails to make or produces inadequate amounts of insulin, a hormone secreted by the pancreas that helps cells metabolize glucose, the common sugar carried in the bloodstream. Without insulin, glucose levels rise in the blood, setting off a chain of events that eventually leads to diabetic acidosis, which results in coma and death. This condition caused the deaths of most type I diabetics prior to the discovery of insulin in 1921. In *type II diabetes,* also known as *non-insulin-dependent diabetes* or *adult-onset diabetes,* the pancreas makes insulin but the cells cannot properly use it. Physicians usually prescribe a special diet and sometimes drugs known as hypoglycemics to control type II diabetes.

Both types of diabetes carry a high risk of serious complications, including coronary heart disease; circulatory problems that may ultimately cause gangrene requiring amputation, particularly of the lower extremities; failing sight and blindness; nerve damage that causes frequent pain; and skin infections.

Why do physicians want diabetics to exercise regularly?

It is a tenet of diabetes treatment that the closer patients can keep their blood-sugar levels to normal, the fewer serious consequences they will suffer from their disease. Another widely accepted tenet holds that exercise helps control blood sugar, especially among type II diabetics.

Soon after the discovery of insulin, a researcher discovered that exercise increased the blood-sugar-lowering powers of injected insulin. Thus, among type I diabetics, physicians traditionally have regarded exercise as one leg of a therapeutic triad that also includes insulin injections and diet. Exercise appears to increase the sensitivity of cells to insulin. Studies also show that exercise further improves blood-sugar control in type I diabetics whose blood sugar is adequately controlled by insulin. However, some recent findings suggest that these benefits fail to last if diabetics significantly increase their food intake either in anticipation of or in response to exercise, which most apparently do. Studies also reveal that otherwise healthy adolescents with type I diabetes, as a group, exercise less than adolescents without diabetes, and that any benefits of exercise on blood sugar continue only as long as the diabetic continues to exercise regularly.

In type II diabetes, physicians want patients to exercise to help them lose weight or maintain their ideal body weight. It is well known that dropping excess pounds helps type II diabetics control their blood-sugar levels.

Does exercise provide diabetics other benefits?

Regular exercise clearly increases physical fitness and helps reduce high blood pressure, blood cholesterol levels, and obesity—major risk factors for heart attacks and strokes. This is important for diabetics, who are more than seven times as likely to die from cardiovascular problems as nondiabetics the same age. Psychologically, exercise can improve a diabetic's sense of well-being, self-esteem, and self-confidence. And for at least some type I diabetics, getting involved in exercise increases their self-monitoring and their control of glucose in the blood.

But before beginning to exercise, diabetics—and absolutely all type I diabetics—must consult their physicians about any program they plan to undertake.

You put that so emphatically. Why?

Exercise without preparation can cause potentially serious consequences in the form of *hypoglycemia,* or too little sugar in the blood. The initial symptoms of hypoglycemia include sweating, flushing, chills, numbness, dizziness, headache, rapid pulse rate, heart palpitations, even fainting. In severe cases, if left untreated, hypoglycemia can lead to coma and death. The risk of hypoglycemia exists during and after exercise for type I diabetics and for certain type II diabetics, particularly those taking the sulfonylurea drugs to lower their blood sugar. Unfortunately, fear of hypoglycemia keeps many young diabetics from exercising or playing sports. A physician can provide a diabetic with the instructions and guidance he or she needs to prevent exercise-induced hypoglycemia.

What steps can a diabetic take to prevent blood-sugar problems when exercising?

Each diabetic needs specific counseling by a physician, and let us give a general example of why. A type I diabetic whose disease is well controlled may respond to exercise by developing hypoglycemia, while a type I diabetic with poor control may respond exactly the opposite—by developing *hyperglycemia,* or high blood sugar. Obviously, these two situations require different prevention strategies. A number of approaches exist to avoid blood-sugar problems associated with exercise. For example, well-controlled type I diabetics can prevent hypoglycemia by decreasing insulin intake and consuming quick-acting carbohydrates before exercise, and by eating carbohydrates during exercise if the activity requires prolonged exertion, such as long-distance running or bicycling. Choosing the site of insulin injection also can reduce the chance of hypoglycemia. A physician should be consulted to choose the right site for an athlete's specific sport. And since diet plays such an important role in diabetes treatment, adding exercise requires careful monitoring and adjustment to avoid blood-sugar problems. The key to safe exercise for a diabetic is to monitor the blood-sugar response and to make the proper adjustments.

Can exercise exacerbate the complications of diabetes?
The danger is essentially the same as for nondiabetics. For diabetics with coronary artery disease, exercise may cause chest pain, irregular heartbeats, or a heart attack. Diabetics with the eye disorder retinopathy face an increased risk of hemorrhage or retinal detachment if they exercise vigorously. And those with peripheral nerve damage are more likely to suffer muscle and joint injuries if they exercise. Fortunately, few diabetics today develop these complications of the disease in their childhood and adolescence.

Does exercise increase the life expectancy of diabetics?
Unfortunately, no one can answer that question at this time. Regular exercise certainly can decrease certain risk factors for heart disease and stroke, and it appears to create no long-term ill effects that diabetics might not otherwise develop. At least one large study suggests a reduced risk of cardiovascular disease among type I diabetics who maintain a program of regular exercise. But only further studies will reveal whether exercise prolongs the lives of diabetics. For now, all that physicians can say is that for most diabetics, exercise begun early in their disease improves the quality of their lives.

What sports do you recommend for young diabetics?
It really doesn't make any difference what sport a diabetic takes up, as long as the youngster is correctly monitored for the demands of that athletic activity.

EPILEPSY

Epilepsy is characterized by seizures triggered by the misfiring of nerves in the brain. The seizures take various forms, depending upon where in the brain the nerves misfire. During petit mal seizures, for example, the person stops his or her activities briefly and may appear to daydream. In the best-known form of the ailment, the dramatic grand mal seizure, a person typically develops a bewildered look, groans or screams, falls unconscious and rigid to the ground, then begins a convulsive jerking of the arms and legs. Such seizures often last less than a minute, rarely more than two minutes. Marked confusion or deep sleep lasting minutes to hours follows the seizure. Anticonvulsant medications can control the seizures of most people suffering from epilepsy.

Will the exertion or excitement of playing in sports trigger seizures?

Chalk that up as one of the many myths surrounding epilepsy. Only one very rare form of epilepsy—so-called tonic seizures—results from activity itself. Studies find no evidence that either the vigorous exercise associated with sports or the fatigue that follows hard play will trigger other types of epileptic seizures. Indeed, a few studies suggest that exercise may even raise the seizure threshold, the resistance of the brain to misfiring. Surveys of large school athletic programs find no differences in the injury rates of players with and without epilepsy. Overall, playing sports seems to offer youngsters with epilepsy many benefits—particularly in helping them feel "normal"—and to pose few risks above those normally associated with their chosen sport. We do not mean to suggest that seizures never happen during sports activities, but that the risk appears to be no greater than at any other time, and may be less.

Does epilepsy rule out any specific sport?

Epileptics get little or no warning of an imminent seizure. Therefore, they should avoid any sport in which even a minor seizure could mean injury or death. These include skydiving, rock climbing, scuba diving, hang gliding, high diving, auto and bicycle racing, and horseback riding.

Can epileptics engage in competitive swimming?

In studies of Hawaiian and Australian children with epilepsy, the risk of drowning proved extremely small. Nonetheless, the risk was slightly higher than in nonepileptics. As a general rule, pediatricians recommend that an epileptic child can swim safely after going a year without a seizure, provided blood levels of anticonvulsant medication are adequate, and he or she swims in a properly supervised pool or swimming area.

What special risks do epileptics face in contact sports?

That question stands in dispute. Traditionally, physicians have feared that a hard blow to the head could precipitate a seizure in youngsters prone to such problems. Given the nature of the disorder and some evidence that seizures sometimes follow nonsports head injuries, this makes sense. Yet no carefully conducted study exists to bear out these concerns, and in a review of some 20,000 seizure patients one physician reported finding no evidence that contact sports increased the risk of seizure recurrence. Still, until researchers resolve the issue, prudent parents might well want to keep a child with epilepsy out of heavy contact sports (the "bell ringers"), such as tackle football, lacrosse, boxing, and wrestling.

CYSTIC FIBROSIS

Children inherit cystic fibrosis, a disease in which the body fails to clear the normal secretions of the respiratory tract. As a result, a thick mucus clogs the lungs, blocking tiny airways and causing breathing difficulties and a chronic cough. Cystic fibrosis was once almost inevitably fatal in childhood, but treatment advances have prolonged the lives of many CF patients into their twenties and even thirties.

A tremendous range in physical fitness and tolerance of exercise exists among youngsters with cystic fibrosis, from the athletic to those bedridden by their disease. Studies indicate that many CF patients can engage safely in sports and exercise programs, with the proper management and monitoring of their disease by a physician. A few CF adolescents have even run in the New York City marathon.

What risks does exercise impose on cystic fibrosis patients?

They have an increased risk of heat problems—cramps, exhaustion, and stroke—and, depending on the severity of their disease, they may experience oxygen desaturation, a reduction in the amount of oxygen carried by their red blood cells.

Cystic fibrosis patients sweat out abnormal amounts of sodium and chloride when they exercise, despite normal temperature, heart rate, and hormonal and kidney responses. Levels of these two elec-trolytes, the constituents of table salt, return to normal within 24 hours with a normal intake of food and beverages. Nonetheless, the excess loss of sodium and chloride in sweat increases the risk of electrolyte problems during vigorous exercise. Moreover, the loss of sodium and water in sweat appears to reduce secretions in the re-spiratory tract, which may lead to breathing problems during exer-cise. To protect against excessive loss of sodium and chloride during periods of profuse perspiration, the CF athlete should be aware of any unusual weakness and be prepared to "salt" himself with salt tablets, following the instructions provided by his physician. The physician should set an exact dosage, determined by the individual's weight, age, and body size.

Studies also reveal that CF patients, as a result of their breathing problems, typically reach the point of exhaustion before they have pushed their heart to the limit. Those with more severe breathing problems also may experience oxygen desaturation. In both cases, physicians should advise CF youngsters at what intensity level they can exercise without experiencing oxygen desaturation and ex-haustion.

What benefits make exercise worth the risks for cystic fibrosis kids?

Exercise appears to reduce the sputum production of CF patients; increase the endurance of the muscles involved in breathing; and improve their exercise tolerance, airflow, and overall health. Some CF specialists contend that no one benefits more from a properly selected and supervised sports program than a young person with this disease. One research team even concluded that regular exercise, in some children, could replace the tedious inhalation-physiotherapy routine used to counter CF's debilitating effects. However, such ben-efits require participating several times a week in an exercise program or sport, or they quickly disappear. Studies indicate that within eight weeks after ceasing exercise, a CF patient reverts to the same level of lung functioning as before beginning to exercise.

Does exercise provide other benefits?

As with so many chronically ill or handicapped children, sports par-ticipation provides the CF child with the twin psychological benefits of a better self-image and greater self-confidence.

What sports do physicians generally recommend for CF youngsters?

Swimming usually ranks first, in part because it involves upper-body exercise. We don't mean occasionally splashing around in a pool, but a regular program of lap swimming for half an hour, three to five times a week. The warm, moist air breathed in during swimming soothes the airways and presents less risk of inducing an airway reaction. One study suggests that canoeing produces beneficial effects equal to swimming, although obviously such a program is far harder to organize and maintain. Some CF patients also jog or get involved in distance-running training and competition. Again, CF youngsters need to work out their exercise programs with their physicians.

CHILDREN WITH HANDICAPS

Nothing has stripped the notion that handicapped children cannot participate in sports of its hold on the public mind as effectively and thoroughly as the Special Olympics program. Through newspapers and magazines, television and radio, the nation has gotten the message that mentally retarded and physically handicapped youngsters can indeed participate in and greatly benefit from sports. To see and hear about handicapped youngsters and adults striving, struggling, and succeeding touches the heart and awakens the mind to these young people's ability to participate at their own level, and to benefit physically, psychologically, and socially.

What are the benefits?

Essentially, the same physical and emotional benefits the nonhandicapped gain from physical exercise and sports participation. Many mentally retarded and physically handicapped individuals are obese and have extremely poor physical fitness levels, and these conditions tend to worsen with age. Sports or other exercise programs can improve their fitness awareness and help them shed pounds. Studies show that wheelchair athletes, for example, can increase their aerobic capacity and decrease their resting heart rate (a sign of cardiorespiratory fitness) to the same extent as people without physical disabilities. Athletics also can improve muscle strength and functioning, sometimes serving as an additional form of physical therapy for some disabilities.

Sports participation also increases a handicapped individual's contact with others, which helps improve his or her social skills. The isolation in which so many handicapped children and adolescents live appears to contribute to their emotional and social immaturity. The human interaction that naturally occurs with sports can help these youngsters develop new social skills and a better level of emotional maturity. Sports gives them, as well, a new sense of freedom and can increase their motivation, self-esteem, and self-confidence. A number of school systems now honor their students who participate in the Special Olympics programs alongside their regular athletic teams—a recognition bound to boost anyone's self-image.

Any sports participation by a mentally retarded or physically handicapped youngster, however, should include consultation with his or her physican.

What sports can the mentally retarded play?

The range of athletic ability varies as widely among these youngsters as it does among any segment of our population. Some have excellent coordination, others are quite uncoordinated. Some correlation also exists between a youngster's level of intellectual development and such things as emotional control, attention span, persistence, and the ability to grasp and follow the rules of the game. But most mentally retarded children and adolescents can and should engage in exercise programs or athletic activities.

As a rule, the mentally retarded do better in individual and one-on-one sports than in team sports; and in activities that require gross motor skills rather than fine motor skills. Track and field events and swimming certainly fit this description. Other sports and physical activities frequently recommended for the mentally retarded include tennis, bicycling, horseback riding, hiking, archery, and folk dancing.

Can the mentally retarded compete against the nonretarded?

It is possible in some sports for some mildly and moderately retarded youngsters. When such individuals can hold their own, in golf or archery, for example, the experience can give them a wonderful psychological boost. But such competition carries risks as well as benefits. Repeated failures will adversely affect their self-esteem and self-confidence.

Does a sport need to be changed in any way in order for the mentally retarded to participate?

This, again, depends in part on the level of mental development. Simplifying the rules does make participating easier. So does changing the rules so that youngsters remain active most of the time, an important point with people with short attention spans. The mentally retarded seem to benefit most when they participate in sports programs organized at the community level that educate coaches and officials to their special needs and problems.

In what sports can the physically handicapped engage?

The overall list runs long, but for any individual the suitable sports depend both on the nature of the handicap and on the person's interests. Never underestimate the importance of personal preferences in sports to a handicapped person's willingness to participate and determination to persist. Equally important to consider are the type, number, and degree of physical handicaps, the person's level of coordination, and the family's financial status. In many sports participation costs considerable money, which many families cannot afford.

For those with disabled upper limbs, the list of possibilities includes tennis, squash, soccer, jogging, cross-country running, track, bicycling, ice skating and ice hockey, tumbling, fencing, karate, bowling, roller skating, table tennis, and badminton. People with lower-limb disabilities may find pleasure in horseback riding, jumping show horses, sculling, canoeing, kayaking, and wheelchair versions of archery, badminton, baseball, basketball, bowling, touch or flag football, golf, handball, softball, table tennis, volleyball, and weight lifting. Many other possibilities exist, depending on the person and his or her handicap, including swimming, downhill and cross-country skiing, dancing, platform diving, water skiing, sailing, snorkeling, scuba diving, rock climbing, and sledding.

What are some of the changes and modifications needed for physically handicapped people to participate in sports?

Some sports may require no changes. Some people with one leg amputated find they can learn to slalom water-ski quite well with nothing more than the standard ski used by people with two legs. Other sports require equipment modifications or additions, either for safety or to make participation possible. For example, a lap belt similar to those used in automobiles can help provide a secure seat in the saddle for people who wish to ride horses. Special harnesses allow individuals with certain handicaps to engage in deep-sea fishing. The list of specialized equipment is almost as long and varied as the sports pursued by the handicapped.

Where can I get further information?
The federal government provides suggestions on planning physical education and recreation programs for the mentally and physically handicapped. Write to the Division of Innovation and Development, Department of Education, 400 Maryland Avenue S.W., Washington, D.C. 20202. The Special Olympics, Inc., provides information on its program upon request. Write them at 1350 New York Avenue, N.W., Washington, D.C. 20005.

INFECTIOUS MONONUCLEOSIS

While not a true chronic disease, mono hits a number of high school and college students each year, and it is a potentially dangerous ailment for athletes, particularly those who engage in sports that involve any body contact. Disappointing and frustrating as it is, physicians have good reason for refusing to allow mono patients to resume their sport until the disease has completely run its often long course.

Infectious mononucleosis apparently results from infection by the Epstein-Barr virus. Its symptoms include fever (sometimes quite high), swollen lymph glands, malaise, muscle ache, a sore throat, and headache. Another aspect of the disease presents a special problem for athletes: the enlargement of the spleen, an organ in the upper abdomen. When enlarged in mono, the spleen can rupture easily if dealt a hard blow, requiring emergency surgery. An athlete whose spleen has become enlarged because of mono needs clearance from a physician before resuming contact sports. Both the degree of enlargement and the nature of the athletic activity will influence the physician's recommendation on when and how to return to competition.

9

The Dangers of Drugs

Ben Johnson of Canada provided the most memorable moment of the 1988 Summer Olympics, not with a spectacular victory or agonizing defeat, but by being stripped of the gold medal he won for his record-setting 100-meter dash. Urine tests performed after the awards ceremony showed that Johnson had illegally used an anabolic steroid to help him achieve his most dramatic victory ever, and investigators later learned he had used banned steroids before almost every major race he had run since 1981. Even after his family physician detected a slight enlargement of his left breast, one well-known side effect of anabolic steroids, Johnson continued using the drugs in hopes of obtaining the edge he needed to beat other world-class sprinters.

The official Olympic motto—*Citius, Altius, Fortius*—translates as "Swifter, higher, stronger." Since antiquity, athletes have pursued these goals, and for probably as long, they have dreamed of finding some magic potion to make them swifter, higher, and stronger than their fellow competitors. Athletes of ancient Egypt favored a mixture of the ground-up rear hooves of an Abyssinian ass, boiled in oil, and mixed with rose petals and rose hips. The Olympians of ancient Greece consumed large amounts of meat, a bit of mythology adhered to even today by advocates of high-protein diets. Nineteenth-century canal swimmers in the Netherlands ate sugar cubes bathed in ether before entering the water. And late in that century, some marathon runners actually got an injection of strychnine mid-race, followed by a swig of brandy, in the belief that this would enhance their performance.

In our own era, with the modern Olympics, worldwide competitions, and star status (and income) for athletes, the use of ever-more sophisticated drugs has increased. Championship-level competitors want to win, first and foremost, and if they perceive that only a performance-enhancing drug will provide them victory, many will risk the humiliation of a Ben Johnson for the opportunity to win. Even the threat of physical damage or death fails to deter many. A Dutch cyclist died and two others were hospitalized during the 1960 Summer Olympics after taking an amphetamine in an effort to improve their performance. Seven years later, an English cyclist died while competing in the famed Tour de France, also after ingesting amphetamines. And a few years ago, a weight lifter died of liver cancer apparently related to his extensive use of anabolic steroids. Too many athletes believe in what Dr. Irving I. Dardik, a former chairman of the U.S. Olympic Committee, has called " 'drug alchemy'—the turning of drugs into gold medals."

DRUG USE AND TESTING

Athletes often call the use of a banned substance to enhance their performance "doping," a century-old term derived from the Boer word "dop"—a South African concoction of cola nut extracts, xanthines, and alcohol. The term includes both taking illegal drugs and "blood doping," a practice also illegal in sports. Sometimes called "blood boosting" or "blood packing," this involves removing blood from an athlete and freezing it for storage. Then, after the athlete has built back a full blood supply, the stored red blood cells are thawed and injected into his or her body shortly before an event. The extra red cells increase the amount of oxygen carried to cells throughout the body, and the extra oxygen increases endurance.

While scandals in the sports world involving performance-enhancing drugs and revelations of their use even among high school and junior high school athletes have attracted considerable attention, studies also indicate that use of illegal street drugs, alcohol, and cigarettes by adolescent athletes parallels that of society as a whole. An annual University of Michigan survey of high school seniors indicated a decline in illicit street drug use by students throughout much of the 1980s, with a smaller drop in alcohol use. Nonetheless, figures released in 1991 showed that 27 percent of high school students who graduated in 1990 used some marijuana during their senior year, 9.1 percent used illicit stimulant such as amphetamines, 5.3 percent used cocaine, and 80.6 percent drank alcohol at least once.

How commonly do athletes use illicit drugs?

Few studies have focused specifically on athletes' abuse. However, one survey of Canadian Olympians, reported in 1983, found that 57 percent drank alcohol, 23 percent smoked marijuana, 10 percent took psychomotor stimulants such as amphetamines, 5 percent used anabolic steroids, another 21 percent contemplated doing so, and 4 percent used cocaine. The expanding use of performance-enhancing drugs by adolescent athletes has greatly distorted two important benefits of sports: Fun is lost in the desire to win at all costs; and improving health is lost in a distorted desire to excel.

What are sports groups doing to detect drug abuse?

Nationally and internationally, sports groups have turned to testing athletes for drugs as the only effective way to detect cheating and enforce their rules against drug use. International Olympic Committee rules ban 68 specific performance-enhancing drugs, including excessive caffeine, and any compounds chemically related to them. These rules apply to all events sanctioned by the IOC and the U.S. Olympic Committee, including the prestigious Pan American Games. Athletes who test positive for a banned drug or who refuse testing are disqualified. The National Collegiate Athletic Association's list of banned substances totals over 80, and unlike the IOC, the NCAA rules include illicit street drugs. Many universities conduct their own mandatory drug tests of athletes, and some people have suggested routinely testing high school athletes for banned drugs.

Has testing foiled the abuse of performance-enhancing drugs?

Unfortunately, drug testing is never perfect, and some athletes spend considerable time finding ways to avoid detection. Existing tests simply cannot detect certain types of cheating—blood doping and the use of human growth hormone, for example. And sophisticated cheats learn how long the body takes to excrete a banned substance, such as an anabolic steroid, and stop using it soon enough so the drug does not show up in a urine test. According to the testimony of his coach, Ben Johnson successfully avoided detection of his steroid use this way for seven years.

Some athletes abuse legally prescribed drugs or over-the-counter medications to get their edge. Wrestlers sometimes use diuretics or diet pills to keep their weight down; other athletes consume a number of nonprescription stimulants to pump themselves up. The International Olympic Committee regards any amount of a banned substance in an athlete's urine, with certain written exceptions, as enough to disqualify an athlete. Perhaps the saddest application of this rule cost U.S. swimmer Rick DeMont a gold medal at the 1972 Olympics in Munich. DeMont was unaware that a medication he took for his asthma contained a banned drug. The IOC stripped him of his medal but later approved several asthma drugs for use by Olympic competitors.

STIMULANTS, STEROIDS, AND GROWTH HORMONE

Athletes today turn to a wide variety of prescription and nonprescription medications in hopes of gaining the extra edge that means victory. Some of these drugs, such as anabolic steroids, are used during training, while others are ingested shortly before or even during competition. Physicians refer to substances that increase strength, flexibility, or endurance as "ergogenics." Studies indicate that some ergogenics can enhance an athlete's work output as much as 7 percent. For world-class competitors, then, a performance-enhancing drug may truly make the difference between narrow defeat and resounding victory. But for most sports participants, whose training (or lack of it) has left them far short of their maximum potential, ergogenics seem of less value than better training methods. Too often lost in the often highly exaggerated descriptions of how ergogenics aid performance are their very real risks, including death.

Is there an acceptable ergogenic?

Inhaling pure oxygen to increase the supply of fuel to working cells represents the purest form of the ergogenics, and the only one that is perfectly legal and acceptable in athletics. Used properly, pure oxygen poses no health threat. Blood doping, however, while effective in increasing the bloodstream's oxygen content, can cause serious problems and is banned in sports. The extra red cells packed into the body increase the blood's viscosity, and thus increase the possibility of clotting, especially in activities that lead to dehydration. Blood clots in the legs can cause tenderness and swelling; clots in the lungs can cause breathing difficulties, internal bleeding in the lungs, and even death. More reccently, some athletes have been injecting themselves with erythropoietin, a drug that boosts the body's production of red cells and that carries the same risks as blood doping.

Why do athletes abuse stimulants?

Many athletes use these easily obtained drugs to boost their energy levels, concentration, and even give them what they perceive as a more positive attitude. The most commonly used stimulants include prescription amphetamines and four drugs sold without prescription in a large number of medications: phenylpropanolamine hydrochloride (an amphetamine-like drug found in many nasal decongestants and appetite suppressants); ephedrine and pseudoephedrine (in asthma medications and nasal decongestants); and caffeine (included in many over-the-counter drugs and found naturally in coffee, tea, and cola drinks). Each of these drugs, particularly the amphetamines, has adverse side effects.

What are the dangers of stimulant abuse?

No drug quite matches the amphetamines' reputation for abuse. Although their level of misuse among athletes appears soundly on the decline, these powerful stimulants continue to attract attention and users, despite their well-known addictive properties and their ability to damage body tissue. Some wrestlers, for example, use them both to enhance their performance and to suppress their appetite and help them keep their weight down. Studies show that amphetamines do increase endurance and help weary athletes fight off fatigue and recover their reaction times, although they do nothing to help a fresh, well-rested athlete. Yet, the degree to which amphetamines improve performance is small. Again, their serious dangers leave no doubt that—morality, ethics, and legality aside—the dangers of amphetamines as performance enhancers go far beyond any benefits. Amphetamines can cause aggressive and/or paranoid behavior, insomnia, headaches, muscle trembling, high blood pressure, potentially fatal irregular or rapid heartbeats, and addiction.

Why worry about caffeine use?

Aware of the physical and legal dangers of amphetamines, a number of athletes prefer caffeine as their stimulant of choice. Indeed, some evidence indicates extensive caffeine use in sports. A number of marathon runners, for example, apparently down many cola drinks before competition to load up on caffeine. This common drug apparently improves performance by stimulating the sympathetic nervous system, increasing the release of free fatty acids from fat cells to provide more energy, and slowing down the breakdown of glycogen in muscle. However, caffeine does not enhance performance in short-duration exercise, such as short races in track or swimming, because such events do not draw on fat reserves for fuel. Heavy caffeine use can cause side effects quite frightening to children and adolescents—agitation, anxiety, confusion, rapid or irregular heartbeats, and in very high doses, seizures. Several falls ago, three high school football players arrived fearfully at an adolescent clinic within a 10-day period, each complaining of rapid heartbeats. Each, it turned out, had been taking heavy doses of a nonprescription, caffeine-based stimulant in hopes of gaining a starting spot on his team. The International Olympic Committee, the U.S. Olympic Committee, and the National Collegiate Athletic Assocation now test athletes for caffeine and disqualify those found with more than a specified amount in their bloodstream.

Do other over-the-counter stimulants cause problems?

Other stimulants popular with athletes have side effects like those of caffeine, and others as well. Phenylpropanolamine's most common side effect is high blood pressure, which may be accompanied by an abnormally slow heartbeat. The drug's other possible effects include a rapid heartbeat—usually when used with other stimulants or antihistamines—irregular heartbeats, chest pain, anxiety, agitation, and rarely, kidney problems. Side effects associated with medications containing ephedrine and pseudoephedrine include high blood pressure, rapid and irregular heartbeats, anxiety, psychosis, and in large doses, seizures.

What are anabolic steroids?

Often called " 'roids," these drugs are forms of synthetic testosterone, the male sex hormone involved in the development of the genitalia, beard, greater male muscle mass, and strength. In the body, anabolic steroids actually prove more effective at building muscles and strength than natural testosterone, and influence sexual organs and hair growth less. Physicians sometimes use anabolic steroids to treat certain anemias, some breast cancers, some cases of starvation, abnormally decreased functioning of the gonads, and hereditary angioedema, an inherited allergic condition that involves swelling of the tissue just beneath the skin. But since the 1960s, some athletes—males and females—have used the drugs to build bigger, stronger muscles and increase aggressiveness. In recent years, some have resorted to taking testosterone itself, since abuse of this natural substance is harder to detect in drug screenings.

Do steroids really pose a problem among adolescent athletes?
The exact usage of these banned and potentially dangerous steroids
remains unknown, but the evidence certainly indicates a soaring
market during the 1970s and 1980s, including among high school
and even junior high students.

The International Olympic Committee added anabolic steroids
to its list of banned pharmaceuticals for the 1976 games, after finding
them widely used by athletes participating in certain events in the
two previous Olympiads. In 1968, all the weight lifters interviewed
on the U.S. Olympic team used anabolic steroids, and at the 1972
Summer Games in Munich, Germany, 68 percent of the runners in
middle- and short-distance events admitted using steroids. Small
surveys elsewhere revealed a growing use of the drugs. In 1973, for
example, a study at five American universities found that 1.5 percent
of all students, including women, took steroids. A 1975 study in
Arizona found that 0.7 percent of all high school students and 4
percent of the athletes used the drugs.

In 1988, a research team reported results from the first nationwide survey of anabolic steroid use among high school males. It
found that 6.6 percent of male high school seniors used or had used
the drugs. Two-thirds began taking steroids when they were 16 or
younger; 44 percent used more than one steroid at a time, a technique called "stacking"; and 38 percent revealed they used both oral
and injectable forms. Just over 60 percent said they got their drugs
from other athletes, coaches, at gyms, or from other black market
sources, but about 20 percent said they most often got theirs from
physicians, pharmacists, or veterinarians. The researchers concluded
that somewhere between 250,000 and 500,000 high school boys in
the United States were then abusing anabolic steroids. As investi-
gations have shown since, young women athletes also abuse anabolic
steroids, although not to the extent of young males.

How do steroids affect athletic performance?
Anabolic steroids increase protein synthesis, which in turn helps
increase muscle size and strength. Abusers typically use 10 to 40
times the therapeutic doses of these drugs in efforts to bulk up their
bodies. For adult males, anabolic steroids can unquestionably increase muscle mass, weight (in part because of water retention), and
strength. The drugs almost certainly increase muscle size and strength
in adult females and adolescents of both sexes as well, although there
is less scientific evidence to support this. Whatever the athlete's age

or sex, however, anabolic steroids do nothing to build up the body unless the abuser engages in a continuing program of weight training, coupled with a high-protein diet. Moreover, these drugs do nothing to increase aerobic capacity, and can increase or encourage aggressive behavior. To date, no one knows whether this greater aggressiveness helps or hinders training and performance, although it may well increase the risk of injury and penalties for rough play or unsportsmanlike conduct. Researchers and physicians still disagree whether or to what extent anabolic steroid use enhances athletic performance. But given their abuse rate, it appears that many athletes harbor no doubts.

Can steroid abuse cause serious injury or permanent health damage?

Anabolic steroids can cause a number of physical problems in athletes, some reversible, some permanent, and some eventually fatal. Usually, these side effects are dose-related: the more steroids taken and the longer the period of abuse, the greater the likelihood of developing side effects and the greater the chance these problems will prove serious. Among males, steroid abuse can lead to lower output of the hormones gonadotropin and testosterone, an abnormally low sperm count, infertility, testicle shrinkage, breast enlargement, suppressed bile flow, sleep apnea (episodes when breathing stops briefly during sleep), and peliosis hepatis, a rare liver condition in which pockets of blood form that can rupture and cause severe bleeding.

What are the effects in females and in adolescents?

Researchers know less about how anabolic steroids adversely affect women and children, but harmful side effects tend to afflict both of these groups more than adult males. Female abusers may develop acne, oily skin, a beard, a deeper voice, irregular and disrupted menstrual cycles, an enlarged clitoris, and reduced breast size. When children and adolescents abuse steroids they risk stunting their growth. The drugs accelerate puberty changes that cause the skeleton to mature prematurely and close the epiphyses, the main points of bone growth. In both sexes, the steroids can produce acne; baldness; serious liver disease, including liver cancer; higher cholesterol levels in the blood, a condition associated with an increased risk of coronary artery disease and heart attacks; an increased sex drive; and stroke.

Although anabolic steroids promote increased muscle mass and strength, they do nothing for the tendons and ligaments, so the risk of dislocation increases. And because steroids reduce pain and thus the signals pain gives an athlete, they increase the danger of over-training and the injuries this can bring.

Can anabolic steroids create personality problems?

Violent behavior, depression, and psychotic symptoms apparently are far more common among steroid abusers than physicians previously realized. A high school football player who began taking steroids at age 13 beat up his girlfriend in his senior year, threatened to kill his sister, and tried to kill himself. One 17-year-old bodybuilder became depressed and began hearing voices six months after he started taking steroids bought on the street. A 22-year-old steroid user came to believe his mind could influence the pictures on his television set and promised to show God to a friend. Psychiatric problems appear most likely when an abuser "stacks," or uses five or six different anabolic steroids together in a regimen.

Do side effects disappear when an abuser stops taking steroids?

Many do, but not all. In adult males, for example, the hormonal balance returns to normal and infertility and testicle shrinkage reverse, but some breast enlargement may remain. Unfortunately, researchers do not know if halting the drugs restores the hormonal balance in adolescent males, nor what future damage might have been done. Among females, the masculinizing side effects are largely irreversible, with increased facial hair, a deeper voice, acne, male-pattern baldness, and an enlarged clitoris often remaining after they discontinue the drugs. In children, once the body's growth mechanism shuts down, nothing can revive it, so stunted growth is permanent. Prolonged steroid use also can narrow heart arteries by raising blood-cholesterol levels that build up fatty deposits in the artery walls. In some cases this requires surgery to shunt blood around the blocked arteries.

Are steroids addictive?

Generally, physicians do not regard these drugs as habit-forming. However, scattered reports by sports medicine specialists suggest that at least some athletes who use extremely large doses and stack anabolic steroids can indeed become dependent on the drugs.

What's the best way to prevent steroid abuse?

Unfortunately, no one knows. Certainly education can help, but to be effective, young athletes must learn the facts before they try the drugs. This means an education program in early high school, or even junior high school, as well as input from the home. Parents, coaches, athletic trainers, physical education teachers, and school nurses all need to be alert to the signs of anabolic steroid abuse and act when they recognize them.

Ironically, people who abuse the drugs for athletic purposes often seem quite concerned about keeping healthy. In one study of steroid abusers—mostly males—recruited from health clubs and gymnasiums, only about 1 in 10 smoked cigarettes and 1 in 7 drank more than four alcoholic drinks a week. So laying out in detail the adverse, sometimes serious and permanent side effects of anabolic steroids should dissuade some adolescents from ever trying them and get others to quit. Parents also should point out that steroid abuse makes the youngster a cheater, and the drugs' benefits aren't worth the humiliation of getting caught. No one knows to what extent drug testing of athletes has discouraged the use of anabolic steroids and other drugs, but the tests are getting better and the penalties for their use harsher. In 1991, possession of anabolic steroids without a prescription became a Federal crime.

What is human growth hormone (hGH), and why the interest in it among grown and growing athletes?

This nonsteroidal hormone, secreted by the pituitary gland at the base of the brain, mediates a number of growth-related activities in the human body, including stimulating the cells' uptake of amino acids (the building blocks of proteins), as well as protein synthesis. Without adequate hGH, a person cannot reach the full growth potential coded in his or her genes. A child with a severe hGH deficiency grows up as a dwarf, and even when treated with hGH, such children do not grow taller than the third percentile of the general population. For years, hGH for treating dwarfism came from pituitaries taken from cadavers, making it scarce and expensive. In 1985, however, genetically engineered hGH became available for medical use, and athletic abuse. The idea spread—unsupported by any scientific evidence—that hGH taken by healthy adults would increase muscle strength considerably. To those inclined to cheat, the drug offered the added appeal that no means existed to identify an athlete taking the hormone.

Does hGH carry the same serious side effects as anabolic steroids?

Exactly what toll hGH will exact from athletes who abuse it remains unknown. But the adverse effects of long-term high levels of hGH are well documented in acromegaly, a disorder in which an excessive secretion of the hormone results in distorted facial features, thickening of the fingers, high blood-cholesterol levels, heart disease, and impotency.

ALCOHOL AND TOBACCO

Simply put, alcohol and the nicotine in cigarettes are by far the nation's two most popular and destructive drugs. They are also, in a sense, illicit drugs when used by youngsters. Within the United States, the sale of alcoholic beverages to anyone younger than 21 is illegal, and a number of states forbid the sale of cigarettes before certain ages. Both alcohol and tobacco, particularly cigarettes, can cause serious and often fatal illnesses. While a number of studies suggest that moderate alcohol use poses no serious health threats, heavy or addictive drinking of alcoholic beverages greatly increases the risk of cirrhosis of the liver, heart damage, cancers of the mouth, throat and pancreas, and accidents of all sorts. As for cigarette smoking, a series of reports by the U.S. Surgeon General says it constitutes the single most important preventable cause of illness and early death. The illnesses linked to cigarettes include coronary heart disease and heart attacks; a number of cancers, particularly those of the lung, throat, mouth, bladder, and pancreas; emphysema and chronic bronchitis, both crippling lung diseases; noncancerous mouth and dental disorders; peptic ulcers; and in mothers who smoke, an increased risk of miscarriages and premature and low-birthweight babies. But alcohol and cigarettes pose immediate problems as well as long-term risks for young people, and can adversely affect performance in sports.

Does alcohol really constitute a major problem among young athletes?

Athletics participation can indeed help reduce or prevent alcohol consumption among some adolescents, but overall, the drinking problems of athletes vary little from their classmates. About 10 percent of 12- and 13-year-olds drink alcohol at least once a month. The University of Michigan's national survey of drug use found that

89.5 percent of the high school seniors graduating in 1990 had tried alcohol at some time; 57.1 percent consumed at least one drink in the month before their interview; 32.21 percent had downed more than five drinks in a row within the previous two weeks; and 3.71 percent drank daily. Alcohol consumption and drunkenness are acceptable to some degree in American society, where for many male adolescents, drinking helps prove their masculinity. Many beer companies link their brews to sports through advertising that features retired stars or through sponsorship of athletic events.

Is alcohol a greater threat to youngsters than to adults?

Generally, young people respond to lower levels of alcohol than adults. They will become significantly impaired or drunk after consuming quantities of alcohol that may not greatly affect an adult— for three reasons. First, children and most adolescents weigh less than adults, and basically, the more body weight, the more alcohol a person can consume without noticeable impairment. Second, young people are inexperienced drinkers. And third, they lack the levels of alcohol-metabolizing liver enzymes that build with alcohol use and increase the body's tolerance to the drug. Given the illusion of immortality that accompanies youth, the bigger bang they get from alcohol can mean serious problems for youngsters. Alcohol-related accidents are the leading cause of death among U.S. males aged 15 to 24. So while not all drinking will cause harm, teenagers do face significant risks from alcohol use, both physical and legal.

Can you predict which child will develop into a problem drinker or alcoholic?

No, but certain things increase a child's risks. First and foremost, children of alcoholics face the highest danger; the risk is greatest if both parents are heavy drinkers. Hanging out with friends who abuse alcohol also increases the risk, for peer pressure really is a powerful force. Other signs that indicate a possible drinking problem ahead or already at hand include the use of alcohol at a young age; a disinterest in school, and bad grades; a strong sense of alienation and antisocial behavior, including fighting, vandalism, and criminal acts; no close ties to family, church, or school; and low self-esteem. None of these things individually, or all of them together, mean inevitable problems with alcohol. But they do constitute risk factors, and many suggest psychological problems that may require help and guidance from trained counselors.

What adverse effects does alcohol have on athletic performance?
Contrary to the belief of some athletes, a drink before competition to "ease the pressure," to stimulate the body, or to provide carbohydrates causes more problems than it solves. For one thing, alcohol is a depressant, not a stimulant. Alcohol also decreases the squeezing power of the heart when it contracts. As a result, it pumps less oxygen-carrying blood to the muscles; makes the muscles burn more sugar and less fat, using up an important store of quick energy more rapidly; and increases sweating, raising the risk of dehydration, heat exhaustion, and heatstroke. A drink or two decreases eye-hand coordination, balance, and reflexes, and dims an athlete's important ability to react quickly to clues provided by sight, sound and touch. The body rids itself of alcohol, breaking down every hour roughly the amount contained in a 12-ounce bottle of beer, or 5 ounces of wine, or 1.5 ounces of bourbon, gin, or vodka. While the body might clear all the alcohol of a heavy night's drinking by game time, excessive alcohol intake can disrupt a night's sleep badly and leave the drinker with a headache, nausea, and a general washed-out feeling the following morning. Neither lost sleep nor a hangover promotes a sharp performance, on the job or on the athletic field. Every young athlete should know that all the evidence shows alcohol harms rather than enhances athletic performance.

How common is cigarette smoking in the teen years?
Again, the best information source is the yearly national survey of graduating seniors conducted by University of Michigan researchers. In 1990, they found that 64.6 percent had smoked cigarettes at least once in their life, 29.4 percent had smoked in the month before their interview, 19.1 percent smoked daily, and 11.3 percent smoked at least half a pack each day. More than half those who smoked daily said they began smoking by age 14. As with alcohol, some teens refrain from smoking because of cigarettes' adverse effects on sports performance. But an unfortunately large percentage of young athletes do smoke.

What performance problems does smoking cause the young athlete?
As far as performance goes, tobacco smoke primarily affects the body's cardiorespiratory system, the intricately entwined relationship between heart and lungs. Evidence from a number of studies shows that inhaling tobacco smoke, either one's own or someone else's,

decreases the lungs' ability to function. Even a small reduction in the ability of an athlete's lungs to deliver oxygen to the body's cells can harm performance. Tobacco smoke contains nicotine, a potent drug that constricts blood vessels. This forces the heart to work harder and raises the systolic blood pressure (the higher of the two numbers in a blood pressure reading, which represents the force against a blood-vessel wall when the heart contracts to pump blood). Cigarette smoke also contains carbon monoxide gas, which binds to the same red blood cell sites as oxygen, but more readily. This means the more carbon monoxide in the blood, the less oxygen reaching the cells that need it. Carbon monoxide in large doses can kill. In smokers, carbon monoxide reduces their ability to perform physically by cutting the flow of oxygen needed to power muscles. Smokers also suffer more colds and other respiratory illnesses than nonsmokers.

Researchers have known for some time that young children who inhale smoke from their mothers' cigarettes suffer more lung-related illnesses and generally have poor lung function compared to children of nonsmokers. But now evidence is mounting that such "passive smoking" can inhibit the performance of nonsmoking teenage athletes. One study, for example, found that passive smoking increased coughs and decreased lung function among a group of 209 high school athletes ages 12 to 17. Boys were exposed to more passive smoke than girls, but the girls in the study suffered more ill effects.

Aren't snuff and chewing tobacco safer than cigarettes?
Only slightly; the smokeless tobaccos still pose a health hazard and an increased risk of death. They can cause nicotine addiction, oral cancers, noncancerous tissue damage, bleeding and shrinking gums, discolored teeth, and decreases in taste and smell. Snuff (cured ground tobacco) and chewing tobacco ranked as the most commonly used tobacco products in the United States at the turn of the century, but lost favor. In recent years, their popularity has returned, particularly with male junior and senior high school students. Smokeless tobaccos now are part of the iconography of sports, from the baseball idol with a plug bulging out his cheek to sponsorship of some of the nation's outstanding stock-car racers.

What can a parent do to prevent a child from using tobacco?
Not smoking yourself helps. Smoking teenagers more frequently have smoking parents than nonsmoking parents. Explaining the harmful

health effects of smoking and its adverse effects on athletic performance, beginning at an early age, may also help. But in truth, we
live in a society in which cigarettes are widely advertised, and in
which young males frequently regard smoking as manly and young
females see it as sexy or as a symbol of independence. Strong pressures, peer and otherwise, exist to entice the young to try cigarettes,
which the U.S. Surgeon General frequently reminds the public can
become addicting. Some success in cutting the number of young
smokers is reported by school systems that include antismoking efforts in their curricula beginning in the fifth grade and continuing
through junior high school. For young smokers who want to quit,
their physicians or local chapters of the American Cancer Society
can provide tips on how to stay the nonsmoking course. A number
of hospitals, health groups, and companies also provide formal stop-
smoking programs, for a fee.

COCAINE AND MARIJUANA

These two mind-altering drugs rate as the favorites of adolescent
"recreational drug" users, and this includes young athletes. Although
illicit drug use among high school students has declined in recent
years, the annual University of Michigan drug-use survey found that
among seniors graduating in 1990, 40.7 percent had sampled marijuana at least once in their life. Fourteen percent of the seniors
reported using marijuana in the month prior to their interview and
2.2 percent said they smoked it daily. Among cocaine abusers, 1.9
percent said they used it in the previous 30 days, and 0.1 percent
described themselves as daily users. The cocaine figures are particularly disturbing because cocaine can create an addiction and can
kill—even, occasionally, on the first use.

What effect does cocaine produce in the body?
Cocaine—a white powder that is generally inhaled by snorting or
smoked in "freebase" form or as particularly addictive "crack"—
produces euphoria and a state of high energy that lasts less than half
an hour. The drug is a central nervous system stimulant, and its
effects on the brain go well beyond creating an altered mood. Users
may suffer anxiety and become agitated as the drug wears off. Cocaine can improve peripheral reflexes for a time, and it does increase
heart rate and blood pressure.

Does this mean cocaine helps performance?
Quite the contrary. Cocaine users may think the drug gives them greater strength and endurance, but that's a myth of the mind. No one has ever documented this alleged enhanced ability from cocaine use; and in fact, the drug can diminish an athlete's ability to react, especially young players. There simply is no conclusive evidence that cocaine can help an athlete, and plenty of evidence that long-term use can harm careers. Cocaine's appeal among today's athletes appears more related to its euphoria-producing properties and its faded image as the drug of the rich and famous than to its ability to improve playing skills.

What are the adverse physical effects of cocaine use?
Addiction and death, to name two serious consequences. The cocaine deaths only days apart in 1986 of two healthy, talented young athletes shocked the sports world and much of the nation. University of Maryland basketball star Len Bias died after celebrating his signing by the Boston Celtics of the National Basketball Association with cocaine. Ten days later, Don Rogers, a free safety with the Cleveland Browns of the National Football League, died after using cocaine. Their deaths served to emphasize the potential tragic consequences of cocaine use. The drug, once mistakenly touted as benign, can trigger seizures, erratic heartbeats that may end in a heart attack, and soaring blood pressure that may rupture a blood vessel in the brain, causing a debilitating or fatal stroke. Cocaine abusers also may suffer breathing problems, bronchitis, and mental depression, and may attempt suicide. Problems primarily associated with snorting the drug include symptoms of hay fever, swelling inside the nose, and ulceration of the tissue separating the two nasal passages.

How does marijuana affect athletic performance?
In a word, badly. Marijuana smokers frequently insist they function as well under the drug's influence as without it, but a number of careful scientific studies have proven otherwise. Marijuana, in amounts typically smoked in social settings, impairs motor coordination, depth perception, peripheral vision, timing, and the ability to track a ball or other object in the air. It also diminishes vigilance and can harm short-term memory. Among frequent users, marijuana can cause concentration problems, apathy, and lowered ambition.

None of these effects helps improve performance, on or off the athletic field.

What other adverse effects can marijuana cause?
The drug can cause conjunctival injection (a reddening and irritation of the membrane covering the eye), rapid heartbeats, lower levels of the hormone testosterone, a low sperm count, breast enlargement in males, acute and chronic bronchitis, and anxiety. A quite serious problem, one with potentially fatal consequences, lies in the not-uncommon practice of lacing marijuana cigarettes with other drugs, frequently phencyclidine (PCP) or crack cocaine.

PART THREE

RISKS AND BENEFITS— SPORT BY SPORT

10

Running and Track and Field

The origins of modern running and field events go back to the first competitions pitting one human against another in tests of strength, skill, and endurance. Sprints and distance running events, the javelin throw, and the discus toss had long histories in antiquity before the ancient Greeks staged their first Olympic games. Still, these athletic endeavors have gotten some mixed reviews over the centuries, from medical and social critics alike. Bernardino Ramazzini, who wrote a Renaissance book titled *Diseases of Workers*, warned that "runners were prone to suffer from hernias and asthma." Pierre de Coubertin, founder of the modern Olympics, invoked a higher power in opposition to the idea of female athletes. "Women's sports are against the laws of Nature," he said in 1902. And even in the 1960s, newspapers published occasional articles about police officers stopping joggers for questioning, on the suspicion that anyone running must be running from some illegal act.

Sports participation by men and women, girls and boys, has come a long way in the last several decades. Nothing testifies to this more than the daily outpouring of Americans who hit the nation's tracks, streets, and roads running. Many youngsters who don't consider themselves joggers, runners, or potential track stars use running as a means of conditioning their bodies for other sports, such as football, basketball, soccer, tennis, even field events.

⊡ *Running*

Many researchers have studied runners, some emphasizing the benefits (considerable) and some the risk of injury (common). Running strengthens the cardiovascular and respiratory systems, reduces

weight, strengthens leg muscles, and may well improve the symptoms of mild depression. At the same time, runners suffer a number
of lower-body injuries. Knee problems appear to rank first, but foot,
ankle, calf, thigh, hip, and lower-back problems also plague runners.
The exact incidence of these various injuries remains unclear, but
research indicates they are common. For example, a study of 438
experienced adult runners at a Dallas health and fitness club, who
ran on average five days a week and averaged 25 miles weekly,
found that 24 percent of these men and women had suffered some
injury from running in the previous year. Studies often disagree on
whether such things as age, sex, degree of stretching before running,
and type of surface or terrain traversed increase a runner's risk of
injury. There seems wider agreement that the greater the number of
miles run weekly, the greater the risk of injury.

Children and adolescents who join the ranks of dedicated runners face risks in addition to those of adults. First, their strength fails
to proportionately match their size, and most youngsters have neither
the will nor the motivation to do the work necessary to condition
their bodies for running or to acclimatize themselves to the heat
runners often face. Second, their more flexible ligaments and their
still-active bone growth plates make them more susceptible to muscle
and skeletal injuries. Third, many young runners pay little attention
to getting properly fitted with quality shoes. Moreover, the first indication of unrecognized congenital problems sometimes appears
when youngsters begin running.

Some studies indicate that there are significant sex differences
in running injuries. One study of 124 boys and girls found that 10
percent of the youngsters suffered stress fractures, but that boys suffered three times as many as girls (9 out of 12). The stress fractures
occurred in those running the highest number of miles weekly, and
the boys tended to run more miles than the girls. Eighteen percent
of the youngsters experienced problems in regions of bone-growth
potential, with those injuries twice as common in the girls as in the
boys. Female runners commonly experience changes in their menstrual patterns, even to the point of a cessation of bleeding (see
Chapter 5), which, if prolonged and unrecognized, increases a girl's
risk of bone loss, particularly in the spine. Most menstrual-cycle
disruptions are reversible with reduced running and/or treatment
with birth control pills, and an increased calcium intake appears to
help prevent bone loss.

Because of these risks, several groups have offered suggestions for children and adolescents who run. The American Academy of Pediatrics notes that youngsters may suffer psychological damage if they set unrealistic goals and fail to achieve them, or if they participate in running for parental approval rather than their own pleasure. The medical group also urges that "immature youth" not run in long-distance races intended for adults, especially not marathons. The International Amateur Athletic Federation of England provides even more specific guidelines. It recommends that children under 12 never run more than 800 meters (0.5 mile) in a day, those under 14 limit their running to 3,000 meters (1.86 miles), and no one run a marathon before reaching age 18.

A woman sought medical attention for her 8-year-old son, who had developed a limp. On examination, the physician found the boy suffering pain in the heel and big toe. Mother and son said he played no sports, but the boy did mention he often "ran around the track" with his father. Further questioning revealed that the boy was running one to three miles at a time. Rest from running cured his limp.

If a boy or girl wants to pursue running seriously, it might prove useful to have a physician examine the youngster's lower body for specific regions of pain, and swelling, and for motion, cartilage, and ligament abnormalities.

PREVENTING INJURIES

Runners stand their greatest risk of injury at four specific times. Not surprisingly, the first comes during the first four to six months they pursue the sport. Flush with enthusiasm and with some progress evident almost every day, fledgling runners push beyond reasonable bounds, with the typical results of foot pain, tendinitis, or shin splints. The adage "Walk before you run" should be heeded by anyone taking up the sport of running. A novice runner does best to walk first and then progress to a combination of walking and running before trying to run during the entire workout. Another high-risk period follows an injury. Too often, returning runners attempt to resume their old pace and distance, mistakenly assuming they have lost nothing during their recovery period. When an injury forces a layoff of two weeks or more, a runner should work back gradually to his or her previous distance.

Finally, runners face their third and fourth periods of increased injury risk when they try either to significantly increase their distance or to better their time over a specific distance. The 2-miles-a-day runner who starts training for a 10-kilometer (6.2-miles) race, or the runner training for a faster time in a 10K or marathon both face a greater chance of injury unless they pay attention to proper running technique, increase their stretching before running, and cool down properly afterward.

Proper and adequate stretching provides runners their single most important protection against injury. Runners should spend at least 15 minutes doing warm-up exercises before taking to the track or street. We described a number of stretching exercises and a typical progression in Chapter 2. The proper way to do warm-up exercises is slow and steady, not fast and jerky. The purpose is to increase the blood circulation, warm the muscles, and improve the muscles' ability to contract. Repeating these same exercises after running reduces the chances of muscle stiffness and cramps and helps increase flexibility. Too much stretching can be harmful, however. Overstretching itself may cause injury. Running with cold, overstretched, undernourished, or damaged muscle fibers can cause tendinitis.

Weight training, within reason, can also help runners. It strengthens muscles and increases the number of capillaries feeding blood to them. Both these effects help increase muscle contraction and reduce fatigue.

Finally, remember the runner's wisdom: "Train, don't strain." Even the most athletic body can stand just so much stress. If performance begins to lag, whether in competition or just street jogging, the body may well be suggesting it needs some rest. That doesn't mean ceasing running totally, but rather cutting back on the pace, distance covered, and frequency of running for a while.

ENVIRONMENTAL CONDITIONS

Weather, the running surface, polluted air, and even high altitudes can adversely affect runners.

HEAT. Heat disorders usually occur in summer, but they may strike in spring and fall, and even in winter if the young athlete runs indoors. The key lies in the body's ability to get rid of the heat generated by exercise. If enough heat isn't dissipated, the body reacts with progressively more serious symptoms—cramps, flushing, fatigue, dizziness, fever, confusion, fainting, coma, and death.

Children burn more energy per pound of body weight while

exercising than do adults. This energy requirement continues into early adolescence. This means that children and younger adolescents produce more heat per pound than adults. At the same time, they have a lower body-surface area per body mass to help dissipate heat than do adults. Thus youngsters stand a greater risk than adults of heat disorders at the same temperature. Young athletes need to drink plenty of fluids (water or unsweetened fruit juices) before running, and some during distance races, particularly in hot weather. Nothing guards against heat disorders as well as proper hydration.

The type of clothing worn can play an important role as well. One of the first rules any safety-conscious runner must follow is to wear clothing appropriate for the weather. Dressing too lightly in cold weather may result in frostnip or frostbite; overdressing in heat could lead to painful cramping, heat exhaustion, or even life-threatening heatstroke. Sweat suits should be avoided in warm and hot weather, because they interfere with the evaporation of sweat, the major source of body cooling. Actually, in the heat, runners should wear lightweight and light-colored clothing and as little of it as possible, within the bounds of decency.

Roadwork should be done before 9 a.m. or after 5 p.m. on hot days, with a bottle of water in hand to replenish fluid loss. And runners should know the early warning signs of heat problems: the hairs of the chest and upper arms standing on end, chills, headache, unsteadiness, nausea, and progressive cessation of sweating. Stop if these symptoms occur, and seek medical assistance if they persist.

COLD. Cold weather, particularly temperatures blew freezing, poses its own potential hazards for runners. Aside from the danger of causing a fall, ice and snow force runners to alter their gait, which may create unusual stresses on the lower extremities and result in an overuse injury. Cold temperatures and winter winds can lead to frostnip (the formation of ice crystals on the skin without tissue freezing) and frostbite (the freezing of the skin and the flesh underneath). In a sense, the underlying problem is opposite that of heat disorders. To maintain its normal thermal balance, the body needs to expel the heat it produces. But in cold weather, too much heat may be lost, leaving the skin exposed to damage by subfreezing temperatures.

Cold-weather joggers should dress in layers—thermal underwear, a shirt, a sweater, a parka or jacket, for example. Layering clothing traps and heats air, helping to keep the body warm, and allows runners to regulate their heat loss somewhat by opening zippers or buttons and even removing an item of clothing if they get too hot. Since the body loses up to 50 percent of its heat through the neck and scalp, winter runners should wear a warm, tight-fitting cap or hat. Mittens give better protection than gloves, and two pairs of light socks work better than a single thick pair. Avoid nylon underwear or running shorts because they lack any real insulating effect. Finally, make sure that both the groin area and the nipples have adequate protection against painful frostnip and frostbite. (See Chapter 6 for a more detailed discussion of heat and cold injuries and how to prevent and treat them.)

SURFACE. Paying attention to where one runs may also pay off in preventing injuries. A surface with some give to it reduces the stresses generated within the body at impact. So a park trail, a footpath, a farm road, or the dirt shoulder beside a road is preferable to asphalt and far better than running on concrete, which experienced runners shun whenever possible. Runners should always run facing traffic, and wear light-colored clothing with battery-powered flashers or reflective tape when running at night.

Whatever the surface, runners need a relatively level and smooth course without a lot of potholes, cracks, bumps, tree roots, or large dirt clods that might cause a strain, sprain, torn muscle, or broken bone. Running up or down hills also poses risks—knee injuries going uphill and foot, Achilles tendon, and knee problems going downhill (caused by forcing the body to decelerate to maintain balance). Running on an indoor track laid out on a concrete floor can lead to shin splints. Runners who use a synthetic all-weather track—a type now popular at many high schools, colleges, and universities—may encounter two specific problems not found with the old cinder or clay tracks. One, appropriately enough, is called "synthetic turf syndrome," which causes pain in the ankle, the tibia (the larger of the two lower leg bones), the kneecap, and the thigh. It appears to result from the shock vibration that occurs with synthetic surfaces. The second ailment results when a runner falls, scraping the skin and embedding tiny particles of the synthetic material in the skin surface. Unless cleaned thoroughly and treated with an antibiotic solution, the wound may develop a long-lasting, annoying reaction in which it oozes a clear fluid.

POLLUTION. Running in smog can cause eye, nose, and throat irritation, headaches, light-headedness, and even nausea, depending on the concentrations of air pollutants. When researchers compared a group of joggers who ran along a highway and through a park in New York City with a group of people who simply stood in the same areas for the same amount of time, they found the runners had three times the amount of carbon monoxide in their blood. This level equaled the carbon monoxide put into the blood by smoking one-half to one pack of cigarettes a day. All this suggests that runners should avoid, as much as possible, routes that will expose them to exhaust fumes, and not run outdoors on days when air-pollution levels soar.

ALTITUDE. When a person leaves the coastal areas or plains and travels into the mountains, it takes his or her body time to adjust to the reduced oxygen levels at higher elevations. For the unacclimated, running in altitudes above 6,000 feet can produce headaches, weakness, nausea, and vomiting. So a youngster enjoying the Rocky Mountain vistas who wants to put in his or her regular roadwork needs to reduce both distance and speed.

SHOES AND ORTHOTICS

Running shoes rank first in the runner's defenses against injury, particularly against sprained ankles. Properly designed, constructed, and fitted shoes provide shock absorption, foot stability, and motion control. A typical runner's feet hit the ground roughly 800 times a mile each, with a force two to three times the runner's body weight. Unless properly absorbed, such forces over time can cause bone and cartilage deterioration, low-back pain, and stress fractures. Slight malalignments of the hips and bones of the legs, knees, and feet can increase a runner's risk of injury. Too often, youngsters who use running as a fitness conditioner for other sports don't wear appropriate shoes, relying instead on cheap canvas high-tops or even, say, their baseball or soccer shoes, which increases their risk of injury while running.

Any child who shows an interest in running should get a physical examination by a knowledgeable physician to assess any alignment problems. Many can be corrected by orthotic devices, "inserts" placed in shoes to compensate for a runner's physical abnormality.

For example, some people grow up with one leg shorter than the other, a potential problem for runners which a "lift" placed inside the shoe of the shorter leg can correct. A physician should look over a youngster's running shoes any time he or she develops an injury. This is particularly true if the shoe contains an orthotic device, which itself can cause problems by overcorrecting an abnormality or when the runner does not fully understand directions for its use. The condition of the shoe and the patterns of wear on the shoe's sole can tell the physician quite a bit about the runner's mechanics.

No running shoe fits everyone's needs. Runners should select comfortable, well-cushioned shoes that keep the foot stable, yet provide enough flexibility for miles and miles of roadwork. Shoes should bend where the foot bends, at the ball of the foot, to help avoid muscle strain, shin splints, and tendinitis in the Achilles tendon. The toe box should be square to provide room for a little toe motion, which reduces blisters, calluses, corns, and nail problems. Good padding running the entire length of the sole will help avoid bruises of the heel and fat pad, foot sprains, and bone spurs on the ball of the foot. Finally, the shoe back should never irritate the back of the heel. Breaking in shoes, rather than running long distances immediately, helps prevent blisters and the bursitis known as "pump bump" (see page 180).

All running shoes lose some of their shock-absorbing power with use. When a research team in New Orleans tested shoes made by 13 manufacturers and worn by frequent runners, they found that the shoes' shock-absorbing qualities varied by as much as one-third when new. Yet the percentage of loss proved quite uniform, with each brand retaining about 80 percent of its initial shock-absorption ability after 150 miles and 70 percent after 500 miles. Interestingly, the weight of the runner made no difference in the shock-absorption deterioration.

DIET AND NUTRITION

We discussed the nutritional needs of young athletes in Chapter 3. A point to remember: Never underestimate the value of an adequate and balanced diet in supplying a runner's energy needs. Far too often, young athletes look to vitamin and mineral supplements and carbohydrate loading to give them an edge. But heavy doses of vitamins and minerals remain of questionable value at best and dangerous in some instances. Some girls and women may need extra iron, but before dosing herself, a female runner should consult her physician.

RECOVERY FROM INJURY

For many injured runners, whatever their age, a physician's order to stop running brings frustration, anger, and sometimes rebellion. Add to that the impetuousness of youth and their sense of healing quickly, and you can understand the problem in getting young runners to lay off long enough to allow an injury to heal. Devoted runners run, and any downtime truly annoys young athletes. Fortunately, not all injuries require total rest. Often a young person can do aerobic walking, bicycle, swim, run in water, or row.

In many injuries, the young athlete need only reduce his or her level of running, not abstain totally. Such a reduced-running rehabilitation program needs the direction of a physician, physical therapist, or professional trainer. Typically, recovering runners cut their usual mileage by half or more, reduce their pace, emphasize certain stretching exercises, and stop running as soon as pain develops or after they've covered a specific distance.

This approach to rehabilitation combines conditioning with healing and allows the body to gradually return to full strength and health. Youngsters must remember that doing too much too fast only threatens their recovery. Impatience can curse the cure.

ICE

Cold kills pain and helps reduce inflammation and swelling. Applying crushed ice wrapped inside a towel to the injury or soaking it in cold water works best. Icing an injury should continue for 15 minutes. In acute cases, ice can be applied every one or two hours. Icing after exercise helps ease the pain of chronic tendinitis and kneecap problems.

ASPIRIN

This inexpensive, nonprescription drug reduces both inflammation—and thus swelling—and pain quite effectively, when the pain is not intense. (Acetaminophin relieves only pain; ibuprofen helps both pain and inflammation.) Most people tolerate aspirin well, although, as with any medication, some suffer side effects. Aspirin reduces the blood's clotting ability and can cause stomach upset and damage to the stomach lining. Taken an hour before competition, aspirin reaches its full power in the blood at the time the athlete begins practice or competition. Anyone taking aspirin or any other non-prescription drug to treat an athletic injury should consult a physician, registered nurse, or certified athletic trainer about the proper dosage. A number of prescription anti-inflammatory drugs exist, but these require careful use under a physician's direction.

SPECIFIC RUNNING INJURIES

ANKLE AND FOOT

Runners commonly suffer injuries to the foot and ankle, the intricate joint that serves as a hinge between the foot and leg. Sprains account for a large portion of ankle injuries. Most sprains result when the foot twists inward and the ankle turns out and drops down toward the ground, stretching or tearing ligaments on the outside of the ankle. Much less common, but often more serious in the time they take to heal, are sprains that result when the foot twists outward and the ankle inward, injuring ligaments on the inside of the ankle. Young females tend to suffer worse sprains for the same amount of stress than young males, for two reasons. First, a female's weight centers over the inside of the ankle, causing more strain on the ligaments when the ankle twists. Second, females usually have weaker leg muscles than males.

Young athletes should never treat sprains lightly. Ignoring the pain and limping bravely around on a sprained ankle will only increase the pain and swelling in the hours ahead. A person who suffers an ankle sprain should think and practice RICE—Rest, Ice, Compression, and Elevation (see Chapter 6). We cannot emphasize enough the importance of keeping weight off an injured ankle until the swelling and pain subside. If the ankle swells immediately, if it becomes discolored, or if swelling and bad pain persist longer than 24 hours, the youngster should consult a physician, who may order X rays to check for a bone fracture.

With moderate or severe sprains, exercises that strengthen the muscles supporting the ankle can often hasten recovery and help prevent future injuries, although once an ankle is sprained it becomes more vulnerable to reinjury. Choosing a relatively smooth surface for running and wearing well-constructed and properly fitted running shoes can help prevent sprains and other injuries to the ankle and foot. We discuss ankle sprains and their treatment in greater detail in Chapter 16.

The Achilles tendon, which attaches the calf muscle to the heel, also causes problems for many runners. Typically, this tendon gets stretched or torn when the heel falls far below the toes, as may happen when a runner steps in a hole or hits a high curb. Runners with a slightly misshapen heel bone, described medically as a superolateral calcaneus, often suffer a bursitis called "pump bump." Pressure from the runner's shoe on the tendon where it attaches to the heel bone causes inflammation and sometimes a painful cyst. If left untreated, a runner may need surgery to ease his or her chronic pain. Pump bump occurs more often in females than in males. Wearing a shoe modified with a ¼- to ⅜-inch orthotic heel lift can usually prevent pump bump.

Youngsters with either high arches (cavus foot) or flat feet (planovalgus foot) run an increased risk of foot injuries. Runners with high arches usually have less flexible and less padded feet. This makes them more prone to metatarsal stress fractures, tendinitis, injuries to the ligaments of the outer side of the foot, stress fractures, and plantar fasciitis (see below). Flat-footed runners suffer more than an average share of calluses beneath the ball of the foot, tendinitis, and ligament injury on the inside of the foot.

Plantar fasciitis, a common condition in runners, results from microscopic tears in the proximal plantar fascia, the covering of the bottom of the foot. Like stress fractures, plantar fasciitis represents an overuse problem. (For further details, see Chapter 7).

Finally, young runners may suffer from ingrown toenails or from a condition known as "black toe." Many ingrown toenails require little more than cutting the nail so it protrudes beyond the soft flesh and placing cotton beneath the edges so they grow up and over the soft tissue. If a toenail is infected, however, a physician may prescribe an antibiotic. Some cases require surgery to provide relief. In black toe, the toe turns black beneath the nail due to hemorrhage, which usually happens because the runner's shoes are too tight. Switching to shoes with a wider toe box generally solves the problem.

BACK AND HIP

Back pain occurs only infrequently among healthy young athletes who use proper running technique—a slight forward lean of the body with the center of gravity over the foot hitting the ground. Pain in such runners usually results either from an injury or from a congenital defect. For example, a runner may unknowingly have spondylolisthesis, a deformity in which a lower vertebra slides onto the sacrum, the shield-shaped bone that forms the back of the pelvis. Some developmental defects will preclude a youngster from running; others, including spondylolisthesis and some spinal malalignments, may only limit the number of miles he or she can run each week. (See Chapter 14.)

Occasionally a runner, particularly a long-distance runner, develops back pain that improves with rest but returns quickly when the youngster takes to the track or street again. This may indicate a stress fracture, which X rays may fail to reveal for months and which may require some sophisticated tests to diagnose. When a spinal stress fracture occurs, the young athlete must stop running until it heals, which usually takes three to six months.

Less common causes of hip pain include a too-rigid foot or orthotic insert, and stress fractures. Exercises that improve the flexibility of a rigid foot or using a more flexible orthotic device often stop the pain. Stress fractures in the hip may occur in the pelvic bone or in the upper reaches of the femur, the long bone that runs from the hip to the knee, and may not show up on an X ray for six to nine months, although a bone scan can spot them much earlier. Treatment obviously bars running and requires the use of crutches to keep weight off the injured hip. Recovery typically takes 6 to 12 months.

BLADDER

Distance runners sometimes suddenly discover blood in their urine. Such blood may signal a serious problem, but in runners, it often represents nothing more than a bruised bladder. Bruising may occur from the repeated impact of the runner's feet, which bangs the soft back wall of an empty or nearly empty bladder against the bladder's thicker, more rigid base. Such bleeding poses no problem for runners, but anyone with bloody urine should quickly consult a physician to rule out any serious disorders.

CARDIOVASCULAR PROBLEMS

Sudden, unexpected death does strike young runners, but is quite uncommon. In older adults, about three-quarters of such deaths result from coronary heart disease, the blockage of the heart arteries by fatty deposits that build up on the vessels' walls. But among runners of high school and college age the cause of sudden death usually stems from other defects, often congenital.

Hours of training for distance racing can affect the heart in ways that may cause a physician to initially suspect heart problems. For example, the heart itself may appear enlarged on a chest X ray or when the physician thumps the chest, but this results from exercise and not disease. And some runners have slight heart murmurs or show a so-called gallop rhythm on their electrocardiograms. Both are benign. Nonetheless, if a physician finds such changes, they should be checked thoroughly to make sure they result from running alone and do not threaten the young athlete.

Knee and Lower-Leg Problems

Unlike football, soccer, or basketball players, whose knee and lower-leg injuries frequently stem from collisions or sudden, twisting turns, distance runners tend to suffer from stress injuries and overuse syndromes. Knee problems occur frequently in runners, but fortunately, most respond well to proper treatment. The knee complaints physicians see most in runners are patellar pain, or "runner's knee"— a group of problems affecting the kneecap—and iliotibial band syndrome, an overuse problem that causes inflammation and soreness along the outside of the thigh and knee.

Most distance runners and joggers suffer at least one episode of kneecap pain. Typically they complain of a dull ache behind the kneecap when they run. In some people the pain comes and goes during their run, in others it persists from beginning to end. The pain usually ceases shortly after the run ends. In some runners, swelling occurs in the synovial membrane lining the knee. Evidence suggests that much of the kneecap pain experienced by runners results from excessive stress forces on normal cartilage, normal stress on abnormal cartilage, or a malalignment of the extensor mechanism, the bones and ligaments that operate to straighten the leg. Current evidence indicates that runner's knee poses little or no increased risk to young athletes for developing osteoarthritis in their knees later in life.

Treatment for kneecap pain obviously depends on the cause of the pain. For many runners, treatment consists of stopping running or reducing their regular mileage for three weeks to three months. Elastic knee sleeves or braces, aspirin or other anti-inflammatory

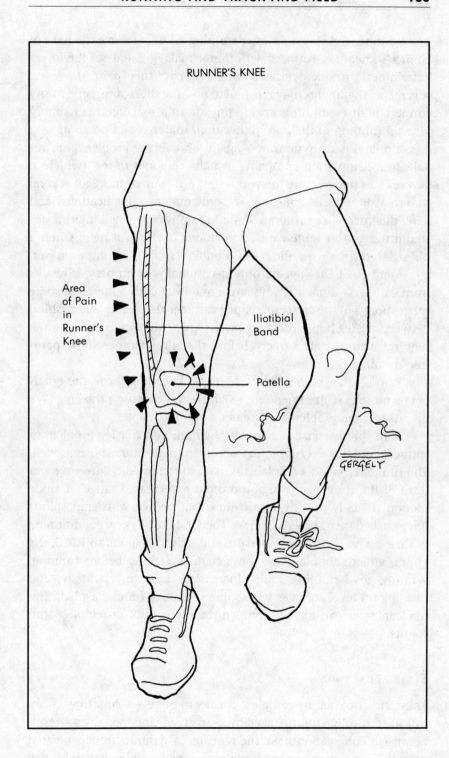

RUNNER'S KNEE

Area
of Pain
in
Runner's
Knee

Iliotibial
Band

Patella

GERGELY

medications, and ice packs after running all help relieve the pain of runner's knee. For runners with minor malalignments of the lower extremities, orthotic devices often can correct their pain. However, severe malalignments may repsond to nothing short of surgery. Many runners with continuing knee pain due to a malalignment simply give up running in the end, rather than undergo an operation.

Iliotibial band syndrome—again, an overuse problem that results in inflammation and pain—usually responds to rest (which in severe cases may require the youngster to give up running for several months) or reduced mileage, anti-inflammatory medications, and icing the knee after running. Sometimes physicians will inject a steroid drug, and in some cases, an orthotic device will help. Often a physician orders a specific set of iliotibial-band stretching exercises.

Meniscus pain appears only occasionally in runners. It results from damage—almost always a tear and frequently suffered in some other sport—to the crescent-shaped cartilage that serves as a cushion between the leg bones that meet at the knee. Meniscus damage often requires arthroscopic surgery before the runner can resume pain-free running.

Pain on the inside or outside of the knee joint or in the quadriceps muscle at the knee often signifies an overuse problem. (We discussed knee problems in greater detail in Chapter 7.)

Shin splints constitute the most common lower-leg problem in runners, and this overuse injury occurs in many other sports as well. The runner typically complains of pain in the middle third or lower third of the front of the leg, and often a decreased range of ankle motion. Usually the physician finds that people with shin splints have pushed themselves to run well beyond the physical conditioning of their body. If such pain persists and fails to respond to RICE, the young athlete should see a physician. Stretching before running, wearing good running shoes, increasing distances gradually, and running on level surfaces with some resiliency (dirt or asphalt, but not concrete) can all help reduce the chances of developing shin splints.

STRESS FRACTURES

These small partial or complete breaks in bone—accounting for up to 1 in 10 running injuries seen by sports medicine specialists—result because a bone cannot take the repeated, rhythmic stress generated as each foot hits the ground again and again, mile after mile, day after day. The runner notices pain, worse when running, which gradually increases in intensity. Stress fractures in bones near the skin surface feel tender and painful to the touch; those in bones padded by muscle and fat produce a more diffuse pain.

Stress fractures in runners may occur in the foot, ankle, leg, hip, and pelvis. The most frequent break site is the femoral neck, the portion of the thigh bone that attaches to the hip socket, and the upper part of the tibia, the larger of the two bones in the lower leg. Stress fractures rarely occur in the growth plates of bones in children and adolescents, but they do happen. A number of things increase the risk of stress fractures from running, including such anatomic deficiencies as gait disorders, malformed bones in the lower limbs, and having one leg shorter than the other. Other factors that increase the danger include poor shoes, poor physical conditioning, a previous stress fracture, running on a steeply banked track or hard surface, and running in excess of 20 miles a week.

Remember that any stress fracture can lead to complications if a youngster tries to tough out its symptoms and continues to run. These injuries belong under a physician's care to prevent further damage, and hopefully, recurrence. Treatment varies with the location of the stress fracture, and physicians try to individualize their rehabilitation plans, but rest remains the key to healing. The length of time a young athlete must give up running and the kind of substitute activities he or she can pursue differ from fracture to fracture. Many physicians, however, regard six weeks' rest as the minimum. Runners who fracture the femoral neck must keep weight off their hip and cease all sports activities. Only when they become pain-free can they pursue substitutes for running, such as swimming and bicycling. On the other hand, many athletes with pelvic stress fractures can engage in substitute sports to keep their bodies conditioned. Youngsters should never resume running until all significant pain has disappeared, and they must resume their roadwork gradually. They should consult their physician about the need for better shoes, orthotic inserts, and changing their running route.

TENDINITIS

This chronic inflammation of a tendon or tendon-muscle attachment occurs commonly among runners. Youngsters may develop an acute episode that basically heals by itself or a chronic condition that produces pain whenever they run. Unless treated, chronic tendinitis will create increasing disability and weaken the tendon, increasing the danger that it will rupture. In runners, tendinitis usually represents an overuse injury. Tendons are made up of a tough, strong material with remarkable recovery powers, provided it gets enough time to heal. But the act of running long distances almost daily can create forces and loads that a tendon cannot withstand. Microscopic tears develop and inflammation follows, creating pain that can reach the point where the runner can no longer run.

As with stress fractures, rest is a central part of tendinitis treatments, although they vary considerably, depending on the tendon involved and whether the inflammation is acute or chronic. The youngster may need to stop running for only a day or two, or for three to six weeks or more. Physicians frequently recommend aspirin for its beneficial effects on both pain and inflammation. Many use corticosteroid injections as well, an effective treatment for inflammation, but one that research suggests lowers the tensile strength of the tendon (its ability to resist tearing) and increases the risk of tendon rupture. A number of physical treatments also help tendinitis, depending on its severity. Icing the injured area for 5 to 15 minutes helps fight inflammation. Ultrasound may help the tendon recover tensile strenth. Heat treatments increase the blood flow to the injury site and reduce stiffness. Electric stimulation can provide pain relief, and physically massaging the area of pain, while painful itself, breaks down scar tissue. Finally, severe cases (rare in young athletes) may require surgery to remove a large buildup of scar tissue. Rehabilitation from chronic tendinitis also should include exercises to rebuild the runner's physical condition (see Chapter 7).

⊡ Track and Field

Running plays an important part in track and field, both in the conditioning of participants and as an actual part of many events. Sprinters and hurdlers run. Long jumpers and triple jumpers sprint to their takeoff points to gain the momentum they need for distance. And researchers Jerome V. Ciullo and Douglas W. Jackson have aptly described the pole-vaulter as "essentially a sprinter with a pole." Many of the points about nutrition, conditioning, and the importance of preparticipation stretching exercises discussed earlier in this chapter hold for these sports as well as for distance running. Each of the track and field events also has its own potential for injury that coaches, parents, and young athletes must recognize. More so than in many sports, the key to preventing track and field injuries lies in learning and following proper techniques. A mistimed step or a limb out of position at the wrong time can result in a painful and debilitating injury.

SPRINTS AND HURDLES

Sprints are short-distance races in which the runner races at full speed throughout. Hurdles are essentially sprints in which the participants run over barriers. In both, the runners begin in a crouched position with their feet placed against starting blocks. Flexibility, a strong lower body, and adhering to proper technique provide the best defense against injury. In particular, the explosive start sprinters seek off their blocks requires powerful quadriceps and hamstrings.

Hamstring strains, or "pulls," rank as the most common injury among sprinters. Exercises to stretch and strengthen the hamstrings and the calf muscles can help prevent this injury (see Chapter 2). Indeed, strengthening and stretching these muscles also can reduce the risk of a variety of knee problems. Tendinitis presents another common problem in sprinters because they run on their toes and the forward part of the foot. Proper stretching lessens the risk. Strengthening the calf muscle and stretching the heel cord can reduce Achilles tendon problems. Sometimes sprinters suffer stress fractures in the two bones of the lower leg, usually because their leg muscles aren't strong enough to absorb the shock of running.

Running around an oval track, as sprinters and hurdlers often do, can produce a variety of stresses that result in knee problems. As an athlete runs around a curve, his or her feet land tilted at the angle of the banked track. This creates unequal forces on the inner and outer portions of the knee, which can eventually lead to injury. Again, strengthening and stretching the leg muscles can help prevent these conditions by strengthening the shock-absorbing properties of the knee's muscles and tendons.

In addition to the problems hurdlers face while running hurdles, soaring over barriers can cause some painful problems in itself. For example, Sean thought he had developed shin splints in one leg, but his physician quickly ruled that problem out, leaving the doctor puzzled at what lay behind the 16-year-old sprinter's obvious pain. Finally, after intensive questioning, the answer emerged: At the request of his coach, Sean had recently begun running the hurdles. His pain came from repeatedly banging his lower leg into the wooden tops of the hurdles.

Learning the proper way to run hurdles takes time and effort, but unless a youngster masters the techniques, he or she faces a high risk of sprains, strains, bruises, or even myositis ossificans, a long-term muscle inflammation that results in formation of a small amount of bone within the muscle itself. Landing too flat of foot or on the heel instead of the ball of the foot, for example, can result in heel injuries. Usually these take the form of a painfully bruised fat pad or, less frequently, a tiny bone fracture that takes months to heal. Landing properly offers the best prevention. Youngsters who fail to master the technique of clearing a hurdle with either foot will have to slow their pace from time to time to add a step so they can leap with their preferred foot forward. This slowing can cause knee-ligament strain.

Hurdlers, even more than sprinters, risk sprains and strains, but they can reduce that risk with diligent muscle stretching. Training early in the season should take place on grass to reduce injuries. Padded hurdles and padding hurdlers at the heel, ankle, and knee in practice also helps.

JUMPING EVENTS

Young athletes and their coaches should personally inspect the ramps, aprons, supporting poles, crossbars, and landing areas used in their event. Each of these can contribute to injuries. The runways used to gain speed should contain no holes or bumps that could twist an ankle or cause a youngster to stumble. Often the approach ramps and aprons for jumping events consist of a synthetic material. Unfortunately, schools and youth leagues, short on cash, may save money by building a path less than four feet wide. This increases the chance of a misstep during the approach run that may cause a fall, cuts and bruises, a sprained ankle, a twisted knee, or a serious ligament injury. Uneven, loose, and excessively worn takeoff boards invite injury and require immediate repair or replacement. Poles holding the crossbars used in pole vaulting and high jumping should be smooth and weighted so they fall away when hit by a participant. Fiberglass crossbars pose less risk of injury when an athlete lands on them than those made of metal. Landing pits for pole vaulters and high jumpers should consist of foam-rubber blocks, elevated well above the takeoff point. They should extend under the high-jump crossbar to protect the jumper who fails to clear the bar and falls straight down, and should extend around the pole-vaulter's planting box to protect those who make a miscue. The landing pit for long jumpers should contain at least 12 inches, and preferably 18 inches, of loose sand or loam, slightly damp and "fluffed," to cushion the impact of the young athlete's landing and reduce the risk of injury.

POLE VAULT

Pole-vaulters must plant their poles properly. A missed plant can result in the pole's spearing the foam rubber of the landing area, a jarring event that can cause a dislocated shoulder or acromioclavicular (arm bone and clavicle) joint sprain. The vaulter who tries to suddenly halt his rapid race down the runway while carrying a heavy pole, for whatever reason, risks ligament damage in the front of the knee. If he must stop, the pole-vaulter should let the pole slide through his hand and slow down rather than stop running abruptly.

A poor plant can throw a pole-vaulter off to one side, an error that often results in cuts and bruises. Other errors of technique include failing to bend the pole properly at takeoff, which can fling the vaulter past the padded landing area. On landing, the pole-vaulter must remember to fall on his back with his arms outstretched at a 45-degree angle, which reduces the risk of spinal damage. Young pole-vaulters today may begin their training with a metal pole, which costs less than fiberglass. The two types of poles require different vaulting techniques, and the vaulter who uses the wrong technique with a pole increases his risk of injury, including strains, sprains, and even broken bones. This most commonly occurs when a vaulter switches from a metal to a fiberglass pole.

HIGH JUMP

The injury most often suffered by running high jumpers is a painful tendinitis commonly called "jumper's knee." Exercises that strengthen and increase the flexibility of the quadriceps and hamstrings help prevent jumper's knee. Young high jumpers may learn any one of several techniques, and the type of injuries that may result will vary according to the one they practice. Perhaps the two most common techniques today consist of the "straddle," in which the jumper rolls over the bar with his face, chest, and abdomen pointed toward the floor, and the newer "flop," in which the jumper passes over the bar with his face up and his back toward the floor, and lands on his back. The kicking, twisting motions used in the straddle technique to help the trailing leg clear the crossbar can cause abdominal- and back-muscle strains. Warm-up exercises that stretch the hamstrings can reduce the injury risks associated with the straddle jump. The flop technique can result in back-muscle spasms or a fractured vertebra. Because the flop ends with the jumper landing on his back, improper technique can lead to back or neck injury, including a compressed vertebra or a fracture. Attention to proper technique offers the best protection for young athletes who use the flop.

LONG AND TRIPLE JUMPS

Participants in these two events move rapidly down a runway, take off, soar through the air, and land. The danger of a muscle strain or of ligament damage to an ankle or knee lurks when the runner misses the mark and tries to stop abruptly, rather than running into the landing pit. But the greatest risk of injury lies in the landing, which should occur with both legs together and ahead of the body, with knees partly bent. This position best absorbs the landing impact, and allows the jumper to spring forward to avoid toppling backward. An improper landing can easily cause an ankle sprain, a twisted or sprained knee, or even a broken bone in the lower leg. Jumper's knee also occurs among triple jumpers, who use a hop, step, and jump to get airborne, particularly if they decelerate when they hit the runway contact board. Triple jumpers should do exercises that strengthen and increase the flexibility of their hamstrings and quadriceps.

THROWING EVENTS

In all throwing events, an uneven throwing surface poses the principal risk of injury, particularly to the ankle. Competitors should check closely for any bumps, holes, rocks, or debris that might cause them trouble.

SHOT PUT

Properly putting the shot, a feat that requires pushing a heavy metal sphere rather than tossing it, produces enormous torque that can cause injury to the back, shoulder, and knees. The shot's weight increases with the age of the shot-putter. Junior high schoolers put an 8-pound shot; high school athletes use a 12-pound shot; and college and adult competitors push 16 pounds. Muscle strains commonly strike shot-putters, often in the buttocks or hip. Other injuries seen regularly in the sport include a sprained wrist, back-muscle spasms along the spine, abdominal-muscle strains, and knee-ligament problems. This last injury results from sticking the toes of the forward foot under the toe bar to stop the body's momentum, an error that can cause an injury so damaging that it can prevent the young athlete from pivoting effectively on the injured leg ever again.

Putting the shot requires strength, speed, flexibility, and coordination. Flexibility and proper technique serve as the best defenses against injury. Preparation for meets should emphasize the development of speed and coordination, with the number of actual throws of the shot limited to avoid injury. Typically, by mid-season, shot-putters put the shot only twice a week, about six times on each of the two days. Shot-putters should warm up quickly, but not with excessive vigor, taking particular care to stretch the muscles of the back, legs, and shoulders.

DISCUS

Blisters and cuts on the fingers, caused largely by nicks and spikes on the discus, account for the most frequent injuries among discus throwers. Sprained wrists occur commonly, particularly among throwers who use too much wrist snap. Again, proper technique helps tremendously in preventing injury. From windup to release, the discus throw should flow in a continuous, smooth movement. Hesitation or jerkiness increases tension on the back, shoulder, hips, knees, and ankles, raising the chance of muscle strains. Proper follow-through is equally important. Without it, the body halts too quickly, putting undue stress on the knees that can cause a sprain.

JAVELIN

The spear-like javelin weighs less than two pounds. The thrower races forward and then stops suddenly, which helps produce the great force necessary to propel the javelin. Again, proper technique is very important to injury prevention. The throwing style used in the United States tends to put considerable torque on parts of the upper body, which can lead to a dislocation of the throwing shoulder. The sport's most common injury is a sprained elbow in the throwing arm, which flexibility and keeping the elbow leading the hand during the throw can help prevent. Strained back or triceps muscles commonly strike javelin throwers, and strains are the most common shoulder injury. Javelin throwers need to do exercises that strengthen their rotator cuff and keep their elbow and shoulder flexible. Thoroughly warming up prior to practice or competition greatly reduces the risk of muscle strains, elbow injury, and shoulder problems.

11

Swimming, Diving, and Other Water Sports

Swimming ranks among the nation's more popular participation sports, at least according to surveys. Inevitably, large numbers of Americans assure pollsters they swim. In fact, many of these people merely splash around in a pool, lake, or river on those occasional days when they even enter the water. Nonetheless, swimming as a sport always draws great attention at the Summer Olympics, where the United States team historically has excelled, and competitive swimming programs have increased in number, from the high school level to the masters teams for adults. Moreover, many adults interested in fitness find swimming an excellent and appealing form of aerobic exercise that, in many urban and suburban areas, they can pursue any time from early morning to mid-evening. Swimming certainly ranks among the sports a person can begin in childhood or adolescence and continue through the adult years.

PREVENTING SWIMMING INJURIES

Many people erroneously think of swimming as an injury-free sport. In fact, accidents happen on slippery pool decks, poorly executed flip turns result in foot injuries, and strenuous training and the repetitive movements used in swimming can lead to overuse symptoms. Studies reveal that about 9 out of 10 swimming injuries involve the shoulder, knee, calf, and foot. Head and neck injuries do occur in swimming and diving, and when the injured athlete is in the water, as usually happens, the threat of drowning adds to the urgency of dealing with such an injury. Rescuers should use a kickboard or similar solid object to keep the injured swimmer's head above water and to support the head and neck while removing the person from the water.

Flexibility provides the main safeguard against injury in swimming and diving, and therefore stretching exercises should always be done before entering the water. Unfortunately, some athletes and many swim-for-fitness adults neglect their warm-ups, or even ignore them altogether. Properly done, pre-exercise stretching not only helps prevent injury, but can improve a swimmer's or diver's strength and performance. Many coaches require their teams to warm up together before a meet, and while the exact exercises may vary from coach to coach, the aim remains the same—to reduce the chance of injury and to improve the athletes' showing. (Warm-up exercises are described in detail in Chapter 2.)

Swimming requires nothing more than goggles as protective equipment, and noncompetitive swimmers can get by without them. In water, the eye's visual acuity falls dramatically—to nearly 20/4000. This means people with "perfect" 20/20 vision will see an object at 20 feet with the clarity they normally see it at 4,000 feet. Goggles, by trapping air between the eyeball and the water, allow swimmers to see normally in water. The better swimmers can see, the better and more safely they can compete. Good eyesight is particularly important in making racing turns. People with significant sight deficiencies can wear contact lenses along with their goggles, or have prescription lenses ground for their goggles or bonded to the goggle glass. One cautionary note: Long use may damage the foam-rubber cups of goggles, exposing the sharp edge of the molded plastic. If the goggles should slip from a swimmer's wet grip as they are being pulled forward for removal or interior clearing, the elastic strap will snap them back onto the face. Any exposed plastic may cut the swimmer, and a few swimmers have suffered a ruptured eye in such accidents. So swimmers must only use goggles in good condition.

Some swimmers simply wear soft contact lenses in the pool, bonding them to the eyes by splashing pool water onto each eye for about one minute. This creates an osmotic bond that lasts as long as the swimmer is in the pool and for about 30 minutes after exiting the water. Removing the lens before the bond dissolves can damage the outer layer of cells on the cornea, so we suggest wearing goggles rather than bonding soft contact lenses to the eyes. Also, this technique won't work in ocean water, because its high salt content allows soft contact lenses to move easily about, resulting in a high risk of loss.

Finally, we have some words about the myth of the "drown-proof child." There is no such thing, no matter what some swimming programs may promise or imply. Young children need continuous supervision in and around pools, lakes, and streams. Too many parents feel their young children can take care of themselves because they have taken swimming lessons. Sadly, about one-quarter of all drowning victims know how to swim. Teaching children to swim provides them a grand pleasure and a wonderful way to stay fit. But the American Academy of Pediatrics advises against group swimming lessons for children under age 3. Swallowing large amounts of pool water at a young age can lead to seizures and other serious problems. If parents insist on teaching a child below age 3 to swim, the training should come from a qualified instructor working only with that child, and with the parent present to watch for any signs of physical problems.

NUTRITION

We discuss in some detail the general nutritional needs of young athletes in Chapter 3. Here we make some specific comments regarding swimmers and divers.

Water sports can require tremendous expenditures of energy, and participants must make sure to eat enough to meet the energy demands of their bodies. World-class swimmers, for example, typically swim anywhere from 5 to 10 miles a day, depending on their workout schedule. Since swimming a mile requires about the same amount of energy as running four miles, you can see why those at the pinnacle of the sport typically consume 5,000 calories—or more—a day. Obviously, swimmers in youth or scholastic leagues who practice only a few hours a week do not need such high-calorie diets. Nonetheless, they may find it more comfortable to eat snacks several times a day in addition to their regular meals, rather than filling up on only three meals.

What to eat is no less controversial in swimming than in other sports. Some authorities recommend extra protein for swimmers during training so that they retain muscle mass, while others argue against this. For youngsters swimming in youth leagues and high school competitions, there appears to be no need to increase protein intake at the expense of other foods. Interestingly, in spite of the energy requirements of swimming, many swimmers still find themselves battling the scales. The best way to win that battle of the bulge is to slightly decrease caloric intake and increase the daily expenditure of energy through more exercise. But increasing exercise may prove impossible or even undesirable for the swimmer or diver already practicing several hours a day. In such cases, the athlete must rely on restricting food intake alone, but without going to a starvation or extremely low-calorie diet.

Eating by swimmers and divers, both prior to and during competition, basically should follow the rules outlined in Chapter 3. However, the precompetition meal may be eaten as late as two hours before competition. On competition day itself, swimmers and divers need to remember to pay attention to fluid replacement and their energy requirements. Because heatstroke and related disorders pose little threat to water athletes, they frequently overlook the need to replenish their body fluids. Yet swimmers and divers do lose fluids through urinating, defecating, breathing, and sweating, especially if a meet takes place in hot weather or a heated gym. And fluid loss will adversely affect performance for these athletes as much as it does for long-distance runners. Some young swimmers even purposely refrain from drinking water, hoping this will prevent them from getting the urge to urinate as they line up to start their race, an effort that rarely works—since the urge represents more a case of "nerves" than an overloaded bladder.

Swimming and diving meets can last hours, sometimes for much of the day, depending on the number of events and competitors. Frequently, participants compete in more than one event, with long breaks in between. During these breaks, snacks can help keep their energy up. It is important that these snacks not contain excessive amounts of sugar. Sandwiches, unsalted chips, cookies, various breads, and unfrosted cakes or cupcakes fit the bill. Diluted fruit juices provide both energy and water.

MEDICAL PROBLEMS OF SWIMMING

DERMATOLOGICAL PROBLEMS

Skin disorders related to swimming occur infrequently and usually prove more an irritating inconvenience than a serious problem. Most problems heal by themselves or respond quickly to medical treatments, usually given in the form of lotions or creams. But some exceptions to this general rule do occur, and swimmers should consult a physician if a skin problem appears unusual or persists.

Dry skin ranks as the most common dermatological complaint among swimmers. Exposure to water, surprisingly to many people, dries out skin and thus irritates it. Salt in seawater and the chlorine used to prevent bacterial contamination in swimming pools only add to the problem of drying. For most people, dry skin requires nothing more than the daily use of one of the moisturizing skin lotions available in any drugstore or supermarket. Swimmers also may suffer from folliculitis—an inflammation of the hair follicles characterized by tiny, raised, reddish areas, and treatable with antibiotics.

"Swimmer's itch" and "seabather's eruption" represent two other water-associated skin disorders. Physicians see swimmer's itch, a rash caused by a freshwater parasite called schistosome cercariae, most often in the states of Illinois, Michigan, Minnesota, Nebraska, North and South Dakota, and Wisconsin. Swimmers develop itching pimples resembling insect bites, and occasionally hives on the parts of their bodies not covered by their bathing suits except the face. The cause of seabather's eruption, seen mostly in Florida among people who swim in the Atlantic Ocean and the Gulf of Mexico, remains unknown. A few hours after leaving salt water, these swimmers develop reddish spots, pimples, and welts on parts of their skin not covered by their bathing suits. Showering immediately after exiting the water appears the best way to prevent both disorders, which usually last a week to 10 days. In particularly bad cases, physicians may prescribe corticosteroid creams and antihistamines to ease the itching associated with these two rashes.

Contact dermatitis, an inflammation of the skin, results from contact with some substance that either irritates the skin directly, such as a caustic compound, or triggers an allergic reaction. In swimming, the cause is almost always a compound used in manufacturing the goggles or the bathing suit. The key to solving contact dermatitis lies in avoiding the substance causing the problem. Without this, treatments won't work. For swimmers, an outbreak around the eyes obviously points to goggles, and one under or around the bathing suit area clearly suggests a problem with the youngster's swimwear. Once you determine the source of the irritation, a physician can treat the problem with an over-the-counter medication, or in serious cases, a prescription drug.

"Blonding" occurs commonly in summer among people who

swim frequently in outdoor pools. This bleaching effect, due to the chlorine used in pools, lightens the hair color and most noticeably affects blonds. But swimmers with light brown and red hair may also notice a lightening. The degree of bleaching depends on the amount of chemicals used to treat the pool, and how much time a person spends in the water and in the sunlight. Shampoos specially formulated to fight chlorine can reduce the problem. "Greening," fortunately, occurs less commonly. In this situation, blond hair turns a greenish color, and even people with red hair or red highlights may notice a green tinge. Greening results from a reaction with the copper-based compounds used in pools to control algae. Shampooing after each swim, and applying a lotion containing 3 percent hydrogen peroxide usually gets the green out; regular application keeps it out.

EAR, NOSE, AND EYE PROBLEMS

EAR PROBLEMS.   Among the medical problems associated with water sports, "swimmer's ear" ranks as the most common. Known medically as *acute external otitis,* this infection of the external ear canal can cause severe pain.

Solutions that dry and acidify the ear canal provide the most effective means of preventing swimmer's ear. A variety of commerical preparations are available, and many drugstores sell at least one. But the same benefit is available at less cost by simply mixing a half-and-half solution of white vinegar and rubbing alcohol, and applying it in the ear with a dropper (which drugstores sell) after swimming. The best results come from using one of these mixtures three times a day—after getting up, after swimming, and before going to bed—and keeping the solution in each ear for five minutes.

The early symptoms of swimmer's ear include itching and a sensation that the ear is plugged. If the condition is recognized promptly, a swimmer can avoid more serious infection by keeping the ear dry, which means not swimming and seeing that no water enters the ear canal during bathing. It also means ensuring that no damage occurs to the skin of the ear canal, such as from probing with a cotton swab or finger, that would allow bacteria to penetrate the protective barrier the skin provides. With care, an infection usually disappears in a few days to one week.

If not treated, this early stage of swimmer's ear moves rapidly to a more serious inflammation, marked by redness, swelling, pain, and some discharge from the ear. Most youngsters don't complain until this point. Pressing on the tragus, the bit of cartilage pointing backward over the ear's opening, causes great pain. Soon, the symptoms include an oozing, foul-smelling, greenish pus, a fullness in the ear that reduces hearing even to the point of loss, and intense, sometimes excruciating pain.

Treating swimmer's ear involves reducing the pain and inflammation. A physician may have to clean the ear of pus and debris to help topical medications reach the surface of the inflammation. These medications are applied as ear drops three or four times a day, often using a cotton earwick that carries the drug to the inner reaches of the outer ear. Physicians will prescribe an analgesic for several days for people with severe pain. It generally takes 10 days to two weeks to cure swimmer's ear at this stage, and during this time the youngster must protect the ear canal from moisture and injury. Many authorities recommend that swimmers stay out of the water totally until their infection heals. Others forbid diving, but will allow swimmers to go into the water using a kickboard, provided they wear a bathing cap and always keep their heads above water. Consult your youngster's physician for his or her recommendation.

Ear specialists treat some children who suffer *chronic otitis media*, an inflammation of the middle ear, by inserting small tubes through their eardrums to drain fluids from the middle ear. The tubes often remain in place for many months, raising the obvious question about the danger to such youngsters of infection if they swim or engage in other water sports. Unfortunately, medical opinion varies greatly. Some physicians say absolutely no water sports allowed; others say go ahead as long as the child uses earplugs and antiseptic drops; still others see no need for either earplugs or drops. Some evidence suggests that divers do stand a greater risk of ear infections if they have the drainage tubes. A study of 53 children with tubes in place found that five of six cases of ear infections occurred among divers. Yet the study also concluded that the infection rate for most of the children turned out to be "reasonably low." Until there has been more research, the prudent course seems to call for the use of earplugs and antiseptic drops before and after swimming in children with these drainage tubes.

NOSE AND EYE PROBLEMS. Swimmers commonly suffer from stuffy noses and sinuses. Chlorine in pools, contaminating bacteria, or tiny particles suspended in the water can irritate the lining of the nose, and cause swelling and an outpouring of mucus. People with hay fever may encounter molds, fungi, and algae while swimming that can trigger allergic reactions. Swimming can block the sinus opening; diving can damage the sinus lining. Nose clips or plugs can prevent or reduce nasal and sinus problems, but in some cases sinus problems may become severe enough to require medical attention and even surgery.

Headaches wouldn't seem to be a problem associated with water sports, except in cases where a swimmer or diver strikes his or her head. But a phenomenon known as "goggle migraine" does occur among people who use tight, ill-fitting goggles. Typically, the swimmer develops an intense, throbbing pain in both temples a couple of hours after swimming. The problem disappears when the swimmer gets properly fitted goggles and adjusts the straps to hold the goggles in place without excessive tension.

Swelling of the cornea, the transparent membrane covering the front of the eye, and an erosion of the eye's surface cells sometimes occurs among swimmers. This results from a variety of things, including the friction of water against the eye, disruption of the tear film over the eye, the levels of chlorine and other chemicals, and foreign substances injected into the water by the filtration system. Lubricating eye drops, commonly called "artificial tears," treat the problem effectively. Using goggles can prevent it.

GASTROINTESTINAL PROBLEMS

Water-borne bacteria pose a threat to swimmers. Swimming in water with a high bacteria content (from, say, sewer seepage) can result in serious illness. As one would expect, swimming in unchlorinated water presents a greater risk than swimming in a chemically treated pool. Nonetheless, gastrointestinal ailments can occur as the result of infections acquired in swimming pools. When Ohio State University researchers compared illnesses among wrestlers, swimmers, and gymnasts at that school, they found one significant difference: swimmers suffered more gastrointestinal problems. Another study of swimming-associated diseases found that gastrointestinal illnesses were second only to respiratory ailments, and ahead of eye, ear, skin, or allergy complaints. These illnesses, however, usually are not serious and rarely last more than one or two days.

MUSCULOSKELETAL PROBLEMS

Today's competitive swimmers, even at the high school level, may swim many miles each day in practice. Some high school swimmers stroke 12,000 meters (7.5 miles) to 18,000 meters (11.2 miles) in training almost daily. This constant repetitive exercise can cause a variety of overuse injuries, many of them related to specific strokes.

BREASTSTROKER'S KNEE. About three out of four competitive breaststroke swimmers develop some sign of an overuse syndrome appropriately called "breaststroker's knee." Depending on the swimmer, the problem may range from mild to severe, and in some cases it can force a swimmer to give up competition. Pain in one or both knees provides the first indication of the problem. The pain gradually increases, which should warn anyone that something is amiss. Unfortunately, many young swimmers, their parents, and their coaches ignore these early symptoms, figuring the athlete will "swim through" the problem. Instead, the problem tends to get worse as the swimmer gets older. Sometimes it reaches the point, usually in the adult years, that a physician orders a total halt to training or the swimmer simply quits.

Specialists disagree on the precise anatomical and biomechanical reasons for breaststroker's knee. But a key factor seems to be stress on the knee's tibial collateral ligament. Some evidence suggests that people who have less internal rotation at the hip joint stand a greater chance of developing knee pain. The breaststroker's kick is an extremely unnatural movement for human beings, and its repeated use leads to knee problems, even in people with good internal hip rotation and anatomically perfect knees.

When knee pain occurs, sports medicine specialists suggest immediately reducing or halting the training distances swum with the breaststroke and its kick. Swimmers often can continue to swim other strokes to keep cardiovascularly fit, and even to pull with the breaststroke, provided they refrain from the pain-inducing breaststroke kick. Physicians treating breaststroker's knee also look to modifying the swimmer's kick, the use of ice after practice, exercises that increase hip rotation and strengthen the quadriceps, and sometimes a nonprescription painkiller to reduce the pain and to counter the physical problems underlying the syndrome. Sometimes, however, treating breaststroker's knee requires weeks or even several months of total rest from swimming.

Obviously, it is better never to suffer breaststroker's knee than to treat it successfully. Prevention starts with stretching exercises that ensure proper flexibility and a sufficient warm-up period. Generally, sports medicine specialists recommend that breaststrokers swim 1,000 to 1,500 yards using a different stroke before they begin serious breaststroke practice or competition. People differ considerably in the training distances they can tolerate while swimming the breaststroke. Coaches should individualize each breaststroker's practice routine. Most specialists recommend that swimmers take a minimum of a two months' break from breaststroke training each year to help prevent breaststroker's knee.

SHOULDER PROBLEMS. "Swimmer's shoulder," also known as "impingement," most frequently strikes those swimming freestyle or butterfly strokes. It results from the overuse of the rotator cuff and typically causes a pain in the shoulder that radiates to the side of the arm. A swimmer may suffer this problem when swimming freestyle, but not when doing the butterfly, or vice versa. Initially, swimmers complain of pain after exiting the water. Then pain occurs both after and during swimming, usually at the point of the stroke when the arm and hand enter the water. Finally, the pain becomes disabling and adversely affects the athlete's performance.

Simply put, nature never designed the human shoulder to take the beating competitive swimmers may give it. Repeated rotation of the shoulder can cause chronic irritation, leading to inflammation of various shoulder parts, including the rotator cuff and the head of the biceps tendon. Very tiny, sometimes irreversible tears may also occur in the rotator cuff, which gives the shoulder its mobility. Many cases of swimmer's shoulder respond to rest, ice treatments, special exercises, and aspirin or a prescription anti-inflammatory drug. If this doesn't work, a physician may try ultrasound treatments and steroid injections. In occasional cases, swimmer's shoulder requires surgery.

Backstrokers sometimes develop an injury called "apprehension shoulder," a slight dislocation that results in pain as the swimmer turns at the end of the pool. Basically, the swimmer has three choices: to live with the pain, to alter his or her stroke so the injured arm and shoulder come over in a forward bend that moves more to the body's midline (although this causes an unusual-looking turn that may increase the swimmer's risk of disqualification), or to undergo surgery.

Preventing shoulder injuries calls for performing exercises that strengthen the external rotation and, before hitting the water, warming up the shoulder area by carrying out a thorough regimen of stretching exercises. Freestyle and butterfly swimmers need to pay special attention to exercises that loosen the shoulder girdle. Furthermore, swimmers should not train with just one stroke, but should use a variety of strokes to reduce the chance of shoulder injury.

BACK, ELBOW, AND FOOT PROBLEMS. Although physicians often recommend swimming as a good exercise for people with lower-back pain, the sport can also cause back problems. The arching of the back that takes place during the butterfly stroke can lead to lower-back pain. So can the "elbow up" position used in the breaststroke. Indeed, both the breast and butterfly strokes occasionally result in stress fractures in the lower back. The basic treatment for such injuries, following diagnosis by a physician, consists of a cessation of swimming, and rest, followed by a program of hamstring stretching and abdominal-muscle strengthening, and then a gradual return to full activity. Occasionally, patients may require a steroid injection to reduce inflammation.

Swimmers also suffer "tennis elbow," the painful inflammation of tendons (tendinitis) in the elbow. It strikes butterfly and breaststroke swimmers most often, and less frequently those swimming freestyle. The problem results from the "elbow up" style of arm pull, in which the swimmer bends the elbow and holds it higher than the hand during the early part of the pull. This type of stroke is highly effective for moving the swimmer through the water, but it also puts great strain on the elbows. This force, when repeated over and over in training, can irritate and inflame the tendons. Treatment includes relieving the inflammation with ice treatments, medication, and sometimes ultrasound; altering the swimmer's stroke to reduce the force applied to the elbow; strengthening the forearms; and increasing flexibility. In some severe cases, swimmers have surgery.

Finally, swimmers of all strokes may suffer foot and ankle pain from stretched and inflamed tendons. The flutter kick used in the freestyle and backstroke most commonly causes this form of tendinitis, but it can occur with the dolphin kick used in the butterfly stroke as well. Continued use of the same kick can result in friction between the tendons, particularly the extensor tendons of the ankle and foot, and the sheathes that surround them, which results in irritation, swelling, and inflammation. Icing the affected ankle, taking anti-inflammatory medication, and wrapping the foot in the neutral position at night generally reduce or eliminate pain, but sometimes treatment requires ultrasound and/or steroid injections. Swimmers rarely need to abandon the water completely, but the return to full activity and kick intensity must be gradual. Proper stretching of the extensor tendons before entering the water can help prevent the problem.

DIVING INJURIES

Diving brings with it the very real potential for serious injury to the head and spinal column. Preventing such injuries should rank tops in coaching any diver. This includes everything from ensuring that youngsters only dive into correctly designed pools with sufficiently deep water, to checking the tension on springboards, to seeing that diving wells have adequate overhead and below-surface lighting, to properly instructing divers in all aspects of the sport—boardwork, takeoff, midair maneuver, entry, and surfacing. Some diving areas, for example, lie too close to the shallow end of a pool and a diver who leans too far forward may enter the water too far out and strike the bottom on the pool's slope or shallow end. Training should also include a year-round exercise program to build strength and maintain flexibility. Coaches should strictly enforce safety rules—no running dives, no double bounces on a springboard, for example—to guard against injuries to high-spirited young athletes.

HEAD

While not common in diving, head and spinal injuries unfortunately are not rare. The origin of most of these injuries lies in the diver's poor boardwork or takeoff, which brings the diver in contact with the springboard or platform. In a reverse dive, for example, if a diver leans too far backward, the force of rotation can twist his head back into the board. Should such an accident occur, rescuers must treat the injured diver with utmost care, supporting his head with a kickboard or some other solid object to keep it above water until he can be removed from the pool, and summon medical assistance immediately.

EYE, EAR, AND NOSE

Eye injuries occur relatively rarely in diving. As a result of the blink reflex, the eyelids normally close just before the diver hits the water. But sometimes a diver's lids remain open at impact, and the sensitive eye itself suffers a blow from hitting the water. Such a blow can cause a detached retina, an injury in which the eye's innermost layer, and the one upon which light rays focus, pulls away from the eye's outer layers. The diver suddenly sees flashes of light, or "stars," and then experiences a sensation as if a curtain were being pulled across the eye. Usually an eye specialist can restore vision with laser surgery, provided the injured diver seeks help promptly.

A growing number of divers use contact lenses to ensure good vision, an important part of good diving. But they should remember to keep their eyes closed after entering the water and not open them until they have slowed and begun swimming to the surface. This reduces the chance of scratching the eye's surface or losing a lens.

Divers with drainage tubes inserted in their eardrums apparently stand an increased chance of developing middle-ear infections, but wearing earplugs reduces this risk. The forceful entry of water into the middle ear via the drainage tube can partially damage the structures that occupy the middle ear. When this happens, the diver feels a fullness in the ear, soreness, and may experience some dizziness. If these symptoms develop, the young athlete should stop all swimming and diving and see an ear specialist (otolaryngologist) promptly.

Aside from the possible bruises, bumps, or fractures caused by striking the face on a board or pool bottom or side, divers suffer few nasal problems other than sinusitis. This usually results from bacteria and algae growing in pool water. Divers can do little to avoid the problem, although careful management of pool chemicals can reduce both bacterial and algal growth.

LOWER-BACK

A number of divers suffer lower-back injuries, largely as the result of poor form, which puts added stress on the lower back. Most often the pain results from straining lower-back muscles, but ruptured discs and even fractures do strike divers. Traumatic spondylolysis, for example, results from a stress fracture created by the physical battering of repeated practice dives, which leaves the young athlete with a low-level but persistent cramping pain. If the diver ignores the symptoms, continued stress will likely cause a dislocation or spondylolisthesis, a painful spinal-column deformity. (See Chapter 14.)

The rules of good form require divers to keep their body vertical during much of their takeoff and entry. This creates so-called vertically direct stress that over time can cause a stress fracture or ruptured disc. Typically, a diver will complain of pain running down one leg. Far less common but equally indicative of a disc problem are the loss of bladder or bowel control or a dropping foot due to an inability to flex the muscles that control the foot, all the result of pressure on a nerve by an inflammation or ruptured disc. If such symptoms ever develop, a diver should stop diving and seek medical attention. Rest is a key element of treatment, and if disc problems are diagnosed early, the young athlete may avoid surgery. Whatever treatment is necessary, many youngsters can resume their diving after appropriate rest and rehabilitation, which usually includes an exercise regimen to strengthen the lower-back and abdominal muscles.

SHOULDER

Divers, particularly those who plunge from high platforms, risk injuring their shoulders. Although the hands break the water first, the force with which the shoulders strike the water remains considerable. Dislocated shoulders may occur if the diver fails to clasp her hands properly and her arms move too far to the side of her body. Young divers in particular, whose shoulder muscles lack full conditioning and strength, may suffer shoulder pain, chronic tendinitis, and dislocations. If an arm gets forced far outside the body line on entry, a rotator cuff injury may occur, and continued cuff injury can lead to serious complications, including tendon rupture. Some diving injuries may require surgery to repair the damaged shoulder. To prevent such injuries, young divers should work to strengthen their shoulder muscles and avoid using entry positions that put particular stress on their shoulders until they have conditioned their muscles.

WRIST AND ELBOW

The repeated physical stress of many practice dives also makes wrist and elbow problems common among diving injuries. The often used "flat-hand" entry technique puts considerable stress on the wrist's carpal bones, which can cause stress fractures or inflammation of the tissue covering the bones. Ligaments can also suffer damage, and bones and cartilage may become inflamed. Warming up the wrists and elbows with light exercise before diving and taping the wrists during practice can help prevent these injuries.

The most common elbow ailment involves inflammation of the joint's bones and cartilage. This often occurs in young divers during their growth spurts, and many sports medicine specialists recommend keeping youngsters off high diving platforms during periods of rapid growth.

INJURIES IN WATER POLO

Water polo, a sport that combines swimming and throwing with physical contact, ranks as the most dangerous of the water sports. The combination of a flying ball and splashing, thrashing, kicking bodies results not only in many of the injuries commonly seen in swimmers, but also in the assorted bumps, bruises, and more serious damage seen in other contact sports. Swimmers and water polo players both frequently wear goggles, but in water polo, eye safety requires that goggles provide more than comfort and clear vision; they must be shatter-resistant so they don't break when struck by a ball or flying elbow. Knees, shoulders, and hands also are frequent sites of injury.

KNEE INJURIES

Water polo players often use a kick called "the eggbeater," which resembles a combination of the kicks used in the freestyle and breaststroke. One leg does the frog kick of the breaststroke while the other remains straight and kicks. This unusual kick puts great stress on the knee ligaments, much like the stress that results in breaststroker's knee (see above). For mild knee pain, ice after practices and games and perhaps aspirin or ibuprofen may take care of the problem. If not, the player may have to give up water polo for a time to let the knee recover. Many players (and breaststrokers) can avoid such knee problems by doing leg extensions and leg curls to strengthen the thigh muscles (hamstrings and quadriceps), and by doing exercises that improve both the internal and external rotation of the knee.

SHOULDER INJURIES

As if swimming did not pose enough of a risk to the shoulder, water polo's throwing element increases the chance of this kind of injury. Physicians who treat water polo players find they often must decide whether the player's pain results from swimmer's shoulder, tendinitis, a dislocation, or a rotator cuff injury. The danger of rotator cuff damage is high in water polo if a player fails to warm up and stretch properly before entering the water.

FINGER INJURIES

Water polo players throw and catch the ball with their fingers, exposing them to injury. Jammed fingers are common, and sometimes the force of the ball dislocates or fractures a finger. Any of the three can cause great pain. A physician can often readily tell a jammed finger from the more serious injuries, but dislocations and fractures may require an X-ray examination for diagnosis.

SYNCHRONIZED SWIMMING

Synchronized swimming, the graceful water ballet so popular at the Summer Olympics, poses far fewer risks to participants than competitive swimming, diving, or water polo. Nonetheless, synchronized swimmers have almost the same rates of swimmer's ear, skin problems, and sinus troubles as competitors in the other water sports. And in recent years, as their routines have grown longer, more intricate, and more strenuous, sports physicians working with synchronized swimmers have noted an increase in overuse injuries, particularly breaststroker's knee (a result of using the eggbeater kick also used in water polo) and swimmer's shoulder.

12

Football

Unquestionably, football ranks high among the world's rough-and-tumble sports, and parents and youngsters alike should realize the risks of playing this hard-hitting game. Studies indicate that young males face a greater risk of serious injury playing football than any other youth or scholastic sport. True, improved equipment and some important rule changes have reduced the number of fatalities and paralyses in football. Nonetheless, as we noted in Chapter 1, more than a half million high school football players each year suffer injuries significant enough to make them miss a game or a day of practice. Yet despite this clear and present danger, football remains a popular sport, both for young athletes and for spectators. According to the National Athletic Trainers' Association, just over 1 million boys play football in more than 14,700 high school programs throughout the United States.

INJURY INCIDENCE

The injury risks associated with football—both in numbers and severity—vary by players' age, position of play, and level of competition. Size, speed, and physical conditioning make important differences, not only in an athlete's performance, but in the risk of injury. As a rule, the older, the bigger, and the faster the players, the higher the risk of injury.

YOUTH LEAGUES

In spite of football's popularity with young boys, only a limited number of studies have explored the injuries suffered in youth leagues. What information exists indicates that youngsters at this level of competition suffer fewer significant injuries than those on high school and college teams. A study of 5,128 boys ages 8 to 15 playing in six Pop Warner leagues in New England found that 5 percent suffered injuries serious enough to keep them out of play and practice for a week or more. Other studies have reported comparable injury rates of 16 percent for high school and 27 percent for college players. No deaths or paralyses occurred among the youngsters, and the researchers remarked on the absence of catastrophic head and neck injuries. But of the 257 significant injuries the researchers tallied, 8 appeared likely to cause some degree of permanent disability. The Pop Warner players faced a higher risk of injury (about 63 percent) during a game than during practice, a fact of football that also applies to high school and college players.

HIGH SCHOOL

Studies at the high school level have provided coaches, trainers, and sports medicine specialists with a clearer understanding of the number and types of injuries suffered by these players. For example, a study conducted for the National Athletic Trainers' Association monitored a total of 21,233 football players throughout the United States during the 1986, 1987, and 1988 seasons. It recorded 12,797 injuries to 7,722 players (36.4 percent of the total) that kept them off the practice or game field for at least one day. Of the injuries, 72.5 percent took seven days or less to heal; 16.7 percent required eight days to three weeks of healing; and 10.8 percent kept the player sidelined for more than three weeks. The study compared the injuries of varsity high school players with those found in an earlier survey of college football players and concluded that the risk of injury during practice was about the same. However, the risk of injury is four times greater during a game than during practice in high school, and eight times greater at the college level.

PREVENTING INJURIES

Learning, and following, the proper way to block and tackle certainly can reduce football injuries. Rules forbid grabbing an opponent's face mask and spearing (hitting an opponent with the head first). Either can do serious harm. Indeed, the rule change in 1976 that outlawed tackling an opponent with the head making first contact, coupled with a 1978 rule requiring the certification of football helmets, sharply reduced the number of deaths and paralyses suffered by high school and college players. However, players need frequent reminders that face-mask infractions and spearing pose the risk of serious injury, as well as a penalty. Even with head tackling illegal, helmets still inadvertently cause a significant number of injuries during tackling and blocking—19 percent of those seen in a study of Pop Warner league players.

A number of other things can help reduce the number of "tackle" league injuries or their severity. For one, children should not play football until at least age 10. Some of the things parents may want to consider before allowing their sons to play football, whether in youth or school leagues, include:

- Does the team warm up for at least 20 minutes before practice or a game?
- Do the coaches stress gradually building to peak physical conditioning, and do they encourage players to participate in one or more fitness activities year-round to keep in proper condition?
- Do the coaches recommend appropriate exercises to strengthen the neck and shoulders to protect against neck and spinal cord injuries?
- Do the coaches have water readily available to guard against heat-related injuries, and do they encourage players to drink freely?
- Are rules against dangerous blocking and tackling techniques taught and enforced at practices as well as games?
- Are the players' helmets certified by the National Operating Committee on Standards for Athletic Equipment (NOCSAE)?
- When an injury occurs, does the player receive proper medical attention and appropriate time to recover before returning to play or practice?
- Is a physician, nurse, certified athletic trainer, or emergency medical technician present at games?
- Does the team have a realistic plan for getting an injured player to a hospital or other emergency medical facility quickly?

Finally, the evidence suggests that an increasing number of junior high and high school football players have turned to anabolic steroids to help them build bigger, stronger muscles. While effective, these drugs are illegal and potentially dangerous (see Chapter 9). While strong muscles help protect against injury, the risks to health and career make the use of steroids a terrible choice in injury prevention.

EQUIPMENT AND INJURIES

Protective equipment seems almost synonymous with football. At a minimum, each player should take the field wearing a helmet, a mouthpiece, shoulder, hip, knee, and thigh pads, and football shoes. Parents should inspect each of these pieces to make certain they are of high quality and in excellent condition to provide their youngsters with adequate protection. Deteriorated equipment should be repaired or replaced to reduce the risk of injury. But protective equipment cannot eliminate all injuries, and sometimes can itself result in harm, an important point for coaches and parents to remember.

HELMET

In the old days, only a thick head of hair protected a football player's skull against opponents' blows. Unpadded leather headgear came into use in the mid-1920s, and designers added an inner suspension system for padding nearly two decades later. Not until the early 1950s did football helmets with hard outer shells, the forerunners of today's impact-resistant models, go on the market.

However, the advent of rigid helmets led to more severe bruises and bone injuries during tackling and blocking, and to the dangerous practice of spearing. And for all the improvements in helmets, they provide far less than ideal protection against head and neck injuries. Moreover, helmets vary considerably in quality, and the explosive popularity of football among elementary and middle school youngsters has seen a proliferation of inexpensive helmets that offer scant protection against concussions and other head and neck injuries. At whatever level a child plays, parents should make certain he wears a helmet certified by the National Operating Committee on Standards for Athletic Equipment, and that it remains in good repair. An improperly worn or ill-fitting helmet increases a child's chances of injury. Perhaps the best type of football helmet now available is the double-crown pneumatic helmet, sometimes called the multichambered pneumatic helmet, which contains an inflatable inner support.

FACE MASK

Face masks in football date to the mid-1950s. They offer a degree of protection against broken noses, lost teeth, and other facial injuries. They also pose a risk of a severe or even paralyzing neck injury, if an opposing player grabs the face mask and jerks a player's head violently. Moreover, the various types of face masks often block some portion of the player's field of vision, which may cause him to miss some part of a play or the approach of an opponent bent on tackling or blocking him. Some experts contend that face masks have allowed players to play far more aggressively. They argue that eliminating face masks, although perhaps increasing some facial injuries, would reduce serious and potentially life-threatening injuries by greatly reducing the overall level of violence in football. Until that day, parents should insist that coaches instruct their players about the dangers of grabbing other players' face masks, and that game officials strongly enforce face-mask penalties.

MOUTHPIECE

Since the National Collegiate Athletic Association first required college players to wear mouthpieces in 1973, these devices, designed to protect players against mouth injuries and lost teeth, have won wide acceptance at all levels of football. However, a player may get his mouthpiece caught in his throat as the result of a violent tackle or block, which can shut off the flow of air to his lungs. Coaches should always have a pair of bolt cutters with them to quickly cut away a face mask so they can remove the mouthpiece, should such an unusual accident occur.

PADS

Today's shoulder pads do a good job of protecting young players, who can add extra padding to improve protection. Elbow and arm pads also help reduce injuries. Various types of neck pads and collars limit the motion of the cervical spine with the aim of reducing neck injuries. Hip pads help prevent or reduce the severity of injuries to the hips and pelvic region inflicted by blows from helmets, knees, or shoulders during blocking or tackling. But for pads to work, players must wear them, as Scott painfully learned. This 15-year-old, who only occasionally wore his pads during practice, took a helmet in his unprotected hip. The boy rested only two days, returned for his next game, and suffered another jolting blow to his hip that left him sidelined for four weeks.

Again, worn or damaged pads increase the risk of injury and require repair or replacement.

SHOES

Football shoes must fit well and players must check daily to make certain their cleats remain tight. Ill-fitting shoes and loose cleats increase the danger of sprains or other foot or ankle injuries.

SPECIFIC INJURIES

HEAT DISORDERS

The potential for heat exhaustion and heatstroke should concern every player, coach and parent. We have discussed heat problems in detail in Chapter 6. But since football players commonly suffer some ill effects from heat, particularly in pre-season and early season when the weather is warm to hot, the dangers of heat need to be restated. The following points are based on recommendations from the National Collegiate Athletic Association:

1. The preparticipation physical should include questioning about previous episodes of heat illness and their duration, which helps spot players at increased risk of heat disorders.
2. Athletes need to gradually acclimatize to heat. Thus, during the first 7 to 10 days, practice should gradually increase in strenuousness, and practice should take place during the cooler parts of the day.
3. Players should wear shorts on extremely hot and humid days.
4. Coaches should be aware of the temperature and humidity, because fatal heatstrokes have occurred with temperatures only in the 60s, but with the humidity close to 100 percent, as well as in temperatures above 90 degrees but with humidity around 50 percent. A sling psychrometer—an inexpensive and simple device that measures both a "wet bulb" and "dry bulb" temperature and gives the relative humidity—is an invaluable tool. If the wet-bulb temperature exceeds 78 degrees Fahrenheit and/

or the humidity exceeds 95 percent, coaches should reduce the intensity of the practice accordingly. (See table on page 111.)

5. In hot and humid weather, players should rest frequently in a cool, shaded area that affords some air movement and should remove or loosen their jerseys. The NCAA recommends resting 15 to 30 minutes out of each practice hour during such conditions.

6. Players should always have easy access to unlimited water, and coaches should see that their players drink enough water to maintain hydration.

7. Athletes need to replace salt lost in sweat. But this should be done by salting their food, never by taking salt tablets.

8. Teams should keep a record of every young athlete's weight, taken daily before and after practice, to learn which players lose excessive weight during practice or a game. In general, as we have noted, a 3 percent loss is safe; a 5 percent loss is borderline; anything over 7 percent is dangerous.

9. To reduce their risk of heat injury, players should wear loose-fitting, lightweight clothing; forget rubberized clothing or sweat suits, double jerseys, long sleeves and long socks; and avoid excessive padding and taping.

10. Coaches should look for players at higher risk of heat problems—those who are overweight, those who lose excessive weight during practice, and those who perform at peak capacity throughout a practice or game.

11. Each coach should keep in mind the symptoms of the various heat disorders and act accordingly when a player shows signs of a heat problem.

When temperatures hang below 66 degress Fahrenheit, coaches and athletes have few worries about heat problems, except possibly those who lose over 3 percent of their body weight during practice. In the range of 67 to 78 degrees Fahrenheit, coaches and players need to remember the importance of adequate water consumption. Temperatures over 78 degrees call for lighter practice routines and players donning shorts. Players who lose over 5 percent of their body weight should remain out of practice. Finally, when the temperature hits 95 degrees Fahrenheit or greater, coaches should postpone practice or greatly reduce the workload of their players, with strict attention to maintaining hydration. For additional information, see Chapter 6.

Head and Neck Injuries

The number of fatal and crippling head and neck injuries suffered while playing football has dropped significantly compared with the first two-thirds of this century. Nonetheless, about a dozen high school and college football players die or suffer permanent paralysis each year from head and neck injuries. The best line of defense against such tragedies remains proper blocking and tackling techniques, and first-rate equipment properly fitted, worn, and maintained.

By its nature as a contact sport, football carries with it the risk of brain concussions. Serious concussions usually get the respect and medical attention they deserve, but many players and coaches too easily dismiss mild concussions, particularly when it comes to returning a player to the field. A brain concussion results when the brain and the bone of the skull bang together, causing brain damage ranging from temporary to fatal. Physicians speak of concussions as mild, moderate, and severe. Typically, the symptoms are as follows:

MILD. No loss of consciousness; little or no confusion; no memory loss; mild dizziness and ringing in the ears; no unsteadiness; mild or no headache.

MODERATE. Loss of consciousness for up to 5 minutes; a brief period of mental confusion; loss of memory for events before or after the injury; moderate dizziness and ringing in the ears; 5 to 10 minutes of unsteadiness; usually a headache.

SEVERE. Unconsciousness for more than 5 minutes; mental confusion lasting 5 minutes or more; prolonged memory loss for events before the injury; severe dizziness and ringing in the ears; more than 10 minutes of unsteadiness; moderate to severe headache.

Often players and coaches accept a mild concussion, "getting your bell rung," as inconsequential and a part of the game, and the player returns quickly to action. But even the mildest concussion should put a player on the bench for a minimum of 15 to 30 minutes. Then, if the player shows no signs of headache, dizziness, ear ringing, or concentration loss, a high school coach might safely allow him to return to the field. However, physicians generally recommend that any youth player who suffers even a mild concussion remain out of play or practice for several days, and that his parents check daily for any lingering symptoms of concussion. If a player shows any continued symptoms, he should see a physician for a neurological evaluation.

Any young athlete who loses consciousness as the result of a blocking or tackling injury should be treated as if he had suffered a spinal fracture. This means removing him from the field on a fracture board with his head and neck immobilized. In the case of severe concussions, he should be kept immobilized and immediately taken to a hospital equipped to treat serious head and spinal injuries. In a moderate concussion, marked by only brief unconsciousness, the player might not need the fracture board for his trip to the hospital, if he has no neck problems after regaining consciousness. Players who suffer moderate or severe concussions should never return to play until cleared to do so by a physician competent to assess neurological injuries.

After one concussion the risk of suffering a second appears to soar. One study of high school football players found that those who had suffered a concussion were four times likelier to suffer another than players who had never suffered a concussion were to suffer their first. Sports physicians have now recognized a rare but deadly condition in which players who return to play or practice while still experiencing concussion symptoms suffer a fatal swelling of the brain after receiving a minor blow to the head. For additional information about head injuries, see Chapter 6.

UPPER EXTREMITY INJURIES

During blocking and tackling, the shoulders and arms take a considerable beating, particularly from opponents' helmets and knees. Dislocated shoulders, either from blows or falls, pose a common problem. Falls and crushing impacts also cause broken collarbones, rotator cuff injuries, shoulder sprains, and hyperextensions—injuries in which a joint, usually the elbow, is forcibly pushed beyond its normal limits of extension, or straightening. Fortunately, serious elbow injuries do not occur as frequently as shoulder and elbow sprains. Bad scrapes and painful bruises, especially where the flesh has no protective padding covering it, rank among the more common football injuries.

Rib Injuries

Badly bruised and broken ribs constitute another painful form of injury. Probably the most common cause is a severe blow to the rib cage from an opponent's helmet or knee. The use of proper technique and enforcement of the no-spearing rule can reduce such injuries. So can the use of lightweight rib and trunk protectors, the so-called flak jackets sometimes worn by college and professional football players, usually after a rib injury. Still, given the size and speed of, and the armaments worn by, football players, rib damage appears a certainty as long as youngsters play the game.

Lower Extremity Injuries

KNEES. Knee injuries rank as the most common serious lower-body injuries, and as the most common permanently debilitating football injuries. Moreover, once a player suffers a knee injury, he stands a high risk of suffering further knee damage. Most of the nonsurgical knee injuries that occur in football are described in Chapter 7 or in Chapter 10 in the section on knee problems in runners.

Interestingly, the percentage of injured football players suffering knee damage appears to have remained remarkably constant. A study of insurance records filed during seven years between 1965 and 1985 showed that the percentage of injured young athletes filing medical claims for treatment of knee injuries ranged from 12.7 percent to 14.3 percent.

Ligament damage stands out as the leading cause of knee injury, with kneecap problems another major source. Since the 1970s, physicians have turned increasingly to arthroscopic surgery to repair damaged knee ligaments. This is a less serious type of operation that usually allows athletes to resume play more quickly. Most ligament damage, however, involves incomplete tears that do not require surgical repair. Nonetheless, no matter what treatment a physician chooses, a player who suffers ligament damage stands a significantly high risk of later knee problems. In the study of knee injuries cited above, only 5 percent of the players with ligament damage said that knee problems restricted their athletic activities four years after their initial injury, and only 22 percent had undergone surgery. After 10 years, however, 25 percent of these men, now in their mid- and late twenties, complained about debilitating knee problems and 52 percent had had a knee operation.

Since Joe Namath led the New York Jets to an upset victory in the Super Bowl in 1969 wearing a knee brace, many players, coaches, and trainers have adopted such braces, both to help speed recovery and to try to prevent injury. Together with physical therapy, braces can help a player recovering from a knee injury or surgery to regain his mobility sooner, which helps him maintain his muscle tone and strength. Moreover, studies indicate that braces can somewhat reduce the chance of reinjury when an athlete resumes play. However, studies generally have failed to find any protective advantage for players who have never suffered a knee injury, and some report that so-called prophylactic braces actually increase the threat. For example, a study of players from 71 NCAA Division I college football teams in 1984 and 61 teams in 1985 found that those wearing braces suffered significantly more injuries than those who did not wear them. A study of 580 New Mexico high school players reached similar conclusions. It appears that exercises that strengthen the muscle supporting the knee do more to successfully prevent injuries than do braces.

HIPS, THIGHS, AND FEET. Besides the knee, blows from opponents' helmets, shoulders, and knees can cause severe, painful bruising of the hipbone (a "hip pointer") and the thigh that can cause painful problems. For example, Mark, a 14-year-old sandlot player, suffered a bad thigh bruise, but toughed it out without treatment and continued playing in spite of several blows to his injured muscle. Two months after his initial bruise, Mark went to a physician with severe pain and was diagnosed with myositis ossificans. A large amount of blood released by repeated bruising had calcified in the muscle, posing the threat of permanent damage.

Hamstring-muscle pulls and ankle sprains are also common; stress fractures in the foot from excessive running and toe sprains are less common. And with the introduction of artificial playing surfaces, "turf toe," a painful hyperextension injury to a toe joint, has become a problem.

Coaches need to remember that a physically fit and well-trained player stands a better chance of surviving the season uninjured. Practice should aim as much at improving the flexibility, strength, endurance, and speed of young athletes as at honing their playing skills. A fit athlete better resists fatigue—itself a risk factor for injury—and is less susceptible to blocking, tackling, and falling injuries. An important part of improving strength lies in working out with weights, but weights require cautious use because they can cause injuries in young athletes (see Chapter 13).

Coaches must teach their players proper blocking and tackling techniques and warn them of the potentially fatal consequences of failing to use them. Many young players want to hit head first, rather than tackling with their heads up and off center, which can help avoid spinal cord injuries and severe blows to the head from the knees of a runner. Coaches should pull any player who spears an opponent for a few downs, and if he does it again, bench him for the remainder of the game. Finally, coaches should evaluate the amount of blocking and tackling that occurs during practice and eliminate unnecessary physical contact as a way to reduce injuries.

The danger of football injuries increases with the age of the players and the intensity of competition. The dangers are real, indeed, but the desire of many boys to play this truly American game is equally real. Players, parents, and coaches need to recognize the dangers of football and do everything possible to reduce the risk of injury.

13

Weight Training

Within the last decade, weight training has come to play an important secondary role in many sports as a way to condition the bodies of young athletes.

Weight training, sometimes called *resistance training*, uses exercise machines, not the massive free weights hoisted by competitive weight lifters. It's designed to improve athletic performance by increasing strength, power, muscle endurance, and speed. Contrary to one of sport's most popular myths, weight training—done properly—does *not* cause muscle-boundedness (an overdevelopment of muscles that reduces flexibility) or lead to slower muscle movements. Indeed, the evidence shows the opposite: increasing muscle strength with weight training can *increase* muscle speed.

Weight *training* differs significantly from weight *lifting*. In the competitive sport of weight lifting, participants try to lift the greatest weight they can—with one try. The lifts come in two categories. The Olympic lifts consist of the snatch and the clean-and-jerk; the power lifts include the squat, the bench press, and the dead lift.

Because of the heavy weights involved, weight lifting carries a potential for serious debilitating injuries, including fractures, and for shoulder, lower-back, and knee damage. As previously noted, the spine is not fully mineralized until a person reaches his or her mid-twenties. In an athlete whose spine is incompletely mineralized, lifting heavy weights repetitively may lead to the development of chronic arthritis-like conditions or spinal fractures.

Weight lifting poses risks serious enough that sports medicine specialists urge athletes not to take it up until they are well beyond puberty. Because of the risk of possible damage to their back, youngsters should avoid weight lifting until they are almost finished with their adolescent growth. Older adolescents are more likely to be able to lift safely—but even this isn't a sure thing. Too often, competitive young athletes want to outshine their peers and "pump iron" beyond their body's capabilities—with injurious effects.

WHO CAN BENEFIT?

Competitive sports, with few exceptions, demand and reward strength, power, and endurance. Done properly, strength training can enhance these physical qualities and reduce a youngster's risk of injury. Strength training toughens muscles, of course, but it also builds tendons, ligaments, bones, and joints, making them all more resistant to the blows, sudden twists, and other stresses that go along with most sports.

The benefit of strength training, however, varies with a youngster's sex and stage of physical development.

As discussed in Chapter 5, females do not have the same absolute strength as males, nor can they build much muscle mass. However, their muscles do have the same qualities, contractile properties, and ability to exert force as those of males. As a result, when males and females devote themselves with equal intensity to the same exercise program, they both make the same percentage gains in strength.

Girls do not significantly increase their strength through weight training until after menarche. Before and during puberty, apparent strength increases result more from "motor learning" than from muscle growth. This motor learning is perceived by coaches and athletes as an actual strength increase. After menarche, females can increase their strength much more, often doubling their strength within three months, and do so without developing bulging muscles. An increasing number of young women who do not participate in team sports have turned to weight training as a means of maintaining muscle tone and controlling their weight.

Prepubertal boys can improve their strength through weight training, but they will achieve small gains compared to those possible for older teenagers. Muscle mass will not increase significantly because at this age boys have insufficient amounts of circulating androgen, the male sex hormone vital to muscle building.

The question of the safety of weight training for prepubescents remains controversial. Only a limited amount of data exists for this age level. The data available indicate that there is no greater risk for prepubescents, provided they work with very light resistances and limit their workouts to sessions planned and supervised by a qualified instructor.

THE MECHANICS OF STRENGTH TRAINING

Muscle *strength* is measured as the muscle's ability to work against a resistance with a single, maximum effort. Typically, this means the maximum weight a person can lift once through a full range of motion. Muscle *endurance* represents the length of time a muscle can sustain its maximum contraction, which bears directly on a person's ability to resist muscle fatigue.

Young athletes can increase both strength and endurance with exercises that force them to work against resistances that their muscles don't normally encounter. This stressing of their muscles, done properly, will make them strong.

Physiologists speak of three types of strength: *concentric*, or *positive*, the strength needed to lift a weight; *isometric*, or *static*, the strength used to hold a weight steady; and *eccentric*, or *negative*, the strength used to lower a weight. In concentric strength, the muscle shortens while contracting; in eccentric strength, the muscle lengthens while contracting. Some experts have expressed concern about the safety of exercises that create large eccentric stresses. Care should be taken, but many sports activities, including throwing a ball and landing after a jump, require eccentric strength.

Strength training divides into two basic kinds of exercises: static (or isometric) and dynamic. Isometric exercises (also called static training) involve contracting muscles with maximum effort, but without visible limb movement—usually by pushing against an immovable object like a wall, a doorframe, or an exercise partner. These exercises do maintain muscle tone and moderately improve strength, and they are particularly useful for very young athletes and those recovering from an injury. However, they are not as effective as dynamic exercises in developing strength. In fact, isometrics can decrease a person's maximum limb speed, reducing his or her quickness.

In dynamic exercises, a muscle group moves a joint through a range of motions against one of three kinds of resistance: accommodating, or isokinetic; variable; and constant, or isotonic.

ACCOMMODATING RESISTANCE

Isokinetic exercise machines force muscles to contract through a full range of motion at a constant velocity. With these machines, a person does not lift weights but instead works against a hydraulic mechanism or a lever moving at a preset speed. To reach personal maximum strength, an athlete should train at a fast machine speed. Studies indicate that training at fast speeds increases an athlete's performance significantly better than training at slow speeds. Isokinetic machines cause little or no muscle soreness, and since a user lifts no weights and the machines accommodate fatigue, the risk of injury remains low.

VARIABLE RESISTANCE

With this technique, the resistance of the exercise machine changes as the user's muscle contracts. The technique is based on the fact that a muscle's force-generating ability changes as it shortens. By varying the resistance to match the muscle's force-generating capacity, the machine stresses the muscle with greater resistance at times when it can produce greater force. This increases the contraction's intensity and builds stronger muscles. Again, the injury risk with these machines is low, although excessive muscle stretching can occur if the user fails to monitor the resistance settings.

While both isokinetic and variable-resistance machines effectively build strong muscles, they also come with high price tags. As a result, most young athletes do not have access to them.

CONSTANT RESISTANCE

By far the most commonly used weight-training machines, these isotonic devices provide a preset resistance that never changes throughout the entire range of motion of the exercise. Actually, weight lifting is an isotonic exercise, and many of the constant-resistance machines used in strength training follow the same principles. The user builds muscle by repeating a series of movements a certain number of times. Each repetition is called a "rep," and the specific number of reps performed before the exerciser rests is known as a set. A person increases the resistance (weight) in each of the exercises as his or her strength grows, thus progressively increasing the stress on the muscle. Often, youngsters will train with both free weights and constant-resistance machines. Between the two, the machines generally pose the smaller risk of injury.

MACHINES, FREE WEIGHTS, AND PLYOMETRICS

For the preadolescent and adolescent athlete, resistance machines provide the safest means of improving their strength. A variety of companies make such resistance machines, but no maker's equipment is clearly superior to another's. In the end, the young athlete holds the most important key to success: he or she must willingly put forth a maximum effort for any weight-training program to yield a significant strength gain.

Resistance machines can greatly improve the strength, power, and endurance of adolescents. Nonetheless, for athletes to reach their full potential, many strength coaches favor a combination of machines and free weights. Young athletes should avoid this pairing, unless working under the close supervision of a knowledgeable strength coach, until well into late adolescence and physical maturity. The use of free weights is particularly helpful in a strength program designed to develop power. However, the introduction of free weights into a strength program also increases the risk of injury and the necessity for additional safety precautions. The most important precaution is a continuing emphasis on using the proper technique for each exercise. Free weights also require a spotter at each end of a weight-laden bar, to grab it if the lifter gives out and begins to lose control; proper shoes and matting to keep the lifter from slipping; and an awareness of the dangers of muscle fatigue.

In one case, a young athlete named Jeffrey arrived at his physician's office complaining of chest pain and pain when inhaling, and was fearful he had suffered a heart attack. It turned out that the 16-year-old had dropped a barbell on his chest while bench-pressing 100 pounds without a spotter. His diagnosis: a fractured sternum, and extremely good luck. Had the barbell fallen on his neck or higher on his chest, Jeffrey's injury might have proved fatal.

In addition to weight training, some athletes pursue *plyometrics*, a set of vigorous exercises designed to increase power for running, jumping, and throwing. While strength depends on muscle-fiber development, power depends on the interaction between the muscles and the nerves that order them to contract. Plyometric exercises increase the speed with which muscles contract.

These exercises involve hops, bounds, jumps—which build power in the legs—and throwing medicine balls or sandbags, efforts that increase upper-body power. In *hops*, the athlete assumes a partial squat and then jumps straight upward as high as possible, without making any effort to move forward, lands into a partial squat, and then jumps again as high as possible. This continues for several more repetitions. *Bounds* also begin with a partial squat, but this time the athlete leaps as high and as far as possible, rebounds, and then repeats. Both hops and bounds should be made with maximum effort, and they should include two-leg, right-leg, and left-leg take-offs. Typically, an athlete should do bounds over 50 meters, then add 5 meters a week until the bounds cover 100 meters. In *jumps*, or depth jumps, the athlete steps off a bench, then rebounds up onto another bench, and continues to repeat this.

Hops, bounds, and jumps are far more strenuous than they sound. Youngsters probably should not engage in these exercises because of the injuries associated with them. Skipping rope and jumping jacks are plyometric-type exercises which youngsters can do. Mature, elite athletes should limit themselves to doing hops, bounds, and jumps every other day at most. Even with that break, many who pursue plyometrics avoid doing hops and bounds on the same day. Finally, to avoid heel bruises or shin splints, these exercises should be done on grass or mats.

DEVELOPING A WEIGHT-TRAINING PROGRAM

Selecting a strength program includes deciding whether to use weight-resistance machines alone or in combination with free weights, and whether to include plyometric exercises. In addition, it requires consideration of such factors as the frequency of workouts, their duration, and their intensity. Such decisions should never be left to an inexperienced and often overexuberant youngster. Instead, the young athlete should work out a program with a school strength coach or certified athletic trainer, or with a knowledgeable counselor at a gym or health club. Making the right decisions can mean the difference between a safe, effective program and an injury or series of injuries that slows the young athlete's progress.

Any weight-training program must consider the youngster's age. Prepubescents and pubescents should use low resistance or light weights and do a larger number of repetitions than older teenagers. The equipment used should be uncomplicated and appropriate to the youngster's size. If the training includes free weights, a trainer or coach needs to devote particular attention to ensuring that the youngster follows proper technique and that the weights are stabilized throughout each exercise. Children and young adolescents should follow a total-body program that concentrates on strengthening the large muscle groups and the most common joint movements. Each workout should feature at least one exercise that builds up a major muscle group. Older adolescents, particularly those playing varsity sports, should include exercises that strengthen the smaller muscle groups, which helps further to protect the joints.

Weight trainers often fail to recognize the importance of stretching exercises. But warming up is as important for someone about to challenge a machine as it is before any athletic competition. We describe a typical stretching pattern in Chapter 2.

Strength coaches sometimes refer to the "overload principle." This simply means that a muscle responds with growth when a person stresses (overloads) it with work or regular exercise. However, the protein synthesis that builds muscle occurs during rest, not during the actual period of muscle stress caused by strength-training exercises. This explains why experienced weight trainers and weight lifters work out one day and lay off the next. We cannot emphasize enough the importance of giving the muscles time to rest, both for preventing injury and for increasing strength. Youngsters, no matter how seriously they pursue a weight program, should work out only three times a week, which usually means Monday-Wednesday-Friday, particularly if they are using school facilities.

Weight trainers talk about reps (or repetitions, the number of times they perform a movement before resting) and sets (the number of times they do a group of repetitions). Since no magic combination of reps and sets exists, choosing a proper exercise pattern depends on the youngster's age, strength, and training goals. Beginners, for their own good, must focus on learning the proper technique for each exercise movement. Trying too quickly to increase the amount of weight they lift only distracts from technique and increases the risk of injury. Beginners should also limit each workout to no more than one hour each. Youngsters ages 9 through 11 should limit their sessions to a single exercise for each body part, and do two sets of 12 to 15 reps each with very light resistance. From ages 12 through 14, young athletes should perform only one exercise for each body part, but raise their sets to three, lower their reps to 10 to 12, and use light resistance. At 15 and 16, youngsters can do two exercises per body part, do three to four sets of 7 to 11 reps, and work against moderate resistance. Finally, athletes 17 years old and older can do two or more exercises per body part, four to six sets with 6 to 10 reps, and use heavy resistance.

The amount of time between sets and between exercises depends on the athlete's sport. The body emphasizes different energy systems in different sports, and how a young athlete carries out his or her weight training can affect different energy systems. While a 50-meter sprinter fares better with no more than 30 seconds between sets, a speed skater should wait 30 to 90 seconds, and a cross-country runner up to three minutes. A knowledgeable coach or athletic trainer can help a youngster select the best resting time between sets and exercises. The best way to increase strength and muscle mass is to train hard. As a youngster's strength and mastery of technique increase, so can the resistance. As a rule, lifters add weight and resistance for a specific exercise after a certain number of consecutive workouts in which they complete the maximum number of sets without reaching the failing point, where they cannot do another rep. Resistance can be increased for only one exercise, without waiting to master all. The number of "perfect" workouts varies by age: those 9 through 11 should go four straight before increasing their resistance; those 12 through 16, three; and those 17 and older, two, provided they have at least two years of resistance-training experience. Typically, lifters increase their weight by 5 to 10 pounds, depending on the exercise. Increasing resistance increases intensity, and so lifters should decrease their number of reps in each set and gradually rebuild it as they gain new strength.

Intensity refers to the amount of effort a person must expend to complete an exercise. Lighter weights or lower resistance require less intensity. People who want merely to maintain a level of strength can exercise at less intensity than those trying to increase strength and build large muscle mass.

WEIGHT-TRAINING INJURIES

The injury rate for weight training appears to be low at any age—when the exercises are properly coached, supervised, and executed. Many youngsters combine strength training with one or more other sports, most of which have a higher injury risk than working out with resistance machines—or even with free weights. Injuries tend to come on gradually and subtly, with the young athlete unable to pinpoint a specific time when he or she first noticed the symptoms. As a result, physicians often find it difficult to tell whether an injury occurred as a result of the weight-training exercises or from another sport.

Most problems that do occur happen when youngsters try too hard or receive inadequate guidance in developing their program. A common fault, for example, is the failure to include exercises to strengthen the rotational muscles of the abdomen and lower back. This omission increases the risk of lower-back pain.

Fractures sometimes occur as a direct result of weight training, usually when a youngster tries to handle more weight than his or her body strength will allow. Lower-back pain also occurs, and physicians occasionally see a ruptured disc. Certain free-weight maneuvers that involve squatting will cause kneecap pain; it's best to limit this type of exercise to a one-quarter squat. And weight trainers should avoid reverse leg curls, if possible (again, to avoid kneecap pain). Some lifters suffer displaced shoulder blades. And improper positioning or holding a weight for sit-ups can cause lower-back injuries. Sit-ups should always be done with the knees flexed.

Youngsters recuperating from an injury, whether caused by weight training or some other activity, must take care not to attempt too much too soon. An overeager lifter may suffer not only reinjury, but a far worse injury. A young athlete whose injury requires a physician's care should never return to resistance training without the doctor's approval, and his or her reentry into a strength program should occur under the watchful eye of someone familiar with the rehabilitation problems posed by resistance machines and weights. The longer the absence, the longer the restrengthening process will take. The injured athlete should start with very little resistance and do a trial series of reps for each exercise, increasing the resistance a bit at a time. If pain occurs, the athlete should stop and return to a lesser resistance. This is not the time for a youngster to fall for that misleading and potentially dangerous adage, "No pain, no gain."

While no evidence exists that weight training can cause hypertension, a permanent and potentially dangerous elevation in blood pressure, working with weights does increase blood pressure during the exercise period. Therefore, physicians advise against both weight training and weight lifting for anyone with hypertension or heart trouble—problems that do affect some children and adolescents. With this important exception, weight training's benefits for young athletes clearly outweigh its risks.

14

Gymnastics and Dance

Interest in gymnastics and dancing, particularly aerobic dancing, soared dramatically during the 1970s and 1980s.

Gymnastics, a sport whose origins go back at least four thousand years, exploded as a result of the extensive television coverage of the sport at the Olympic Games and the dramatic victories of such young talents as Olga Korbut, Nadia Comaneci, and Mary Lou Retton.

Men's competitive gymnastics consists of six events: parallel bars, horizontal bar, rings, pommel horse, long horse vault, and floor exercise. Women compete in four events: uneven parallel bars, side horse vault, balance beam, and floor exercise. Most gymnasts compete as members of independent clubs—where training begins as early as age 5 or 6—or as members of scholastic or collegiate teams. The U.S. National and Olympic teams consist almost exclusively of gymnasts who began with independent clubs.

Gymnastics stresses strength, agility, and grace. Success in this sport requires coordination, balance, rhythm, flexibility, speed, and stamina, as well as determination, self-discipline, and a sense of showmanship.

Dance—ballet, theatrical, modern, jazz, and, to a lesser extent, aerobic—requires a combination of athletic and artistic skills. While ballet long has had its enthusiasts, especially among girls, aerobic dancing—a combination of stretching, calisthenics, dance steps, and jumping in place done to rhythmic music and led by an instructor—rode the crest of the U.S. exercise boom to enormous popularity. Today it ranks as the nation's largest organized fitness activity among women. The movements required in gymnastics' floor exercises resemble those of dance, and the two activities share another, less pleasant similiarity—the types of injuries their participants suffer.

INCIDENCE OF INJURIES

Injuries to both dancers and gymnasts occur largely in the lower extremities, and usually result either from stress or from trauma, such as excessive twisting or a fall.

Studies reveal that the greater the skill or competition level, the greater the risk of injury. In gymnastics, interestingly, the greatest number of injuries to females apparently occurs during floor exercises, with the balance beam second. A recent study that followed 50 highly competitive young female gymnasts (average age 12.6 years) for a year found that they suffered 147 injuries during that 12-month period. Nonspecific pain—general pain in the ankle, knee, wrist, elbow, or lower back, for example—accounted for 40.1 percent of the girls' complaints, followed by sprains (19 percent) and muscle strains (17.7 percent). A study of 873 male and female gymnasts found the knee to be the most frequent site of injury, with the ankle, foot, and wrist essentially tied for second.

Dancers' injuries often develop slowly and many dancers live with their pain for long periods before seeking medical attention. Shin splints and foot and ankle injuries represent the most common complaints of dancers, who also frequently suffer knee problems and lower-back pain. Certain factors in dance—the floor surface, the shoes worn, and the type of dance—appear more likely to influence the dancer's risk of injury than such things as age, height, weight, and gender.

SAFETY GUIDELINES FOR YOUNGSTERS

GYMNASTICS

Youngsters can reduce their injury risk by warming up properly, following proper technique, and increasing their workload slowly to avoid overuse problems. The use of spotters during gymnastic maneuvers also can help significantly to reduce serious injuries from slips and falls.

A number of factors enter the safety equation in gymnastics, ranging from the condition of the gym and its equipment to the physical and emotional condition of the young athletes and the attitudes of their coaches. When children express an interest in pursuing gymnastics, parents should make certain their offspring have both the physical skills and the emotional strength the sport requires, as well as a qualified coach with whom they can communicate and who understands and accepts each child's goals. In our opinion, a coach should have performed as a gymnast at one time, hold a current certification from the U.S. Gymnastics Safety Association, and have had certified training in first aid and the emergency treatment of serious injuries.

Among the questions parents should ask are the following:

- Does my child have the strength, flexibility, quickness, and stamina needed to do gymnastics? If you have doubts, ask a physician or the coach the child will work with for an evaluation.
- Is there any existing medical problem that may predispose the young athlete to injury?
- Does the youngster harbor fears of injury or doubts about his or her ability that will hinder development of gymnastic skills? Safety anxieties and self-doubt can themselves contribute to injuries.
- Does the coach stress safety? For example, are spotters used during all practices? Is discipline maintained and horseplay discouraged? Are the gymnasts pushed to continue when fatigued? Does the coach have a copy of the *Gymnastics Safety Manual*, the sport's safety bible?
- Does the coach recognize when a child is emotionally as well as physically ready to attempt a more difficult maneuver?
- Is the gym well maintained and is damaged equipment immediately taken out of use and repaired or replaced?
- Is the lighting bright? Inadequate lighting poses a major safety threat in gymnastics.
- Are there enough mats, and is chalk resin always available for the young gymnasts' hands?

Gymnasts typically peak in their late teens, and two decades ago, participants consisted largely of postpubescents. Today, especially in women's gymnastics, prepubescents and pubescents dominate. This has led to considerable concern about the ill effects of the sport on the very young. Growing evidence indicates that the growth patterns of prepubescent and pubescent athletes—particularly their growth spurts—greatly increase their risks of injury over those of postpubescents. Certain measures can be taken to cut this risk: these include doing a musculoskeletal screening and a maturity assessment as part of the annual preparticipation physical, and keeping height charts to alert coaches to sudden growth spurts. Coaches should consider reducing the training activities of girls during periods of rapid growth and not allowing them to resume a full load until growth slows again.

DANCE

Dancing rarely results in a growth-plate injury, even in very young girls. However, dance does carry risks. Whether theatrical, modern, jazz, ballet, or aerobic, dance at its best is physically strenuous and demanding. A child can pursue several levels of dance without great concern of injury. But as the skills and maneuvers needed increase, so do the risks of injury, although to a lesser degree in aerobic dancing.

Often injuries result because the child's body fails to meet the demands of the technique. Consider ballet. Females should not begin dancing on their toe tips, a position called "on pointe," until about age 11 or 12, and then only after at least three years of training in the basics of ballet technique. Dancing on pointe requires strength and stamina, balance and coordination, and feet structurally suited for the stressful task. If a child's feet aren't built for dancing on pointe, the risk of injury soars. Many dance specialists discourage such children from pursuing ballet beyond the beginning level.

All dances require external hip rotation. Dancers with hips that naturally turn out poorly often compensate by forcing an excessive external rotation of the knees and ankles, a misalignment that accounts for many dance injuries. Dance teachers should not only stress correct technique with their young pupils, but take into account their anatomic differences.

NUTRITION

While we discussed the nutritional needs of young athletes in detail in Chapter 3, dancers and gymnasts can pose special concerns. Both activities put a premium on slender, lithe figures, a requirement not found in other sports. This puts tremendous pressures on dancers and gymnasts and leads many of them to excessive and unhealthy dieting. Medical studies typically find that many top performers in both activities, particularly females, consume an unbalanced diet that contains too few calories to support their physically strenuous routines. These dancers often take large, sometimes potentially unhealthy doses of vitamins to try to compensate for their nutritional deficiencies.

These practices often start early. For example, a study of 97 competitive female gymnasts, aged 11 to 17, found that they averaged 300 calories *less* than their daily energy needs, and that more than 40 percent were getting less than two-thirds their recommended amounts of calcium, folic acid, vitamin B_6, iron, and zinc from their diet. Such chronic poor eating results in the loss of electrolytes, minerals, glycogen stores, and lean tissue, and can lead to vitamin and mineral deficiencies, reduced performance, an increased risk of stress fractures, and menstrual irregularities.

Anorexia nervosa, a potentially fatal eating disorder, represents the most serious consequence of an unhealthy preoccupation with thinness. Studies have shown a high incidence of the disorder among top-level ballerinas, and evidence now suggests that anorexia nervosa also poses a problem for many female gymnasts. Those suffering the disorder invariably perceive themselves as too fat, no matter how emaciated their bodies, and deny the existence of the problem even when confronted with evidence. The causes remain unclear, but appear to involve both physical and psychological dysfunctions.

Certainly not all thin dancers and gymnasts suffer from anorexia nervosa. But parents and coaches should be alert to the early warning signs, which include a progressive weight loss that continues even during vacations and other periods of inactivity; self-induced vomiting; and the abusive use of diuretics and laxatives. (These latter symptoms also may indicate bulimia, a related eating disorder characterized by binge eating followed by purging the body of food and liquids.) As anorexia nervosa progresses, more serious symptoms develop, including an abnormally slow heart rate, low blood pressure, hair loss, and rarely, bleeding from the mouth and/or rectum. The disorder is difficult to treat, and the further it progresses, the more difficult it becomes. About half the anorexics who require hospitalization relapse at least once after their release.

Menstrual concerns also trouble many young female dancers and gymnasts. These include delays in the initial age of menstruation, irregular cycles, and cessation of menstruation. Weight loss, low body fat, extensive exercise, and emotional stress have been linked as causes of these reproductive system problems. But no one has yet determined the exact reason. Some experts argue that the physical activity required of young female dancers and gymnasts leads to late menstruation. Others suggest that the typical physique of successful dancers and gymnasts—they tend to have long legs and hips that are narrower than average—is more of a factor than the early physical activity. Women with this body type may have an inherent predisposition to delayed menstruation and irregular menstrual cycles.

PHYSICAL CONDITIONING

Gymnastics and dance demand flexibility and strength. Indeed, beyond its importance to performance, flexibility is one of the things that judges evaluate in gymnastics. Flexibility also helps prevent soreness and decreases the chance of injury. By themselves, the moves and movements of gymnastics and dance fail to provide or maintain the flexibility these endeavors require. Only a regular routine of stretching exercises can do that.

There are two types of stretching exercises. In *static* stretching, the youngster holds the stretch's final position for a period of time. *Ballistic* stretching flows right through the final position without a stop. Both increase flexibility, but the evidence suggests that static-stretching exercises pose less risk of tissue damage. Although we discussed the importance of flexibility and described some important stretching exercises in Chapter 2, we urge anyone interested in gymnastics or dance to consult closely with his or her instructor, and to obtain one of the books available that outline specific stretching exercises for gymnasts and dancers.

Body strength also plays an important role in the success of dancers and gymnasts. Many gymnasts and some dancers have turned to weight training to improve their strength. During gymnastic routines, males spend about 60 percent of their time holding their positions; females spend about 30 percent of their time in support holds. These holds require strength and muscle endurance, which has led to the interest in strength training among gymnasts.

The types of strengthening exercises best suited for gymnastics are whole-body lifts, which strengthen all of the joints. These include rowing, one-quarter squats, latissimus pulls, bench presses, and military presses. Donald T. Kirkendall of the Cleveland Clinic Foundation recommends that the workout routine change with the athletic season. During the noncompetitive (or nonperforming) part of the year, the youngster should do low-intensity, high-repetition exercises, between 8 and 20 repetitions for four or five sets. With the approaching season, intensity should increase with 3 to 6 repetitions for three to five sets. During the competitive (or performance) season, the youngster should do only one, two at the most, high-intensity workouts a week.

Unfortunately, gymnasts and dancers and their instructors too often forget a simple fact of nature: the human body has its endurance limits. Athletes need to rest their bodies, both during practices and rehearsals and between performances and meets. A fatigued athlete has less body control, and therefore a greater risk of suffering some injury.

SHOES

The issue of shoes is moot for modern dancers, who typically wear none. Ballet dancers perform wearing only thin slippers, which provide essentially no support. Calluses, blisters, corns, bunions, and ingrown toenails commonly afflict ballet dancers. Tap and jazz dancers need well-fitted, well-made shoes to avoid similiar problems.

Aerobic dancers, who seek physical fitness far more than a graceful performance, should wear shoes with excellent shock absorption. Some people do their aerobic dancing barefoot, which significantly increases their chances of hurting themselves. In one study, those who danced barefoot had one-third again as many injuries as those who wore shoes. Athletic shoe companies market a variety of models designed for aerobic dancing. Such shoes should protect against the impact of aerobic dancing, which is equal to about three times the dancer's body weight with each strike of the foot. They should also help protect the feet against twisting inward or outward. Running shoes and those designed for court sports fail to offer the full protection aerobic dancers need. Properly fitted viscoelastic insoles— made from a polymer material with excellent shock-absorbing properties—appear to provide more comfort and greater pain relief than foam insoles, but whether they actually reduce musculoskeletal injuries among aerobic dancers remains unknown. Properly designed and fitted orthotic shoe inserts can help in treating dance injuries, but never try to use them to compensate for poor training or improper technique.

SURFACES

GYMNASTICS

Safe gymnastics requires proper floor matting and a layout of run-ways and landing areas arranged so that collisions between gymnasts don't occur. Gymnastics rules call for a 1¼-inch base mat covered by a 4-inch mat during competition. But during practices, coaches should use extra matting, especially when students are learning a new skill or a more complicated maneuver. Gymnast coaches have a saying: "Expect the unexpected and put a mat there." But mats tend to slide. So beyond the crucial act of thinking ahead, coaches must anchor mats in place by either tying them down or affixing ropes to the mat handles and tying the other ends to secure objects.

Runways should provide good traction so that youngsters don't slide and hurt themselves. While rubber runways usually remain in place by themselves, coaches must make certain that other kinds of runways (for example, a rolled-out carpet) are secured to the floor. If a runway surface provides less than firm traction, gymnasts should wear shoes that give them a good grip.

DANCE

Whatever type of dance they choose, dancers risk injury from rough, irregular, uneven, or poorly maintained floors. Inflexible dance sur-faces, such as a concrete slab, also raise the injury risk because they fail to absorb the energy of the dancer's impact. This added stress on the lower extremities may result in shin splints or stress fractures. On the other hand, a surface with too much give, such as a thick, loosely filled mat, can also lead to a greater risk of a strain or sprain. So the quest is for a surface that combines flexibility with stability. One study of aerobic dancers found the lowest injury rate among those who danced on a concrete floor covered by heavy padding and a well-secured carpet. The second fewest injuries occurred among those who danced on a wooden floor with an air space below.

SPECIFIC INJURIES

Injuries among gymnasts and dancers usually occur in the lower extremities, in dancers most frequently as the result of a fall or twisting motion, in gymnasts, as the result of a fall or faulty dismount. However, the middle and upper body suffer their share of problems, particularly from falls. Elbow injuries from a spill off the balance beam are not rare in gymnastics, for example, and pelvis bruises commonly occur among female gymnasts working the uneven parallel bars.

Unfortunately, some gymnasts and dancers try to hide their injuries for fear they will lose their place on the team or in the company. For example, Alison sought medical assistance after her gymnastics coach accused her of losing her commitment to the sport. The 14-year-old had twisted her ankle a month before and quickly returned to practice when the swelling subsided. But the pain persisted and her performance suffered. In an emotional conversation with a physician, Alison said she had never told her coach of her continuing pain for fear she would lose her spot on the team.

ANKLE INJURIES

Ankle sprains rank high among the injuries to gymnasts and dancers, and constitute the most common acute injury seen in ballet and modern dancers. Most often, these sprains result from a faulty landing that twists the ankle and stretches or partially tears a ligament. Mild sprains often need no treatment beyond RICE (see Chapter 6) and perhaps a nonprescription anti-inflammatory drug such as aspirin, and taping or an air cast to immobilize the ankle. Moderate sprains may require putting the injured ankle in a cast.

Gymnasts and dancers must take care not to rush back to practice before their sprain heals. Both activities require absolute stability of the ankle, and returning early only increases the risk of a more severe injury. Swimming, when approved by a physician, provides an excellent way to help restore the sprained ankle's range of motion. After that has been accomplished, the goal becomes restoring the ankle's strength and endurance by exercising the muscles that support it. A mixture of isometric and isotonic exercises (see Chapter 13), recommended by a physician or physical therapist, works best.

Dancers, particularly ballet dancers, sometimes complain of tenderness and swelling in the ankle, and an inability to execute certain positions properly. If the problem is talar impingement, it usually can be diagnosed from X rays and treated by a physician.

Ankle fractures usually result from a false step. Treatment, obviously, requires a physician's diagnosis and wearing a cast for about a month. Rehabilitation takes longer; it will sometimes take as much as two years before a ballet dancer can fully resume pointe dancing.

FOOT INJURIES

The ability to rotate the hips and lower extremities outward plays a more important role in a dancer's success than in a gymnast's. "Turn-out" receives great emphasis in ballet, but also in other forms of performance dance. Unfortunately, many people do not have the natural anatomical configuration needed to rotate their lower body well, and their efforts to force a perfect turnout generate stresses that can end in injury. Two improper techniques often used to compensate for poor natural turnout are "rolling in" and "sickling." Rolling in involves gripping the floor with the first three toes and forcing the foot away from the body while lifting the outside edge of the foot. Sickling can occur in demipointe or full pointe and involves inward or outward movements of the forefoot and heel in improper body alignment. These poor techniques result in excessive strain on the middle of the foot, which can cause acute and chronic injuries to the hind, middle, and forefoot. The best prevention—and treatment—for such injuries is to correct the improper techniques that create them. But physicians and podiatrists also use anti-inflammatory drugs (usually ibuprofen), elastic bandages, and orthotic devices to treat these foot injuries. Only rarely is surgery required.

Prolonged, intensive dance training can affect a child's skeletal structure. The stresses thicken the femur (upper leg bone), the tibia and fibula (the two bones of the lower leg), and the metatarsals (the long bones of the foot). Some dancers develop *exostoses*, noncancerous tumors that bulge from the bone. In some cases, exostoses interfere with a dancer's ability to perform, and the tumors may require surgical treatment.

Bunions, corns, and *calluses* commonly afflict dancers and sometimes gymnasts. Bunions, the inflammation of a saclike cavity called a bursa at the big toe, appear to strike child dancers more often than adults. They usually don't cause significant problems, but in severe cases, they can produce a deformity that hinders a dancer's career. Bunions are best prevented by properly fitting ballet slippers or other shoes used by dancers, strengthening the muscles that support the foot and ankle, and ensuring that the young dancer uses proper technique. Only a knowledgeable health care professional should remove corns and calluses; they should never be cut off by the youngster, a parent, or a friend. Infection could result, causing far more serious problems.

"Knuckling down" and a pinched os trigonum are two other situations common among the problems seen in young dancers. Knuckling down occurs in young ballet dancers who attempt to dance on pointe before they are physically capable. The toes collapse and curl under inside the ballet slippers, which throws the body off, thus increasing the dancer's risk of a sprained ankle or knee. Knuckling down may go unrecognized for some time, because the curling of the toes is hidden by the dancer's slippers. When knuckling down occurs, the dancer should cease dancing on pointe until physically ready.

The os trigonum is a small bone that usually causes no problem. But in dancers who dance on pointe or on the balls of their feet, as most dancers sometimes do, the bone may get pinched between the calcaneus (heel bone) and the tibia, causing an inflammation. Stretching exercises often alleviate the problem by increasing the flexibility of the foot and ankle. But if symptoms continue, the dancer should consult a physician.

KNEE INJURIES

Most knee injuries in gymnastics result from the twisting, bending, and jumping associated with the sport, particularly when a participant makes a faulty landing. A 6½-year study at the Cleveland Clinic Foundation found that knee injuries to gymnasts accounted for about 1.3 percent of all injuries seen at the clinic's sports medicine section. The most common knee injuries involved patellofemoral problems (see below), manifested by pain at the kneecap. Sprains followed, with tears of the meniscus (the crescent-shaped cartilage within the knee) third. Over half the sprains (53 percent) involved the medial collateral ligament. The 170 knee injuries included 28 among males and 142 among females, with most of the injuries in "full-bodied," mature women gymnasts attempting particularly difficult maneuvers.

Dancers also commonly suffer knee injuries, often as the result of twisting the joint. Dancers can reduce their risks of suffering such injuries by doing exercises that strengthen the quadriceps and the hamstrings, muscles that support the knee.

In both gymnasts and dancers, a variety of problems can produce pain that appears associated with the kneecap. (We discussed the overuse syndromes that cause such patellar pain in Chapter 7.) Chondromalacia (softening of cartilage) poses another threat to gymnasts and dancers. This problem characteristically strikes people whose activities require a lot of running, jumping, or prolonged bending of the knees. Typically, it causes pain that seems vaguely located around the front of the knee or beneath the kneecap. Sometimes swelling occurs within the joint. When the kneecap is pressed against the bone behind it, a person suffering chondromalacia experiences tenderness. Interestingly, chondromalacia may occur without pain; while doing arthroscopic or other knee surgery, physicians sometimes find even severe cartilage changes in athletes that had produced no symptoms. Again, strenthening the quadriceps helps reduce the risks of such injuries. If the injury does occur, the coach should analyze the athlete's routine carefully to determine what activity or activities most aggravate the pain and should modify or eliminate them whenever possible.

Finally, the problem of patellar instability, or "floating kneecap," creates a situation in which the knee gives out, causing the athlete to fall. This condition not only causes pain, but creates considerable apprehension in the young athlete, and a physician should treat it.

BACK INJURIES

Most back pain that comes on suddenly during or after a gymnastic or dance workout results from muscle strain. When questioned, the young athlete often can describe a specific reaching or twisting motion that sent pain stabbing through his or her back. Such pain requires a rest from activity. In addition, physicians usually recommend ice-pack treatments, lasting no more than 20 minutes (see Chapter 6), for the first 48 to 72 hours, and heat treatments after that. Once the pain subsides, the young athlete can resume workouts, but a concentrated effort to warm up and stretch the body should precede any gymnastic or dance activities. Generally, it takes young athletes one to two weeks to recover from a muscle strain. If pain persists longer than two weeks, the physician should reexamine the youngster for other possible problems.

Young dancers whose training emphasizes straightening the spine sometimes suffer subtle ligament strains, which cause a vague pain in the back. A program of stretching exercises that increases the body's flexibility helps decrease the risk of such pain. If the problem does develop, physicians generally treat it with anti-inflammatory medications and a training program to promote greater flexibility.

Serious spinal injuries appear more commonly among gymnasts than among dancers. Such injuries always require a physician's attention. These can result from either a single major injury or an accumulation of microscopic tissue injuries. Two debilitating problems bear quite similar names: spondylolysis and spondylolisthesis. *Spondylolysis* refers to a radiologically demonstrable defect that involves the dissolution of the spine's pars interarticularis. Essentially, this creates a stress fracture of the back. Spondylolysis may or may not be symptomatic. In *spondylolisthesis,* one vertebra slips forward over another and the stress fracture may become painful and debilitating, requiring a long recovery time. Spondylolisthesis also may or may not produce symptoms. Heredity can predispose certain people to either disorder, but in many cases, overstressing the spine serves as the immediate cause of the injury.

Typically, youngsters who develop spondylolisthesis complain of a continually aching lower back that interferes with their performance and gets worse with activity, particularly when they twist or overextend their back. In young athletes, most cases result from defects of the pars interarticularis. The initial defect may occur between ages 5 and 7, but may not create a problem until the child becomes heavy enough and active enough to aggravate the tiny break and create symptoms.

Sometimes, however, the defect doesn't develop until adolescence or even adulthood. A developing stress fracture of the pars interarticularis may not show up on an X ray and may require more sensitive and expensive imaging techniques to confirm. Spondylolisthesis may require treatment, but in many cases, youngsters can return to their sport under a physician's guidance.

Spondylolysis occurs about twice as often among boys as it does among girls. For reasons yet unknown, spondylolisthesis—one vertebra slipping over another—appears to be twice as common in girls as boys. Its more frequent occurrence in girls is puzzling because spondylolisthesis in young athletes often occurs in those who have already suffered spondylolysis.

Most of the slippage in spondylolisthesis occurs sometime between ages 9 and 14, and slippage rarely takes place *after* the completion of the vertebrae's growth. Physicians speak of two types of

SPINE ANATOMY

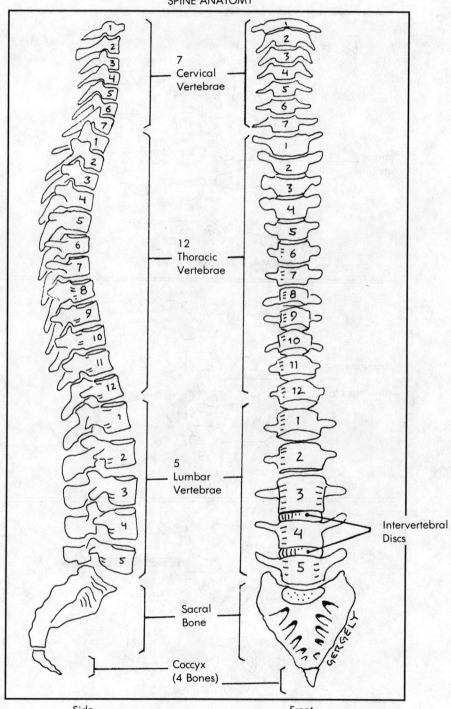

7 Cervical Vertebrae

12 Thoracic Vertebrae

5 Lumbar Vertebrae

Intervertebral Discs

Sacral Bone

Coccyx (4 Bones)

Side   Front

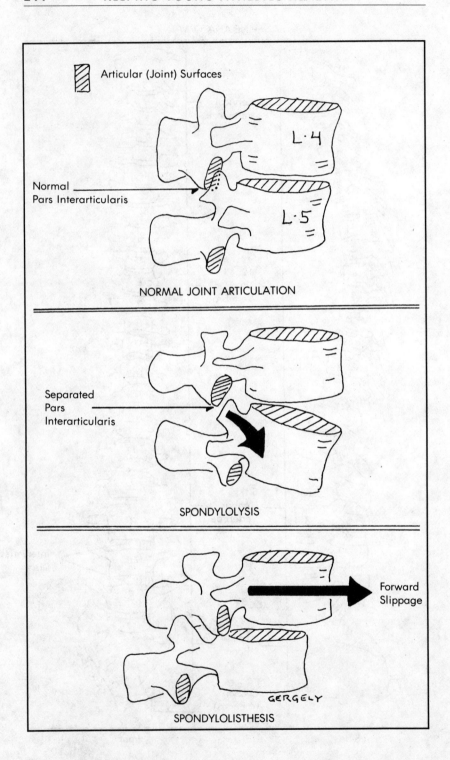

Articular (Joint) Surfaces

Normal
Pars Interarticularis

L·4

L·5

NORMAL JOINT ARTICULATION

Separated
Pars
Interarticularis

SPONDYLOLYSIS

Forward
Slippage

GERGELY

SPONDYLOLISTHESIS

the disorder. In one, the slippage follows a stress fracture in the pars interarticularis; in the other, the slippage occurs because of an abnormal elongation of the pars interarticularis. Either can cause intense pain and muscle spasms, or may be asymptomatic. Treatment requires refraining from vigorous activities until pain and spasm disappear and, often, medication in the acute stage. Unfortunately, some young athletes suffer a recurrence when they return to action.

Young athletes, like adults, may suffer damage to the *discs* between vertebrae. Treatment typically requires bed rest, and pain and anti-inflammatory medications for a time, and a break from vigorous athletic activities for six months to a year.

Finally, *scoliosis*, an abnormal curvature of the spine, occurs in young athletes and nonathletes alike. Often it is noticed at very early stages in young gymnasts and dancers because of the emphasis these activities put on form and grace. Both disc injuries and scoliosis require a physician to adequately diagnose and treat.

HIP INJURIES

Dancers often develop hip problems as a result of forcing their turnout. Ballet dancers in particular work on their turnout throughout their careers. However, after about age 11, developing the turnout occurs only by stretching the ligaments of the hip and the knee, and this may lead to arthritic problems in young adulthood. Also, young dancers and gymnasts occasionally suffer stress fractures of the femoral neck, the part of the long thighbone that fits into the pelvis at the hip. This requires them to stop their athletic activities, rest, and usually to use crutches. Rehabilitation typically takes six months to a year.

Far more often, gymnasts and dancers develop tendinitis or inflamed muscles at the hip. When they do, physicians restrict some of their athletic efforts, prescribe anti-inflammatory medications and sometimes heat or ultrasound treatments, and put them on special stretching exercises to increase their flexibility. Again, a very flexible body may help prevent these problems.

UPPER-BODY INJURIES

While injuries to the upper extremities occur in both gymnasts and dancers, gymnasts run the greater risk.

Muscle strains rank as the most common shoulder problem for

gymnasts, followed by tendinitis. The major causes of strain include overstress, improper technique, and poor rehabilitation from an initial strain. Males suffer shoulder strains from overstress far more commonly than females, largely, it appears, because of the different grips they use. These injuries may result from a single episode of overstressing the muscle or from a long period of overstress. Muscle strains from improper technique go with the territory, in that they commonly occur among inexperienced gymnasts just learning the sport. But they also strike more experienced gymnasts. At any level, an emphasis on proper technique can help prevent either an initial strain or a recurrence. Treatment requires getting rid of the pain and inflammation, followed by an adequate and supervised rehabilitation program.

Elbow problems most frequently occur in female gymnasts because their sport requires the frequent use of the "locked-out" position. This position forces the end of the ulna (the longer of the two forearm bones) into a small hollow space called the olecranon fossa, resulting over time in inflammation and pain. Strengthening the biceps may help prevent this problem, or, along with ice treatments, assist in treating it. If, however, this fails to solve the problem, a physician should check for a fracture.

Dislocated elbows also occur in gymnasts, particularly among females, usually as the result of falls. With proper medical care and rehabilitation, this painful injury usually causes no lasting problems or increased risk of another dislocation. However, in some cases, the injury leaves the young gymnast unable to fully extend the elbow. This can end a career, especially that of a female, since the lock-out position requires full elbow extension.

Both male and female gymnasts commonly experience pain at the back of the wrist—so often, in fact, that some regard it as just part of the sport, rather than a true injury. The pain usually results from inflammation of the wrist capsule caused by repeated forced extension of the wrist. Ice helps relieve the pain. If pain persists at rest, especially in the skeletally immature athlete, a physician *must* be consulted. Bone growth problems in the ulna—the small bone in the forearm—have been reported in younger gymnasts.

Sometimes pain develops on the side of the forearm, most often among males working on the pommel horse. Gymnasts often call this pain "wrist splints," and the cause usually cannot be determined. Treatment essentially follows that for pain on the back of the wrist.

OVERUSE SYNDROMES IN DANCE

STRESS FRACTURES

Dancers commonly suffer stress fractures in the tibia and fibula, the two long bones of the lower leg. These fractures can also develop in any of the bones in the foot and ankle, but they most commonly occur in the foot's second and third metatarsal bones. Stress fractures can strike the beginner or the pro; the harder, the more unyielding the dancing surface, the greater the risk. The injury may take several months to develop, and may go undiagnosed for a year or more.

Once a stress fracture is recognized, the dancer must stop dancing until it heals, which typically takes about two months. Leg fractures require the use of crutches; foot or ankle fractures may require a cast. Rehabilitation often includes swimming or exercising in water. If a dancer returns to dancing too early, he or she runs a high risk of another stress fracture and another, even longer period of rehabilitation.

PLANTAR FASCIITIS

This painful inflammation of connective tissue between the toe bones and the metatarsals typically occurs three to five days after a dancer returns to a strenuous practice schedule following a long layoff. Usually it indicates that the dancer failed to exercise properly during his or her period of inactivity. Treatment generally requires whirlpool baths and anti-inflammatory medications. The symptoms may last up to four weeks. Sometimes soft arch supports in a dancer's shoes can help prevent recurrences.

ACHILLES TENDINITIS

Inflammation of the ankle tendons occurs very commonly among dancers, and the most commonly affected is the Achilles tendon. Dancers usually first notice pain when they land from a leap, or after long periods of pointe dancing. Males and females suffer equally, although some experts regard ballerinas' tying their shoes very tightly as a contributing factor in their tendinitis.

Exercises designed to stretch and strengthen the ankle may help prevent tendinitis, or its recurrence. Treatment includes rest (with jumping forbidden until symptoms disappear), elevation of the ankle, and anti-inflammatory medications. A dancer should never ignore an inflamed Achilles tendon. To do so is to risk rupturing the tendon, a far more serious injury that requires surgery and may take more than a year for complete recovery.

SHIN SPLINTS

Most often, this soreness along the shinbone strikes dancers practicing on a hard floor with no give. Shin splints can also develop as the result of fatigue or improper technique. Typically, the dancer notices the pain developing over several weeks and has difficulty walking after a workout. Rest eases the soreness, but it returns as soon as the youngster begins dancing again. Maintaining a high degree of flexibility and dancing on a surface that absorbs some of the shock of landing help prevent shin splints, but not in everyone. Treatment generally consists of elevating the leg; some people find that ice helps if heat doesn't. Physicians sometimes recommend whirlpool treatments and/or anti-inflammatory drugs. If shin splints fail to respond to treatment after several weeks, the dancer should be examined for a possible stress fracture and, if possible, change the surface on which she dances.

HEEL PAIN

This may result from a stress fracture or an inflammation of a branch of the plantar nerve of the foot. Nerve involvement may prove extremely painful, but often requires little more than rest and wearing a felt heel pad with a hole cut in to fit around the sore area. If X rays reveal no fracture, but pain persists for more than a month, more sophisticated imaging may be needed to check for a stress fracture.

15

Racquet Sports

To many people, the term "racquet sports" brings tennis instantly to mind. But other sports in which participants wield racquets to smash a small object at one another fit into this very popular category. They include racquetball, squash, and badminton.

These sports put considerable stress on all of the musculoskeletal system—making the entire body vulnerable to some form of injury. The majority of racquet sports injuries stem from a force overload of the body's muscle-tendon-bone units. The shoulder, elbow, feet, and ankles are particularly susceptible to such overuse problems as tendinitis, bursitis, and plantar fasciitis. Among adolescents, common problems include Osgood-Schlatter disease, Sever's disease, and chondromalacia (see Chapter 7).

Eye injuries also plague racquet sports players. A tennis ball may explode off a racquet in the hands of a professional player at speeds up to 140 mph, and release speeds of 90 mph, 100 mph, and higher are common among amateurs. While somewhat slower-moving, the balls used in squash and racquetball still can do severe damage if they strike a player in the eye.

PHYSICAL CONDITIONING

Properly conditioning and strengthening the body, and warming and stretching the muscles before taking the court, can help tennis and other racquet sports players improve their game and prevent injuries. These sports require the use and power of many muscle groups, the ability to go quickly from rest to maximum effort for brief bursts of intense activity, and the endurance to maintain this stop-and-go play for long periods. With the burgeoning growth of racquet sports it has become clear that simply playing regularly does not in itself provide the protective fitness level needed by young athletes. Indeed, evidence suggests that players who play intensely and often, without also working at improving their strength, may suffer microscopic muscle tears that can lead to scarring, inflammation, and ultimately a loss of strength and flexibility—which increases the risk of more serious injury. Children don't need the same strength and endurance training as a member of a high school tennis team, but they do need to warm up and stretch before they play.

The intense, brief bursts of effort and the often-long durations of matches force the body to draw on both its anaerobic and aerobic energy-generating systems (see Chapter 2). Tennis players (henceforth we shall use "tennis" to refer to all racquet sports) need a strong capacity in both systems to do well on the court, and thus need to train to improve both. Anaerobic exercises require a brief, all-out effort, followed by a short recovery period, followed by another energetic burst. These may include running sprints, bicycling, riding a stationary exercise bicycle, jumping rope, or plyometric burst exercises (see Chapter 13). Aerobic exercises require prolonged, sustained effort. Playing long tennis matches can improve aerobic capacity, and so can long rides on a bicycle or stationary bicycle, jogging, and sustained lap swimming for at least half an hour.

A team of Philadelphia researchers—Ezra Deutsch, Susan L. Deutsch, and Pamela S. Douglas—has developed an anaerobic and aerobic training regime on a stationary bicycle for college-level tennis players already in good condition. Its basic timing pattern can be adapted by adolescents to do a variety of conditioning exercises. On Mondays and Fridays, the player begins with a 5-minute warm-up ride, followed by a 1-minute sprint at the fastest speed the rider can pedal, followed by a 4-minute recovery period, followed by another 1-minute all-out sprint and a second 4-minute rest. Then the rider pedals three 30-second sprints, each separated by a 2½-minute recovery period. The workout ends with a final 1-minute sprint and a 4-minute recovery. On Wednesdays, the player rides the stationary bike for half an hour at a constant speed of between 25 to 30 miles an hour. It is important to remember that this program was developed for athletes already in fine physical condition, and youngsters less fit need to ease into any exercise program.

Tennis also requires strength, both to hit the ball hard and to help protect the body from injury. The shoulder obviously demands special attention, but the elbow, forearm, wrist, trunk, and lower extremities also require strengthening for success in competitive tennis. We discussed strength training for athletes in Chapter 13, and books detailing specific strengthening exercises for tennis players are available. However, any young athlete embarking on such a program should do so in consultation with a knowledgeable coach or athletic trainer who can guide them in the proper exercises for their sport.

It is important to note that conditioning and strengthening exercises themselves may cause injury, unless the young athlete warms up and stretches his or her muscles. (Both topics receive special attention in Chapter 2, including a list of suggested stretching exercises.) Equally important, players need to warm up and stretch before taking to the court. A few minutes of easy jogging or jumping jacks, just enough to break a sweat, followed by slowly practicing a few times the major movements used in the game—such as serve, backhand, and ground strokes—get the muscles warmed and ready for stretching exercises. Some coaches have specific stretches they prefer to emphasize. The key point is to increase the body's flexibility. This is important at any age, but growing youngsters need to pay particular attention to stretching, because their growth spurts tighten their muscles.

Finally, tennis players must guard against dehydration and the dangers of heat-related disorders (see Chatper 6) as much as any athlete. Not only do they often play in hot, humid conditions for prolonged periods, but the emotional stress of competition can increase sweating and therefore the loss of body fluids and electrolytes. Tennis players need to drink a lot of water before and during their matches. They should avoid electrolyte-fortified beverages, at least prior to and during play, because these can cause nausea during play.

EQUIPMENT

Tennis requires relatively little equipment—essentially, a racquet with strings, balls (feathered "birds" in badminton), and shoes. Tennis pros and sports medicine specialists increasingly recommend wearing goggles to protect the eyes. Tennis togs usually consist of a shirt and shorts or a skirt. Light colors reflect sunlight, reducing heating and sweating, and cotton best absorbs perspiration and thus aids cooling by evaporation. The racquet size, material, and string type and tightness, as well as the playing surface, can all play a role in tennis injuries.

RACQUET

Tennis racquets come in light, medium, and heavy weights. Among experienced players, their style of play in part determines their racquet weight: those who prefer a serve-and-volley game tend to use a lighter racquet than baseline players. The heavier a racquet's head, the greater the stress on its user's shoulder, elbow, and wrist; even a small increase in weight translates into a significantly larger force on the elbow. Larger racquet heads require greater string tension, and tighter strings increase the stress on the elbow, forearm, and wrist. However, the greater surface area of a large racquet head disperses the tension better, and larger heads mean fewer off-center hits, which also increase stress on the elbow. In racquet frames, certain materials—graphite and epoxies, for example—provide less vibration and diminish the forces that stress the elbow. Moreover, the strength of these materials allows the construction of lighter-weight racquets that don't cost the player stroke power and ball control.

Strings come in three types: gut, nylon, and synthetic materials that mimic many advantages of gut. Gut and synthetic materials appear to create less stress on the upper extremities and help reduce the chances of overuse problems; so does playing with a looser-strung racquet.

Finally, young players often pay too little attention to the length of their racquet handle and the size of its grip. If either is too small, the end result is an increased torque on the arm, which increases the risk of injury.

The evidence suggests that beginners and young players do best with a light racquet made of graphite or an epoxy material that has a large head strung with gut or a synthetic material at two or three pounds less tension than the manufacturer recommends, and a properly measured handle size and grip. While perhaps more costly in initial outlay of dollars, buying a racquet from a tennis pro shop or sports store specializing in racquet sports may save a young athlete pain in the future.

BALLS

A worn or "dead" ball requires a harder hit to get the same return speed as a new ball. So hitting worn balls increases the stress on the upper extremities and the risk of an injury. As for color, no one has yet determined an optimal color that allows players to see balls best.

Certain colors will blend in against or contrast with different colored backgrounds, affecting how easily and quickly players will pick up and judge balls coming at them. Tinted eyeglasses and sunglasses also will affect a player's vision. So it helps to keep a variety of ball colors in a tennis bag and see which works best on any given day.

SHOES

Tennis players can choose from a variety of shoes, although any style chosen must be well made to support the foot against the stresses generated by such a fast-paced game of running, hitting, twisting, and turning. In part, the surface on which a young athlete plays can influence the choice of shoe. Lighter-weight shoes work well on softer surfaces, such as clay, for example. Players with feet that turn in or out excessively should consult a physician or podiatrist about the proper shoe for them, and perhaps the use of a corrective insert (orthotic) in their shoes. Indeed, a physical evaluation and corrective measures can sometimes prevent overuse and other injuries to the foot, ankle, and knee.

SURFACES

Tennis players take their game to a variety of court surfaces—grass, clay, outdoor carpeting, wood, and asphalt. The softer surfaces put less stress on a player's feet, ankles, and knees. If a lower-extremity injury occurs, it is best for a young athlete to play on a softer surface whenever possible when he or she first returns to the court. The surface type also affects how the ball bounces, which itself can affect the risk of injury. Hard surfaces produce shots that bounce closer to the ground than shots on clay or grass. This gives the ball increased speed and causes greater stress to the upper extremities when players hit a return. Grass surfaces, on the other hand, cause more erratic bounces, which result in more stress to the upper extremities.

SPECIFIC INJURIES

EYE INJURIES

Racquet sports account for about 10 percent of sports-related eye injuries, according to the National Society for the Prevention of Blindness. Some evidence indicates that inexperienced players stand a greater chance of such injuries than court veterans; nearsighted players also appear to be at increased risk. While no firm figures exist, estimates place the annual number of eye injuries in racquet sports that require medical treatment at between 70,000 and 96,000, many of them quite serious. They include hemorrhages of the eyeball and eyelid, tears of the iris and retina, retinal detachments, corneal scratches, lacerations of the lid and cornea, and eye-socket fractures. One study of racquet-sports eye injuries found that 10 out of 848 players lost an eye as a result. Such a toll seems all the more regrettable since wearing protective eyegear can prevent most eye injuries in racquet sports.

The velocity of a hard-hit ball can easily shatter eyeglasses, whether the lenses are hardened glass or plastic. So eyeglass wearers were among some of the earliest converts to protective goggles. For a time, some players favored an open-eye guard that provided a plastic frame around the eye but contained no lens. But experience showed that balls striking the frame, and in some cases hitting the opening with enough force to lodge there, caused serious injuries. Today, racquet sports enthusiasts can choose from a variety of safety goggles. Indeed, an increasing number of clubs, associations, leagues, and sanctioning bodies now require such protective eyewear for all players. In the United States, the Eye and Face Protective Equipment Certification Council (EFPECC) issues its approval only to protective goggles that meet safety criteria set by the American Society for Testing and Materials (ASTM). And in Canada, the Canadian Standards Association certifies eye guards for use in racquet sports. Players should avoid uncertified goggles.

SHOULDER INJURIES

Tennis players suffer a number of the same shoulder injuries as baseball players, particularly pitchers. We detail these problems and ways to help prevent them in Chapter 17. But we want to highlight several problems here.

Adolescent tennis players commonly suffer shoulder pain, sometimes as early as age 12, from an injury called *subacromial impingement*. The youngster typically complains of an ache at the front of the shoulder during and/or after playing. Most often the young athlete feels pain while serving and hitting an overhand return. In some cases, the pain also occurs at night. The source of pain in this impingement syndrome is the subacromial bursa, a sac of soft tissue that acts as a cushion between a bony structure at the top of the shoulder called the subacromial arch and the shoulder's rotator cuff (see Chapter 17). The injury develops as the player repeatedly swings the racquet forward in an overhand motion.

Although physicians divide subacromial impingement into three stages, adolescents suffer only the first. In this, the bursa swells and hemorrhages. Treatment requires about a two-week break from tennis, and physicians usually prescribe a nonsteroidal anti-inflammatory drug. The young athlete may continue anaerobic and aerobic conditioning, so long as it involves no overhand motions, such as swimming. A recovering player can return to the court when swelling and pain subside, but should omit overhand shots until after completing a prescribed regimen of strengthening exercises and receiving clearance from his or her physician. Particular attention should be paid to a player's swing to ensure that he or she is using proper technique and not a motion that will guarantee a recurrence of subacromial impingement.

Adolescents who practice long and hard at perfecting their hitting, particularly their serve, may develop a painful shoulder that results from tendinitis of the supraspinatus and biceps tendons. Repeated hitting motions can also lead to a bruising of the rotator cuff, but rarely to an actual tear of the cuff in youngsters. Pain occurs when the young athlete swings his or her hitting arm in an overhead arc. Typically, testing reveals a weakness in the shoulder's supraspinatus muscle. In mild cases, the inflammation usually disappears with the aid of an anti-inflammatory medication and a two-to-three-week break from smashing balls and other overhead motions. But the youngster should then begin a program of shoulder-strengthening exercises prescribed by a physician or physical therapist.

A problem unique to still-growing youngsters results from an excessive pulling by muscles on the growth plate of the humerus, the bone of the upper arm. It is sometimes called Osgood-Schlatter disease (see Chapter 7) of the shoulder. Typically, an adolescent will complain of pain with an overhead motion and a tender shoulder. X rays generally reveal the cause quite readily. Again, the young athlete must avoid tennis, other overhead movements, and training with heavy weights for about three weeks for the pain to subside. But many physicians refuse to allow a player with this problem back on the tennis court for months afterward.

Finally, repeatedly hitting tennis balls over a long period of time can result in "tennis shoulder"—also known as "King Kong arm"—on the side holding the racquet. The body builds an excessive amount of bone and muscle, and that causes the shoulder to droop. The exact cause of tennis shoulder remains unknown, but it may result from chronic stretching of the shoulder muscles.

ELBOW INJURIES

The elbow forms the joint where the humerus (the upper arm bone) connects with the radius and ulna (the two bones of the lower arm). Tennis and other racquet sports place considerable stress on this hinged joint, and frequent playing, poor conditioning, or using an improper stroke can lead to an elbow injury. Fortunately, young players can avoid many of the overuse problems associated with the racquet sports by strengthening the muscle groups supporting the elbow and by properly stretching these muscles before taking the court.

Few sports injuries match the name recognition of "tennis elbow," also known as *epicondylitis*, the most common elbow injury among athletes. The term serves as a catch-all diagnosis for various problems of the elbow's epicondylar region—the bony protrusion on the outside of the elbow. Most often, however, it means an inflammation of the elbow tendons that attach to the outer forearm's extensor muscles, which bend back the wrist and fingers. The inflammation affects the lateral (outside) part of the tendon area most commonly, the medial (middle) part much less frequently, and only occasionally the posterior (back) part of the tendon.

Among those who play tennis throughout much of their lives, about one in two will develop tennis elbow, with males and females at equal risk. While any player can develop the ailment, poorly conditioned players definitely have a higher risk; so do older players, those who play frequently, those playing with a handle grip too large or too small, and, it appears, those who use an aluminum racquet. Tennis elbow can strike any athlete whose sport applies a lot of force to the muscles of the forearm. Racquet sports players usually develop the lateral form; baseball pitchers and javelin throwers more often suffer a medial tendinitis. Golfers develop an inflammation of the tendon that attaches the flexors, the muscles on the inside of the forearm, to the elbow.

Tennis elbow results because a player repeatedly overtaxes the shock-absorbing abilities of the extensor muscles at the elbow. This results in microscopic tissue damage and degenerative changes that cause inflammation of the tendon. Symptoms include pain and tenderness on the outside of the elbow and pain in the outer forearm's

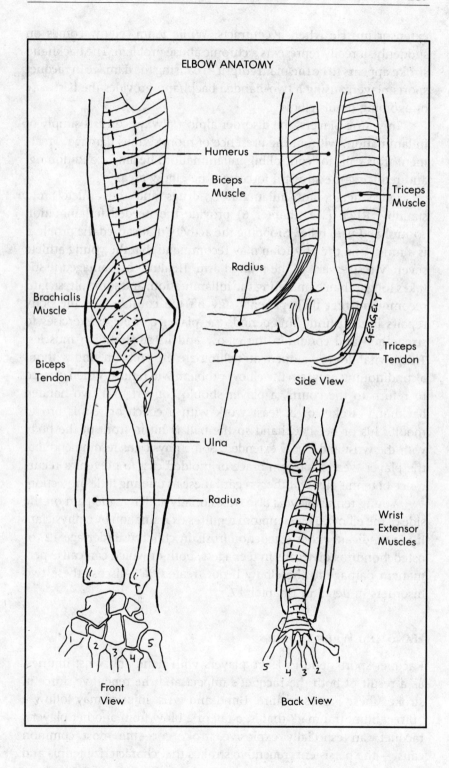

ELBOW ANATOMY

Humerus

Biceps Muscle

Triceps Muscle

Radius

Brachialis Muscle

Biceps Tendon

Triceps Tendon

Side View

Ulna

Radius

Wrist Extensor Muscles

Front View

Back View

extensor muscle when it contracts. While tennis elbow comes on suddenly, it really represents a chronic abuse problem. The backhand stroke appears to be the main culprit in causing the damage in racquet sports players; using a two-handed backhand provides the best way of avoiding tennis elbow.

In young players, the disorder almost always consists simply of inflammation, without the presence of more serious damage. Treatment thus calls for controlling inflammation, healing, conditioning, and reducing the stressful forces on the elbow area.

Once again, anti-inflammatory drugs and the athlete's old standby, RICE (see Chapter 6) provide the needed inflammation control and pain relief. Stopping the activity that caused the problem is a must, and the physician may recommend that the young athlete severely restrict use of the injured arm. Healing the damaged tissue takes longer than eliminating the inflammation, and some physicians recommend that their patients stay off the courts while the body repairs itself. During this period, the player can begin exercises to strengthen and condition the elbow and its surrounding muscles. This is vital, for rest alone won't eliminate the problem, and without a conditioning program the elbow problem will return. When cleared to return to the courts, a player should convert to a two-handed backhand stroke, or at least work with a coach or tennis pro to modify his or her backhand so the ball is hit in front of the body with the wrist and elbow extended. Some physicians recommend that the player wear a forearm brace or molded cast to prevent a recurrence of tennis elbow; others regard these as offering little protection.

Young tennis players also occasionally suffer vague pain on the side of the elbow. This symptom requires examination by a physician. It may indicate either osteochondrosis in children under age 12, or osteochondritis dissecans in teenagers, both of which can cause permanent damage to the elbow if not treated. We discuss these two disorders in detail in Chapter 17.

HAND AND WRIST INJURIES

Racquet sports tend to leave players with hand and wrist injuries, as a result of both the racquet's impact and the repetitive, forceful strokes these games require. Hand and wrist injuries may follow a "direct blunt trauma," that is, a fall or a blow from another player's racquet; an especially explosive stroke; or—the most common cause—the persistent, repetitive strokes that characterize tennis and

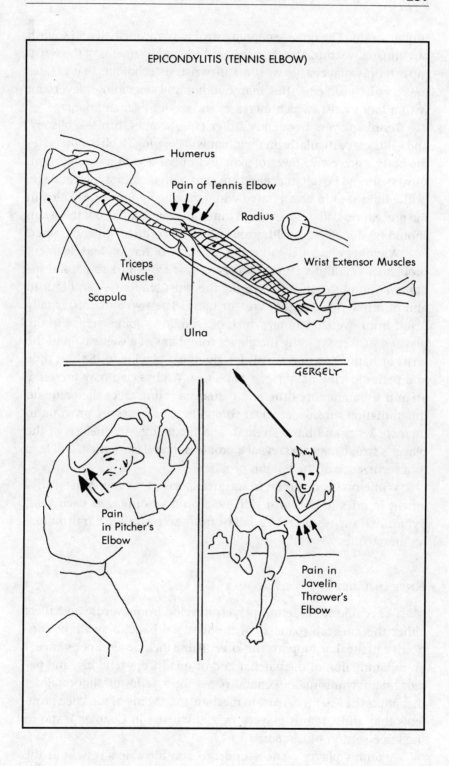

EPICONDYLITIS (TENNIS ELBOW)

Humerus

Pain of Tennis Elbow

Radius

Triceps Muscle

Wrist Extensor Muscles

Scapula

Ulna

GERGELY

Pain in Pitcher's Elbow

Pain in Javelin Thrower's Elbow

similar sports. The quick, snapping strokes of racquetball and squash put unusually strong stress on the tendons and ligaments of the wrist. Most tennis players hit with a stiff wrist, a technique that creates fewer wrist problems. But many young and beginning players hit with a loose wrist, which increases the risk of ligament damage.

Tennis players frequently suffer cuts, scrapes, bruises, blisters, and calluses, particularly on their hands. "Popping" a blister breaches the body's protective layer of skin and opens a wound to infection. Blisters should be left intact and covered with a cushioning bandage, or the fluid should be aspirated with a needle by someone skilled in the procedure. Calluses may need trimming with a knife, but this again should be done by a health professional or certified athletic trainer.

Wielding a racquet can cause a variety of tendon and ligament problems. Tendinitis and *stenosing tenosynovitis*—a more painful inflammation of the sheath covering the wrist tendons—can occur in almost any tendon of the wrist or hand. The two ailments usually result from overstretching, which often follows some change in the player's stroke. Typically the player complains of a vague pain in the wrist or hand. Treatment calls for giving up playing for a short time and periodic icing daily (see Chapter 6). A physician may prescribe an anti-inflammatory drug and perhaps a splint. Once the pain and inflammation subside, a player should begin an exercise program to increase wrist and hand strength and flexibility. An analysis of the player's stroke may also reveal a problem that, if continued, will lead to a recurrence of the tendon problem.

While not as common in racquet sports as tendon damage, ligament injuries to the wrist sideline a number of players each year. Typically these result from a fall or from excessive force transmitted by the racquet.

Knee Injuries

Most knee injuries in tennis players develop from overuse and affect either the kneecap (patella) or the iliotibial band, a swath of connective tissue that supports the knee. These include "jumper's knee," an inflammation of the patellar and/or quadriceps tendons; and patellar pain syndrome, a general name for a series of abnormalities that affect the knee's extension mechanism. (Many of the knee problems that afflict tennis players were discussed in Chapter 7 and in the knee section of Chapter 10.)

A tennis player's knees undergo considerable stress from the rapid starting, turning, and stopping required by the sport. Exercises that stretch and strengthen the muscles and tissues supporting the knee can help prevent a number of injuries, or their recurrence.

LOWER-LEG INJURIES

Older tennis players sometimes suffer a rupture of the gastrocnemius muscle in the calf, an injury commonly called "tennis leg." Stretching the lower-leg muscles and the Achilles tendon prior to taking the court can help prevent the muscle damage and some ankle injuries. A player who suffers from tennis leg should embark on a program of stretching and strengthening exercises to guard against a recurrence.

TRUNK INJURIES

When, and for whatever reasons, the sequence of actions involved in the flexing and uncoiling of the trunk muscles goes awry, a tennis player can suffer a painful abdominal-muscle strain. Groin-muscle strains commonly result from a player's attempt to stop his or her sideways movement by sliding. On clay, this can literally cause the player to "do the splits," landing with one leg in front and one behind. It is not uncommon for players who suffer abdominal- or groin-muscle strains to stop playing for a few days and then try again, frequently with the return of the pain. Some will repeat this cycle a number of times before finally seeking medical attention.

Treatment depends on the severity of the injury and how soon the youngster sees a physician. When a player seeks aid after the initial strain, treatment typically calls for stopping all strenuous activities for one to two weeks, taking an anti-inflammatory medication, and icing the injury several times a day for a few days. Proper rehabilitation requires a player to adopt a program of stretching and strengthening exercises.

BACK INJURIES

While lower-back pain typically afflicts adult tennis players, young athletes also can suffer from this common problem. Unfortunately, at least one study suggests that using a two-handed backhand stroke, which reduces the risk of tennis elbow, appears to increase the risk of lower-back pain. Exercises that stretch and strengthen the back and abdominal muscles may prevent low-back pain, and they can help in treating a player who suffers from the problem.

16

Basketball

Basketball may not match football as a contact sport, but as players from youth leagues to the pros can testify, the game today involves its share of hard knocks. Just how hard for young athletes became clear in studies conducted for the National Athletic Trainers' Association by John W. Powell, now at the University of Iowa. In the late 1980s, Powell did a three-year study of girls' basketball and a two-year study of boys' basketball involving a total of 8,700 high school players. He then projected their injury rates to provide a picture of injuries nationally. In high school, girls participate in basketball almost as avidly as boys, with about 380,000 boys and 333,000 girls participating each year during the late 1980s. The two sexes also suffered remarkably similar injury rates, with 22.1 percent of the boys and 22.8 percent of the girls suffering injuries that put them out of action for at least a day during the two study periods. Nationally, Powell projected the total average annual basketball injuries to be 119,056 injuries among 84,066 boys and 110,473 injuries among 75,873 girls.

More than half the injuries occurred in the lower extremities, suggesting that some of them could have been prevented. Among the injured boys, 42 percent suffered damage to the ankle or foot, 11 percent had a hip or thigh injury, and 10 percent had knee trouble. Among the injured girls, the comparable figures were: ankle or foot, 32 percent; knee, 18 percent; hip and thigh, 12 percent. Conditioning exercises specifically designed to strengthen the quadriceps can protect the knee, and other strengthening exercises can help protect the legs, ankles, and feet against injury. Powell's findings also suggest that an overall improvement in physical conditioning might help prevent some injuries. His studies showed that 63 percent of the game-related injuries in girls and 59 percent in boys occurred during the second half of a game, indicating that fatigue plays an important role. Indeed, among the boys, 35 percent of the game-related injuries occurred during the fourth quarter, compared to 10 percent during the first period.

EQUIPMENT

Clearly the foot, ankle, and knee rank high on the injury-risk list in basketball. One obvious defense against lower-extremity injuries is the player's shoes. Youngsters should wear high-quality shoes designed specifically for basketball, not cheap sneakers or even expensive shoes intended for another sport. Top-grade running shoes, for example, are designed to give support along the longitudinal arch and are built up to pad the heels and support the toes, but they offer relatively little support against side-to-side movements. Basketball shoes provide more side-to-side protection, giving the player steadier support during the jumping and turning movements so common in basketball.

Coaches and athletic trainers have long recognized that basketball carries a significant risk of ankle injury and have sought to counter this problem. Basketball players can choose between three different types of ankle support: tape, lace-on braces, and reusable thermoplastic supports. The assumption is that an external support reinforces the ankle's ligaments, increases its stability, and restricts motions that can damage the joint. At this point, none of the three types of support appears to be clearly superior to the others, although only a few comparative studies have been done.

Tape, used to support the ankles of athletes for more than 100 years, appears to provide the best initial support. But tape quickly loosens and loses its advantage as a result of body sweat and the movements of the foot and ankle. Proper taping also takes considerable time, and over a season its costs add up. Lace-up braces, while they do not limit unwanted ankle motions as effectively as newly applied tape, provide more consistent support throughout a game. They also have the advantage that the player can easily tighten them during time-outs or other brief periods off the floor. But a player who opts for lace-up braces should wear low-top shoes, because it is impossible to tighten the braces quickly if high-top shoes are covering them. The semirigid, reusable thermoplastic supports also offer good protection, but they are bulky and custom-fitting them takes time and equipment not always available to young athletes and their coaches.

Although any of these three approaches will provide support, young athletes must remember that none of them is an adequate substitute for ankle-strengthening exercises. Good physical conditioning remains the best safeguard against ankle injury.

Knee pads can certainly protect a player against scrapes and bruises, but their value and the value of knee braces in preventing more serious injuries remain controversial. Studies have failed to find an advantage to wearing a knee brace to protect against an initial injury, and some evidence suggests that such prophylactic bracing may increase a player's risk of injury. However, when combined with physical therapy, braces do help players regain their mobility more quickly after a knee injury or surgery. And some studies do indicate that knee braces can help reduce the risk of reinjury when a youngster resumes play. (See the discussion of the use of knee braces in Chapter 12.)

SPECIFIC INJURIES

Young athletes can do more to help protect themselves against injury than carefully selecting their equipment. We discussed the importance of proper nutrition in Chapter 3 and the need to warm up and stretch the muscles before play or practice in Chapter 2. Keeping a proper fluid balance by drinking adequate amounts of water, which we detail in Chapter 6, also poses a challenge to basketball players. Finally, weight training (Chapter 13) has become a major part of the on- and off-season training regimen of many basketball players. All together, close attention to these details in an athlete's life can improve performance and help cut his or her risk of injury. Nonetheless, as the Powell studies indicate, lower-extremity injuries take a heavy toll in basketball.

ANKLE AND FOOT INJURIES

Lower-extremity sprains, particularly of the ankle, constitute a major risk in basketball. A sprain results when a ligament gets twisted or wrenched so badly it stretches excessively, tears, or ruptures. Sprains can run from mild to severe. They usually happen when a player pushes off, runs, jumps, or stops suddenly.

The ankle serves as a hinge between the foot and leg. It is an intricate joint composed of three bones and three ligament complexes crossed by 10 tendons. Studies indicate that the joint can experience a stress equal to five times a person's body weight each time the heel hits the ground. Some physicians and trainers regard the ankle as the body's ultimate example of Murphy's Law: If something can go wrong, it will. Most ankle sprains occur when the foot twists inward and the ankle turns out and drops down toward the ground, damaging the ligaments on the outside of the ankle. The severity of the injury depends on the severity of the force generated on the ligament. The greater the force, the more serious the sprain. In young athletes, a severe sprain of this type, called an *inversion* injury, can cause a small piece of bone to tear away from the tip of the outside malleolus, one of the rounded projections of the ankle. Less often, a sprain results when the foot twists outward and the ankle inward, injuring ligaments on the inside of the ankle. These *eversion* sprains usually prove more serious and slower to heal than inversion sprains. Sometimes a spiral fracture of the fibula, the thinner of the two lower-leg bones, accompanies an eversion sprain.

An ankle sprain causes immediate pain, often followed by swelling, soreness, and sometimes discoloration. Physicians have several different ways of grading a sprain's severity, but basically, we can classify them as mild, moderate, and severe. Mild ankle sprains involve some tearing of ligament fibers, but little or no internal bleeding; the player suffers no loss of ankle strength or function. In moderate sprains, a portion of the ligament tears and some bleeding and swelling occurs; the injury causes some decrease in ankle motion, but no noticeable loss of ligament strength. Severe sprains result from a ligament rupture, accompanied by internal bleeding and swelling, which may become quite diffuse. A severe sprain causes a total loss of ankle function. The medical treatment for an ankle sprain depends on its severity, but quick action courtside by a coach or trainer can help speed a player's recovery.

A sprain calls immediately for RICE to reduce any internal bleeding, control swelling, and ease pain. Studies show that recovery occurs faster when swelling is prevented or greatly reduced by icing and compression. The player must keep his or her weight off the injured ankle. If the swelling and/or pain increases after icing, if the ankle becomes discolored, if ankle function is greatly reduced or lost, or if swelling and severe pain remain after 24 hours, the young athlete should consult a physician, since such symptoms may indicate a bone fracture or dislocation. Depending on the severity of the sprain, a physician may order hydrotherapy in a cool whirlpool bath, put the patient on crutches, encase the ankle in a cast, or rely on tape

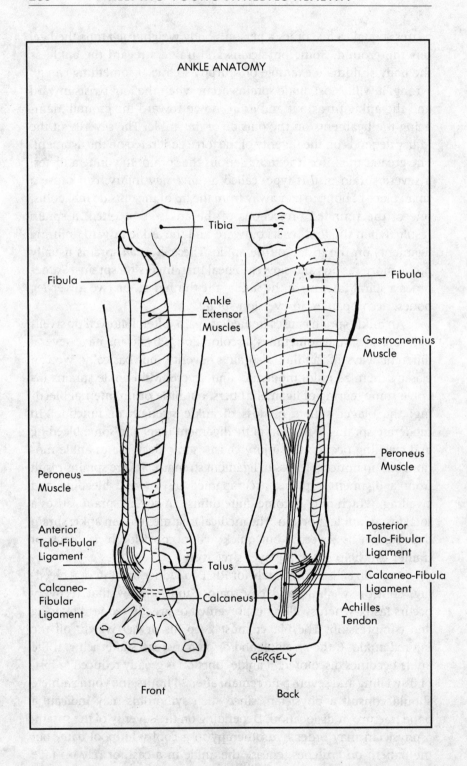

ANKLE ANATOMY

Tibia

Fibula

Fibula

Ankle Extensor Muscles

Gastrocnemius Muscle

Peroneus Muscle

Peroneus Muscle

Anterior Talo-Fibular Ligament

Posterior Talo-Fibular Ligament

Talus

Calcaneo-Fibular Ligament

Calcaneo-Fibular Ligament

Calcaneus

Achilles Tendon

GERGELY

Front

Back

ANKLE SPRAIN

Mechanism of Injury

Mechanism of
Lateral Ankle Sprain

or other support materials, such as compressive stockings. This treatment phase normally lasts up to 48 hours, but can run longer.

Once the swelling and pain decrease and mobility begins returning, the focus shifts to restoring normal ankle activity, often with further hydrotherapy treatments and special exercises. Finally, the rehabilitation effort turns to strengthening the muscle groups that serve the ankle joint. While such exercises can help, the unpleasant fact remains that once sprained, an ankle remains more vulnerable to injury. So once again, prevention is better than cure.

The way ankles sprain—by twisting or wrenching—is the same for children and adults, but the pattern of internal damage frequently differs considerably. In young people who have not finished growing, the ligaments and capsular tissues of the ankle attach to the growth centers at the ends of the two bones in the lower leg. Youngsters still growing should always have a sprained ankle examined by a physician if pain persists, if they limp when walking, or if the joint cannot bear their weight. It is important in such cases to make sure the child has suffered no significant or subtle bone injury.

Evidence suggests that a condition called *tarsal coalition* predisposes young athletes to sprained ankles. Tarsal coalition is the general name given to one or more fusions of the small bones at the back of the foot. This often-painful condition usually makes itself known between the ages of 11 and 18, particularly among youngsters engaged in sports such as basketball that require a lot of running and jumping. These activities put excessive stress on the fused bones, which results in pain—usually directly above the bone fusion, but sometimes in the heel and up the calf—and a progressive loss of mobility in the affected foot. And this lack of mobility appears to increase the danger that a youngster with tarsal coalition will suffer recurrent ankle sprains and/or muscle strains. About 1 percent of the population apparently has tarsal coalition. For years, physicians tended to equate tarsal coalition with flat feet. But recent studies indicate that most people with the bone fusions do not also suffer from flat feet. The cause remains unknown, but studies indicate that in many cases the condition is inherited. Physicians can often resolve the problems of tarsal coalition by inserting a wedge, counter, or some other orthotic device in the young athlete's shoe. Sometimes, however, the condition requires surgery if a youngster wants to seriously pursue sports.

The most common foot problems among basketball players include blisters, calluses, and corns, particularly early in the season. Players can help prevent these ailments—which result largely from the game's quick starts, stops, and pivots—by wearing properly fitted shoes and two pairs of clean socks, by conditioning their feet with skin-toughening compounds, and by using adhesive bandages to minimize rubbing of the skin. Blisters that break must be cleaned and watched for infection; only people with proper training should remove calluses or corns.

KNEE INJURIES

The Powell studies show that knees account for 1 in 10 basketball injuries in high school boys and nearly 1 in 5 in high school girls. These may result from collisions or sudden, twisting turns, or they may signify overuse syndromes. Collisions or twisting motions can cause ligament damage or even a fracture in the knee. Given the potential for permanent damage, any knee injury that causes swelling or more than passing pain should be seen by a physician. Again, RICE should be applied immediately at courtside in knee as well as ankle injuries. Players also suffer episodes of patellar pain, a group of problems affecting the kneecap that basketball players and other athletes sometimes call "jumper's knee." We discuss patellar pain and its treatment in greater detail in Chapter 10. The overuse syndromes of the knee that hit many basketball players as well as participants in other sports—such as iliotibial band syndrome and Osgood-Schlatter disease—are covered in Chapter 7.

TENDINITIS

Not surprisingly, given the amount of running required in basketball and the fact that many players keep in condition by doing roadwork, this tendon inflammation is common in basketball. We discuss the causes, prevention, and treatment of running-related tendinitis and stress fractures in detail in Chapter 10.

WRIST INJURIES

Most wrist injuries result when a player falls on his or her outstretched hand. Sprains happen this way, and in children, growthplate fractures from falls occur with some frequency. A wrist injury should receive immediate splinting and icing (see Chapter 6), and the child should then be taken to a physician for examination and further treatment.

HAND INJURIES

Hand injuries occur regularly in basketball, with jammed fingers and finger sprains the most common. Most often these injuries result from the ball hitting the fingertips, and physicians often can treat them simply by taping. Sometimes, however, a splint is required. Broken fingers may require additional therapy.

EYE INJURIES

A speeding basketball can damage an eye, particularly if a player wears eyeglasses. Soft contact lenses have sharply reduced eye injuries for players who wear them. Players who wear eyeglasses should cover them with protective plastic goggles.

MARFAN'S SYNDROME

Finally, we will make note of a life-threatening condition that is sometimes found in athletes in sports that emphasize unusual height and reach. Marfan's syndrome, an inherited defect in the body's connective tissues resulting in many physical abnormalities, affects about 1 in 20,000 people. Perhaps the best-known victim of Marfan's syndrome in recent years was Flo Hyman, who sparked the U.S. women's volleyball team in the 1984 Olympics.

Marfan's syndrome can involve eye, bone, and cardiovascular abnormalities. Marfan-associated heart defects, particularly an enlarged ascending aorta (the section of artery just above the heart), create an increased risk of early death, and youngsters diagnosed with the disorder should not play vigorous, competitive sports. Any child with a family history of Marfan's should be tested for the syndrome. Clues—but not certain diagnostic signs—that should alert physicians to Marfan's syndrome include flat feet, extra-long fingers and toes, an arm span longer than the youngster's height, and joints that can straighten beyond the normal range. Medical and surgical treatments exist to reduce the risk of early death in people with Marfan's syndrome, provided their disorder is recognized.

17

Baseball and Softball

Generations of youngsters have grown up knowing baseball as "the National Pastime." From an early age, many kids play sandlot baseball or softball and many play in organized leagues. By one estimate, some 2.3 million children between ages 6 and 12 play on organized amateur baseball teams each year, and millions more play softball. Aside from their other appeals, the two sports carry a relatively low risk of injury, although certain injuries—sometimes serious ones—do happen. Several studies, including one that covered some five million Little League players, have found that the incidence of injuries requiring medical attention runs about 2 percent. While baseball and softball injuries result from running, sliding, and throwing, catching, and hitting a ball, the majority of injuries stem from throwing.

INJURY PREVENTION

Baseball and softball players often spend considerable time simply standing and waiting. Then, with the crack of a bat, they must shift almost instantly from inactivity to running at full speed. This places great demands on even healthy young muscles and cardiorespiratory systems, demands that require a year-round conditioning program if the player hopes to fend off fatigue, turn in a peak performance, and reduce the risk of injury. During the off-season, a player should work on maintaining heart and lung endurance and leg strength. A regular program of bicycling or running (see Chapter 10)—particularly one that includes both long distances and sprints—does both. Increasingly, young baseball players have also turned to weights to build both upper- and lower-body strength (see Chapter 13). But when they do, baseball players must avoid the temptation to "bulk up," build enormous muscle mass, which can reduce their flexibility and range of motion and increase the risk of throwing injuries. Playing baseball doesn't maintain the fitness achieved with a conditioning program, so a player must continue with such a program, perhaps modified somewhat, to keep in peak shape throughout the season. In addition, baseball players need to eat a proper diet to help keep fit (see Chapter 3).

Prior to taking the practice or playing field, young athletes should warm up and stretch their muscles to help guard against injury. This is true in all sports, but particularly in baseball, where periods of inactivity increase the risk of injury when a player must respond suddenly and quickly. That is why you see players, particularly pitchers, putting on jackets when off the field and stretching and jogging in place after returning to the field following their turn at bat. Initially, jogging lightly or doing jumping jacks warms the muscles. Once players break a light sweat, they should begin their stretching exercises to increase their flexibility and range of motion. During play or practice, players and coaches must remember to keep players properly hydrated to prevent heat-related disorders (see Chapter 6). Plenty of water should be on hand and should be drunk.

Proper equipment properly used also reduces the risk of injury. The introduction of the batting helmet, which helps protect against a severe blow to the head by a wild pitch, has helped cut serious injuries in baseball. These hard-plastic caps should fit well, should have a thin compressible liner and earflaps extending down over the temples, and should be worn whenever the player is in or around the batter's box. Shoes, obviously, should fit well, and should have nonsteel spikes. Catchers, because of their vulnerable position behind the batter, require considerable protective equipment. They should wear a plastic cap to avoid injury if struck by a flying or wildly swung bat. Their wire face mask must fit correctly and should include a throat protector. Catchers should also always wear a well-padded chest protector, properly fitted shin guards, and a cup in their athletic supporter to protect the groin. Finally, a variety of precautions on the field can reduce injuries, including the use of breakaway bases that come free when a player slides into them hard, moving the on-deck circle far back from the batter's box, and placing screens in front of dugouts.

THROWING INJURIES

The shoulder ranks first among the body's joints in mobility and range of motion. Greater mobility means less stability, and this increases the potential for injuries, particularly to the muscles surrounding and supporting the shoulder. Overhand throwing, because of the high velocity and frequent stress it places on the shoulder, poses a greater risk than underhand throwing. This explains, for example, why baseball pitchers tend to suffer more shoulder problems than softball pitchers.

Sports specialists generally divide the act of throwing into three or four phases: windup and/or cocking phase, acceleration, and follow-through. As described by orthopedists Frank W. Jobe and Gordon Nuber, the windup constitutes the initial readying to throw that flows into the cocking phase, during which the arm is bent and the shoulder goes through its maximum external rotation. In the acceleration phase, the arm is brought from the back to the front of the body with increasing speed that continues until the player releases the ball. During the follow-through, the arm continues through its arc with the palm down, but with decelerating speed. Injuries, particularly overuse injuries, can develop in any of these phases. Often, overuse produces microscopic damage and shoulder instability. If not recognized and treated, this can progress to greater problems, including slight dislocations and rotator cuff damage.

SHOULDER INJURIES

Adolescents risk the same shoulder injuries as adults, but they also are vulnerable to some injuries not seen in older players. Because the growth plates in the bones of their shoulders have yet to fuse, an injury that normally would sprain a ligament in an adult may result in a fracture in an adolescent. Overhand pitching commonly results in shoulder injuries. One rare but often-mentioned problem is "Little Leaguer's shoulder," which appears to involve damage to a growth plate and usually resolves itself if the player stops throwing for a year.

Tendinitis and bursitis in the shoulder occur commonly in sports that require frequent overhead arm motions. Tendinitis is an inflammation of the sheaths surrounding the tendons; bursitis is an inflammation of the bursa, a sac that acts as a cushion, usually between bone and muscle. Repeated overhand throwing makes baseball pitchers particularly vulnerable to both problems. Typically, the player feels pain at the tip of the shoulder and down the deltoid muscle into the upper arm during the cocking and acceleration phases of throwing, with pain easing during the follow-through. Tendinitis and bursitis usually develop in the shoulder because the upper arm bone, its tendon, and its bursa fit beneath a narrow arch of bone and ligament. When the arm is raised, the opening through the arch narrows and this can pinch the tendon and bursa, eventually resulting in irritation and inflammation.

Treating tendinitis and bursitis requires rest—and that means no throwing—and icing the shoulder at least twice a day (see Chapter 6). A physician may prescribe medications to relieve pain and inflammation and may order physical therapy and exercises to strengthen the joint to prevent a recurrence. Chronic tendinitis or bursitis may require surgery. Once a player can return to throwing, he or she should begin slowly and gradually increase speed over a number of days. How long depends on the degree and location of the injury and must be worked out with the physician.

The shoulder is a ball-and-socket joint, in which the rounded top of the humerus (the long bone in the upper arm) fits into a shallow cavity in the scapula (the shoulder blade). The rotator cuff consists of four muscles that help hold the humerus in place and, working together, give the shoulder its great range of mobility. Damage to one of these muscles or anything that disrupts their function constitutes a rotator cuff injury. Such injuries can result from falling on an outstretched arm, but more often they evolve from overusing the shoulder.

A portion of the rotator cuff lies between the humerus and a portion of the scapula called the acromion. Repeated use of the shoulder, particularly hard throwing, can increase the muscle size of this part of the rotator cuff, causing it to rub against the acromion. Repeated rubbing leads to inflammation, swelling, and pain, generally localized over the front of the shoulder. When such pain occurs, a young athlete should cease playing and seek medical treatment to prevent irreversible damage to the rotator cuff. The player who continues throwing in spite of his or her pain, or who returns to the playing field prematurely, risks small tears in the muscles and eventually a rupture in the rotator cuff or the biceps tendon.

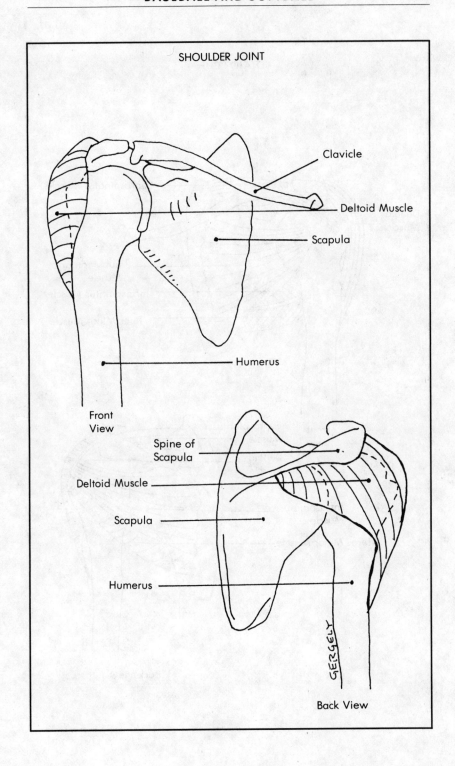

SHOULDER JOINT

Clavicle

Deltoid Muscle

Scapula

Humerus

Front
View

Spine of
Scapula

Deltoid Muscle

Scapula

Humerus

GERGELY

Back View

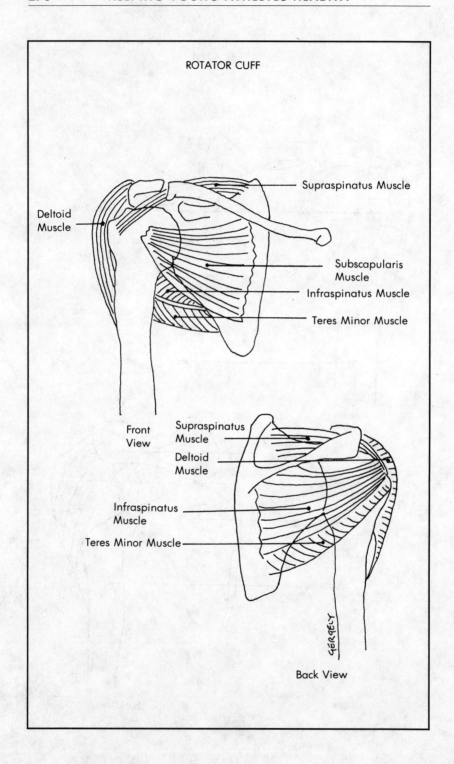

ROTATOR CUFF

Supraspinatus Muscle

Deltoid Muscle

Subscapularis Muscle

Infraspinatus Muscle

Teres Minor Muscle

Front View

Supraspinatus Muscle

Deltoid Muscle

Infraspinatus Muscle

Teres Minor Muscle

Back View

Shoulder dislocations and subluxations also constitute less-than-rare injuries among baseball players. And indeed, adolescent athletes appear to suffer more shoulder dislocations than adult athletes. A dislocation occurs when the humerus moves out of its socket. Generally, a dislocation requires physically forcing the bone back into place. More often than not, a dislocation results from a fall or from a collision with another player or with a stationary object, such as a wall.

A shoulder subluxation, or partial dislocation, typically involves the humerus slipping out of alignment and then spontaneously returning to its proper place. In baseball, pitchers sometimes develop subluxations as a result of the wear inflicted by their overhand throwing motions. Any player who suffers a dislocated or subluxed shoulder has an increased risk of recurrence.

Some players, whatever their sport, can sense when they have an "instability," or a tendency for their shoulder to sublux. Their bodies almost instinctively respond by moving in ways that protect the shoulder. For example, basketball players prone to subluxations will keep their arms close to their bodies when rebounding to protect against having their arm pulled, which might cause a subluxation. Baseball pitchers prone to partial dislocations change their pitching motions to prevent subluxation, which some sports medicine specialists suspect increases the risk of rotator cuff injury.

Both types of injuries require resting the shoulder, and some physicians feel that using a sling for up to three weeks reduces the risk of recurrence. If any instability remains, the player should consult a physician before attempting to return to the diamond.

Rehabilitating a shoulder injury so that a player can return to pain-free throwing with full flexibility, strength, range of motion, stability, and endurance usually requires a strengthening program (see Chapter 13), supervised by an athletic trainer or knowledgeable coach. As noted earlier, baseball players should limit themselves to low weights and high repetitions, which build strength without adding bulk.

ELBOW INJURIES

The elbow, known anatomically as a hinge joint, connects the arm's two long bones. In baseball, adult pitchers suffer shoulder and elbow injuries about equally. Younger hurlers, however, develop elbow injuries slightly more often than they do shoulder problems.

Sports as a rule, and overhand pitching in particular, stress the elbow and require a joint that is functioning properly. Overuse problems (see Chapter 7) stemming from repeated throwing are common among pitchers. They may develop enlarged forearm and shoulder rotator muscles and a thickening of the humerus (upper arm bone) on their throwing side. These growths may not cause problems, but in some pitchers, they appear to lead to a valgus—or turning out at the elbow—deformity.

In 1965 a physician coined the term "Little League elbow" to describe the accelerated growth, separation, and fragmenting of the bone growth area at the end of the elbow seen in some adolescent pitchers. Today the term is used to describe an even broader range of bone and soft-tissue injuries. Little League elbow can result from repeated excessive throwing without enough rest, overuse of off-speed pitches, or improper pitching form.

Because adolescents still have active growth occurring in the bones of their arms, elbow injuries may affect them differently—and more seriously—than they affect adults. Adolescents stand a greater risk of deformity and disability resulting from their injuries. And, unfortunately, once they suffer an elbow injury many young players are unable to return to their peak levels of pre-injury performance.

Young players can prevent many elbow problems with proper conditioning, with sufficient rest between pitching performances, and by paying attention to proper throwing mechanics. Parents and coaches can help by insisting that players follow these guidelines.

Occasionally, very young ballplayers suffer from *osteochondrosis*, a degeneration of the bone growth centers. Adolescents can develop *osteochondritis dissecans*, an inflammation which involves both bone and cartilage and which can result in an abnormal bone growth that can fragment within the elbow. Some physicians regard the two as separate entities; others regard them as separate stages of the same disorder. In the elbow, the two problems occur most often among players of throwing and racquet sports. They can result from a trauma, such as a fall, or from a tiny disruption of the blood supply brought on by the stress imposed on the elbow by the two types of sports. Both disorders cause a vague pain and swelling at the elbow; in addition, the young athlete with osteochondritis dissecans may have restricted motion of the inflamed joint. Osteochondrosis may resolve itself with rest, or it may grow more serious.

Osteochondritis dissecans can progress to the point where the elbow requires surgery, and even then some permanent damage may remain. Those who see the two disorders as parts of the same problem often divide osteochondritis dissecans into three stages. The first (osteochondrosis) responds well to rest and sometimes splinting. The second, which almost always occurs after age 13, may require an arthroscopic examination and perhaps securing bone within the elbow with a metal pin. The third stage is seen in adults who have ignored their condition for years and often requires surgery to remove bone fragments, insert a pin, or graft new bone to the elbow.

The elbow's ligaments and tendons are probably stressed more by baseball pitching than by any other athletic activity, and may also suffer an injury. In children and adolescents, too much stress on a ligament may result in a strain or sprain, as it does in adults, or it may cause the elbow's growth center to fracture (which may or may not show up on an X ray).

Elbow ligament problems often emerge as overuse injuries, and occur in four typical stages. At first, the player notices mild pain from an inflammation, and perhaps some swelling of the elbow. This can progress to stage two, in which scar tissue forms in the ligament. In the third stage, calcium deposits form amid the scar tissue, which makes the elbow tender to the touch and may restrict its range of motion. Finally, the calcium hardens to grains of bone, creating pain, greater motion limitations, and the sound of bone rubbing on bone. These changes within the ligament can lead to permanent damage.

Baseball and softball players also suffer the tendinitis popularly known as "tennis elbow," an inflammation brought on by repeated tiny injuries to the joint's tendons (see Chapter 15). Although this overuse problem—which frequently occurs after small changes in throwing technique—usually strikes adults, it can affect adolescent players as well.

Players who suffer ligament or tendon injuries should cease throwing, ice the injury (see Chapter 6), and see a physician if pain continues after three days of resting. As a rule, a ligament or tendon injury requires about two or three weeks of rest before the player can begin throwing again.

The elbow's muscles and bursas also stand at risk among athletes and among baseball players in particular. Overuse injuries, again, constitute the major threat to the muscles associated with the elbow. Players often feel pain and tenderness after practicing or playing, along with some swelling along the flexor pronator muscle group below the elbow on the inside of the arm. Sometimes the elbow will not fully extend the arm. Typically, treatment requires rest from throwing, ice treatments, anti-inflammatory medication, and sometimes splinting. Once the tenderness disappears, the player should begin exercises that strengthen the elbow-area muscles and increase their flexibility.

A blow to the elbow can damage a bursa, creating acute pain, tenderness, and swelling that sometimes requires the removal of fluid with a needle. Recovery usually takes a week or two. More often, bursitis develops more slowly from the stress applied to the elbow in throwing. Symptoms develop during play or practice, and continue for some time afterward. Unless treated, this can develop into chronic bursitis that may require surgery to treat.

Elbow and shoulder pain, while common among baseball and softball players, signals a problem of some sort, which may grow worse and even cause permanent disability. Ignoring pain is never wise. A short break in athletic activity may well prevent a more painful future.

PLAYING INJURIES

Hitting

Obviously, the greatest danger to a batter lies in the thrown ball, whose speed may exceed 90 mph even in high school games. Softball players appear to have a lower incidence of serious hitting injuries than baseball players, in part because the ball is usually thrown with much less velocity. Injuries can range from a lingering sting to a broken bone, or even a fatal skull fracture. A batter hit with a baseball commonly suffers a painful bruise; bone fractures most commonly occur in the hand and forearm. Baseball is also a leading cause of sports eye injuries (see Chapter 15) that require emergency-room treatment. Not only can the batter get hit in the eye, but a line drive can hit the pitcher, or a player at another position, or a runner on base. A study of injuries among five million Little Leaguers found that 38 percent of all their injuries requiring medical treatment involved the head and that batting injuries accounted for 22 percent of the total. For that reason, players should always wear batting helmets at the plate—advice now readily accepted by youngsters because they see major league players wearing the protective headgear.

FIELDING

Two types of injuries dominate among players in the field: collisions and muscle damage. Players sometimes collide with each other, or with a wall, a pole, a railing, or a dugout while trying to make a play. The end result can range from nothing more than embarrassment to a concussion, dislocation, or broken bone. It is important for fielders to remember and pay attention to the team's prearranged signals for who will catch a ball.

Often, baseball and softball players must quickly sprint to full speed to sweep up a grounder or grab a fly ball. This can strain or tear a muscle, with the hamstrings particularly vulnerable. Shoestring catches also can cause hamstring damage, and other injuries—to an arm or shoulder, for example—if the player falls. It is important that players warm up and stretch before a game and throw the ball around each time they return to the field.

CATCHING

Bad bruises and broken fingers are well-known legacies of a catching career. The catcher risks injury from badly thrown or poorly caught balls, foul tips, and wildly swung bats. The position requires squatting to catch the thrown ball—which stresses the quadriceps and knee-caps—and then springing quickly erect to chase a foul ball or to throw out a runner trying to steal. The repeated return throws to the pitcher can stress the shoulder, and tagging out runners at home plate can result in violent collisions.

Guarding against debilitating or serious injuries requires a catcher to be in excellent physical condition, to warm up and stretch well before taking the field, and to keep his or her muscles warm and flexible during the game. Catchers, because they encase much of their body in protective gear and are involved in every play of a game, run a greater risk than other players of dehydration. So they must drink plenty of water during a game to protect against heat disorders.

SLIDING

This integral part of baseball carries with it significant risk of injury, both to the runner sliding and the player covering the base. Spikes can catch in the dirt or the bag, wrenching the slider's ankle, leg, or knee. In today's game, the slide used most often sends the player into the base in a half-sitting position, with one leg tucked under the other, and arms thrown into the air. The upper leg, lifted about six inches off the ground, makes contact with the base. If the player's spikes dig into the bag or dirt, the result may be a sprained or broken ankle. If the player fails to raise an arm, his or her hand can get jammed against the dirt.

Sometimes, players will go to a hook slide, which carries them to one side of the bag and just beyond the base. The toe catches the base as the player slides past. Unfortunately, the hook slide is difficult to perfect, prone to catching spikes, and causes more broken legs in baseball than any other slide.

The headfirst slide, popularized in this era by "Charlie Hustle," Pete Rose, should never be used by young players, and probably not by players of any age. While it appears simple—the player dives headfirst for the bag and lands on the hands and chest—the slide can cause serious head, neck, and shoulder injuries. Some players have died or suffered permanent paralysis as a result of such injuries.

Infielders and catchers also can suffer injuries as the result of a runner's slide. Spikes can gash a defender, sometimes inflicting debilitating damage on flesh and bone. Another common injury occurs if the runner slides into an infielder whose foot is planted firmly on the bag. This can break the fielder's leg or can twist the fielder's knee and cause severe ligament damage.

Sliding requires a lot of practice to master. Players should start without spikes, preferably in canvas shoes or even socks, and do their practice slides under the watchful supervision of a knowledgeable coach. The practice bag should be loose, not anchored, reducing the risk of injury. Safe sliding requires getting the correct mechanics down to the point that they come automatically, without thought. Beyond that, coaches must watch their players to make certain some error in sliding technique doesn't develop.

18

Wrestling

Wrestling, an athletic endeavor popular with the ancients of Egypt, Greece, and Rome, ranks among the world's oldest sports. It divides into two basic types: freestyle, whose form traces its origins back to the wrestlers of antiquity, and Greco-Roman, a style developed in Europe in the late nineteenth century that bars holds on the legs or the use of the legs to trip or hold an opponent. Basically, the style of wrestling used in U.S. high schools and colleges is a modification of the freestyle form used in international competition. A wrestler wins with a "fall," in which he pins both of an opponent's shoulder blades against the mat continuously for one second. If no fall occurs, the win goes to the wrestler with the highest number of points, awarded for such things as a takedown or forcing one shoulder of his opponent to the mat. Among high school athletes, wrestling stands as the fifth most popular sport, with around 275,000 young-sters competing each year. More than 350 colleges and universities also field wrestling squads for intercollegiate competition.

INCIDENCE OF INJURY

A study conducted for the National Athletic Trainers' Association by John W. Powell during two seasons in the late 1980s provides our best insights into injuries among high school wrestlers. He found an injury rate of 26.8 percent. Projected nationally, Powell's data in-dicate that among an average of 277,965 boys wrestling in each of the two seasons, 73,110 suffered a total of 123,960 injuries annually. Two-thirds of the injuries sidelined a wrestler for one to seven days, while 33.4 percent prevented a return to the mats for eight days or longer. Sprains (30 percent), strains (23 percent), and bad cuts, scrapes, and bruises (28 percent) accounted for just over four out of five injuries. Fractures accounted for another 7 percent, slightly less than Powell found in his separate studies of boys' and girls' basketball teams.

The sources of injuries ranged from direct blows by an opponent, to falls, twisting the body, and friction injuries caused by the mat. Overall, Powell's studies indicate that high school wrestlers face a smaller risk of injury than scholastic football players, but a greater risk than either girls or boys playing high school basketball.

NUTRITION

We discuss sports nutrition in Chapter 3, but wrestling presents problems that deserve added attention.

Wrestlers perform best with a diet high in carbohydrates, which the body uses as the compound glycogen (a sugar rapidly converted to energy). This diet provides greater endurance. Adequate protein intake is vital for building and repairing muscle, but excessive amounts can get stored as fat. Dietary fat provides energy for muscles, yet a high-fat diet not only increases the risk of eventually developing heart disease, it can reduce a wrestler's endurance. Generally, athletes do well on a diet that consists of 55 to 60 percent carbohydrates, 12 to 15 percent protein, and 25 to 30 percent fat. However, some sports nutritionists suggest that wrestlers do better with a diet of 70 percent carbohydrates, reduced fat, and the same 12 to 15 percent level of protein. This will prove effective only if the young athlete eats as many calories as he expends. Unfortunately, wrestlers have notoriously bad, if not harmful, eating habits.

Scholastic and collegiate wrestlers compete according to weight classes, which largely eliminates size as a factor and provides a more equal level of competition. Still, many wrestlers rely on starvation diets and dehydration to help them "make weight"—that is, reduce their weight so they can compete in a specific weight class. They typically do this because they feel they would do better at the high end of the weight class below their current weight status or because the team has no one who can wrestle at the lower weight. Reducing weight, as described in Chapter 3, can be done within reason. Unfortunately, most wrestlers use methods that do more harm than good—severely restricting their food intake and fluids, inducing excessive sweating, and using diuretics and laxatives.

Though used widely, often with the knowledge and sometimes the encouragement of coaches, such weight-reduction methods can prove detrimental to performance and perhaps to health. Interestingly, most wrestlers weighing under 190 pounds are not fat by any means; studies show that a majority carry less than 8 percent of their weight in fat. Nonetheless, wrestlers may reduce their pre-season weight by 10 percent (and in some cases, as much as 20 percent), often losing much of it in one or a few days before their weigh-in for a match. Most choose dehydration as their main method of rapid weight loss. Often they severely restrict their intake of fluids for 12 to 24 hours before stepping onto the scales, then drink large quantities of fluids in the one to five hours between their weigh-in and match. But this amount of time usually proves too little for the wrestler to restore his proper balance of fluids and electrolytes. Studies also show that young wrestlers who severely restrict their food intake fail to consume enough nutrients. For example, one study of 42 college wrestlers found that between 25 percent and 59 percent (depending on the nutrient) failed to get two-thirds of their recommended dietary allowances of vitamins A and B_6, thiamine, magnesium, and zinc.

Evidence suggests that any weight loss over 10 percent can significantly reduce strength, endurance, and athletic and classroom performance. The American College of Sports Medicine warns that even smaller weight reductions, done on a crash basis, can reduce muscle strength and performance times; lower blood volume; reduce heart function and the amount of oxygen-rich blood pumped; impair the body's ability to regulate heat; decrease blood flow to the kidneys; and increase the amount of electrolytes lost from the body. At this point, no one knows whether these problems cause permanent damage, although some authorities worry that starvation diets may stunt an adolescent's growth and that repeatedly reducing blood flow to the kidney may do subtle damage that surfaces in middle age.

The American College of Sports Medicine urges that daily caloric intake requirements be obtained from a balanced diet and be determined on the basis of age, body surface area, growth, and physical activity levels. Coaches, school officials, physicians, and parents all share the responsibility for discouraging wrestlers from consuming less than their minimal needs without medical approval, and for discouraging fluid deprivation and dehydration.

PREVENTING INJURIES

As they do in many sports, coaches serve as the key link in injury prevention among wrestlers. They train, educate, and supervise the proper execution of the sport, oversee their athletes' physical conditioning, maintain the discipline needed for safety, and make the ultimate decision as to whether an athlete is healthy enough to practice or compete. A coach who fails in any of these roles risks injury to his wrestlers.

Flexibility and strength both serve to protect wrestlers. Flexibility, or the range of motion of the body's joints, comes into play frequently. A wrestler with tight shoulders, for example, must yield to an opponent's hold more often than one with greater flexibility—or suffer an injury. Prior to any sports participation, properly warming the muscles and stretching them to promote flexibility (see Chapter 2) helps protect against injury. Strength, particularly upper-body strength, also may make the difference between escaping a hold safely or injury. Weight training (see Chapter 13) can greatly increase a wrestler's strength, but youngsters should never undertake such a program without the aid of a knowledgeable coach or trainer. Not only can strength training itself cause injuries, but different sports demand different training techniques. For example, wrestlers benefit most by doing their repetitions rapidly.

Protective equipment can also help prevent certain injuries. Knee pads guard against painful scrapes that can become infected (see below), and they appear to reduce the risks of prepatellar bursitis in the knee. Headgear, now required in high school and college wrestling, helps protect against ear hematomas—a hemorrhaging under the skin that can cause cauliflower ear, a characteristic and permanent injury among the wrestlers of old. Mouth guards protect the teeth from damage, and these devices are even more important if the young athlete wears dental braces. Finally, mats cushion falls, though their protective advantage lessens as their resiliency declines with use and time. Safety necessitates replacing old, worn mats.

The rules of wrestling themselves serve to reduce some injuries or limit their severity. Certain holds—one that might choke an opponent, for example—are barred. If a wrestler suffers an injury that prevents him from continuing as the result of an illegal hold, he wins the match, an incentive for all participants to wrestle by the rules. Referees interrupt matches to prevent potentially dangerous holds and after an injury occurs. If the injury is serious, the referee halts the match. Nonetheless, as statistics show, injuries do happen.

SPECIFIC INJURIES

SKIN INJURIES

Wrestlers wear uniforms that expose a considerable amount of skin and, as a result of their close, frequent body contact, run a considerable risk for dermatologic ailments. Communicable skin diseases can spread throughout a team. "Mat burns," scrapes caused by rubbing the body against the mats, readily become infected, posing the threat of spreading the infection to others. Impetigo may also strike in adolescents and spread to other wrestlers. The herpes simplex virus, primarily known for causing cold sores, can infect the eye's cornea—and this may cause blindness. Folliculitis, an inflammation of the skin's hair follicles; atopic dermatitis, an allergic reaction that causes chronic itching; and acne occur commonly among wrestlers and should receive prompt medical attention when they erupt. Indeed, coaches should make certain that wrestlers who develop skin disorders see a physician and should bar those with infectious ailments from wrestling or other physical contact with other team members until they are no longer contagious.

Good personal hygiene plays a key role in preventing skin problems among wrestlers. Team members should shower before and after taking to the mats, whether in practice or competition, and should wear a clean uniform daily. Mats should be washed frequently and treated with an antiseptic solution.

HEAD AND NECK INJURIES

These injuries range from nosebleeds (common) to paralyzing injuries (rare). A study of injuries incurred over eight seasons by members of the University of Iowa wrestling team revealed that more than one in four affected the neck (12 percent), face (8 percent), ear (5.5 percent), or head (3 percent). The most common neck injuries involved nerve pain—such as the so-called pinched-nerve syndrome—strains, and sprains. Wrestlers who suffered neck injuries lost an average of 10.7 days from their sport as a result. Neck injuries frequently occur during a takedown.

Sports medicine experts believe that a stronger neck is a safer neck. Today, many coaches include specific neck-strengthening exercises as part of their training programs, with the twin aims of enhancing performance and preventing injury. These programs may use weight machines, or they may require nothing more than two wrestlers helping each other through a series of resistance exercises. Any program, however, should have the supervision of someone knowledgeable about strength programs.

A neck, or cervical, strain results from a tear where a muscle and tendon join. In wrestling, strains generally prove mild or moderate, with a complete rupture a rare event. Symptoms include pain, tenderness, and an inability to fully control voluntary muscles at the injury site. It takes several hours for maximum pain, swelling, and reduction in range of motion to occur. In mild strains, the youngster may notice no problems—once the immediate pain of injury subsides—until awakening the next morning. Physicians generally treat neck strains with anti-inflammatory medications, ice treatments followed after several days by heat, and rest from any activity that will aggravate the injury, until the young athlete has a pain-free, normal range of neck motion.

Sprains result from damage to ligaments, and the type that occurs most commonly in wrestling is called the "jammed neck syndrome," a mild, transient sprain resulting from compression of the neck vertebrae. Pain is confined to the neck and shoulder blades, and sometimes the upper arm. The injury causes no reduced reflexes or loss of motor activity, but it limits the neck's range of motion considerably. Neck sprains generally require anti-inflammatory drugs and brief immobilization with a neck collar or brace until the range of motion returns to near normal. Rehabilitation usually calls for exercises to strengthen the neck. It is important that a young athlete not return to the mats until his pain and tenderness have disappeared, and his neck has regained its full maneuverability. Returning earlier heightens the risk of sustaining another sprain. Some wrestlers appear prone to sprains, a tendency that increases their chances of suffering disabling nerve damage. Anyone who suffers a series of sprains should consult a physician about the dangers and the possible need to give up the sport.

LOWER-BACK INJURIES

Most back injuries in wrestling involve strains or sprains. Disc ruptures do happen, but these are quite uncommon. As with neck injuries, back injuries typically occur during takedowns. The grappling between opponents before a takedown frequently occurs with the back mildly hyperextended (overstraightened). Prolonged moving in this position, combined with the twisting motions of wrestling, can inflict painful strains and sprains, as can lifting up a struggling opponent and overflexing the back in a roll or in trying to escape a hold. Sometimes, however, a low-back injury results not from a single event but from a series of tiny tissue damages that finally create a painful injury.

Sometimes the pain resides on one side of the spine, other times on both sides. The wrestler has a limited range of back motion. Usually the pain centers in a small area of the back, and grows worse, reaching its peak 24 to 48 hours after the injury. Treatment typically includes anti-inflammatory medications, ice packs for several days, and rest from any activities that will aggravate the injury. Sometimes a physician will order other treatments, such as massage, deep heat, ultrasound, and electrical stimulation of the nerves. Most wrestling-related low-back injuries resolve readily, and young athletes can return to practice and competition when their pain subsides and they have regained their full range of motion. However, it is wise in such cases to add some back-strengthening exercises to their daily routine.

KNEE INJURIES

Wrestlers use their legs in takedowns and on the mat, and this exposes the knee to some potentially serious injuries. John W. Powell, in his study of high school wrestlers, found that 15 percent of their injuries involved the knee; in the study of University of Iowa wrestlers, knee problems accounted for 24 percent of all injuries. Sprains, particularly of the medial collateral ligament, account for many knee injuries in wrestling. Wrestlers also suffer a significant number of injuries to the meniscus, the knee's crescent-shaped cartilage. (We discussed both these types of injuries in more detail in Chapter 12.)

Prepatellar bursitis, sometimes called "housemaid's knee," is an inflammation of a small sac (bursa) that acts as a cushion in the knee. It can result from an infection, but in wrestling it usually stems from an injury to the bursa when a wrestler strikes his knee on the floor or an opponent delivers a blow to it. As noted earlier, wearing knee pads reduces the risk of prepatellar bursitis, whose symptoms include pain, swelling, tenderness, and limited motion of the knee. Physicians frequently prescribe anti-inflammatory drugs and pain-killers to treat it. But this injury, which usually sidelines an athlete for around three weeks, also calls for resting the knee until pain and tenderness subside to the point where some movement can be accomplished comfortably. It is important to work the knee, without overstressing it, to prevent the buildup of adhesions that can permanently limit the knee's range of motion. Rehabilitating a knee with prepatellar bursitis should be done with a physician's advice.

SHOULDER INJURIES

The functioning of the shoulder and the reasons why athletes often suffer shoulder injuries are described in Chapter 17. In wrestling, these include dislocations and subluxations (partial dislocations), strains and sprains, and tendinitis. Wrestlers risk dislocations and partial dislocations because of the upper-body holds used in the sport.

19

Soccer

Soccer in the United States exploded during the 1970s and 1980s from a game of extremely limited appeal among young athletes to one played by nearly two million persons under age 19. Worldwide, soccer is the most popular sport, and although it has yet to win a major following at the professional level among U.S. sports fans, the nation's youth show no signs of losing their enthusiasm for the fast-paced game. Perhaps one reason for their enthusiasm is the fact that practice sessions more closely resemble games than they do in such sports as baseball, basketball, or football. Another reason may be the fact that soccer requires a variety of skills—speed, endurance, power, agility—yet excelling in only one will not make a player a star, as, say, speed will in football. Soccer rewards the all-around athlete more than many sports, yet allows plenty of room for the player of only modest ability to enjoy the game.

INCIDENCE OF INJURIES

While we lack precise statistics for injuries suffered by young soccer players in the United States, several studies suggest that they get hurt only about one-fifth as often as U.S. football players and that they sustain less severe injuries overall. Nonetheless, injuries do happen, primarily to the lower extremities. Studies in North America and Europe typically find that between two-thirds and three-quarters of all soccer injuries involve the lower extremities, and a Danish study reported in 1989 found that 84 percent of soccer injuries occurred in the lower extremities, including the groin. Head injuries also occur regularly in soccer, primarily as a result of "heading," a technique peculiar to the game in which a player uses his or her head to hit the ball. A study of injuries sustained by members of the 1,016 boys' teams and 332 girls' teams competing one year in the Norway Cup, an annual international youth soccer tournament held in Oslo, revealed that 17.3 percent affected the head and neck. Hyperventilation, an excessive deep breathing that can lead to fainting, also occurs in soccer. The Norway Cup study reported seven girls and one boy hospitalized because of the problem. Indeed, girls generally suffer more injuries of all types in soccer than boys.

Most soccer injuries involve severe bruising, strains, and sprains. More often than not, strains and sprains occur while the player is running or turning, not from contact with another player. A Danish study suggests that ankle injuries and strains of all types pose the greatest risk of reinjury; 56 percent of the ankle injuries in that study occurred in players with a previous history of a sprained ankle.

A sharp increase in soccer injuries occurs about the time players reach age 14. This appears to result from the more aggressive and riskier style of play that youngsters adopt as they mature. Strength and flexibility always give a player a safety advantage, but certainly by age 14, serious soccer players need to pay more careful attention to their bodies. Studies find that for unknown reasons, soccer players tend to have tighter muscles than other athletes and even some nonathletes. In Chapter 2 we described the importance of warm-ups and stretching to injury prevention and suggested a series of exercises to improve and maintain flexibility. An increasing number of adolescent soccer players have embarked on weight-training programs (see Chapter 13) to build strength, but these should be supervised by a knowledgeable coach or athletic trainer. Soccer players need to build strength without building a lot of muscle, since excessive muscle can reduce flexibility.

PROTECTIVE EQUIPMENT

SHOES

Some soccer shoes can provide players a definite protection against ankle and foot injuries. But fashion and performance often clash with protection in the minds of young soccer players, with safety the loser. Well-padded soccer shoes that lace to above the ankle provide the best protection. However, such shoes are bulky and many young players refuse to wear them because they look unfashionable and do reduce a player's ability to perform. Whatever style soccer shoe a player wears, it should be well made, keep the ankle stable, and have a symmetrical pattern of cleats. Players who wear cleats of different heights on one shoe increase their risk of injury.

Many players now wear elastic ankle bandages or tape to help support their ankles. The ankle supports available at sporting goods stores and drugstores often fit somewhat poorly, readily get soaked with sweat, and lose some compression, but they slip on easily and take less time to apply than tape. Also, while anyone can slap tape on an ankle, effective taping requires skill and experience (see Chapter 6).

SHIN GUARDS

Soccer involves a lot of kicking and dueling for the ball with feet and cleats flying. Shin guards can greatly reduce the risk of lower-leg injuries, a common and painful problem in the sport. Sharp cleats can cause severe flesh injuries. In a study of 1,139 boys and girls attending a summer soccer camp, researchers found that players who failed to wear shin guards had nearly five times the number of leg injuries as those who wore them. Parents should inspect their youngsters' shin guards regularly to make certain they are in good shape and fit properly.

EYE GUARDS

Flying balls cause most eye injuries in soccer. A kicked soccer ball travels more than 35 mph and can reach 75 mph. At high speeds, a soccer ball can cause a detached retina, which may end in permanent vision loss. Young soccer players, whether they wear eyeglasses or not, should protect their eyes with the unbreakable eye guards used in racquet sports (see Chapter 15).

SPECIFIC INJURIES

HEAD INJURIES

While serious head injuries represent a tiny fraction of soccer injuries, "heading" poses the threat of a rare fatal injury and can cause concussions, neurological problems, and, if the fears of some experts prove correct, permanent loss of mental functioning in some longtime players. A kicked soccer ball, especially one that strikes a player at close range, delivers a significant blow to the head, and heading means players can suffer a great many blows over years of play. Since evidence from other sports—notably boxing—indicates that the effects of such blows are cumulative, some sports medicine authorities have questioned whether longtime players risk developing the sort of brain damage seen in "punch drunk" boxers. As yet, no one has answered that question.

Clearly, however, a player falling on his or her head, or two players banging heads as they battle each other to head a soccer ball can have serious consequences. Cuts, bruises, neck injuries, and concussions can result. Several studies indicate that young soccer players are more likely than older players to suffer head injuries, probably because the youngsters lack experience in heading the ball. Any player who complains of dizziness, headache, and/or nausea after a blow to the head should see a physician quickly for an evaluation. Any player who loses consciousness or becomes disoriented during play should be treated as if he or she has suffered a serious head or neck injury. We discussed the symptoms of these injuries and how to handle them on the field in Chapters 6 and 12.

KNEE INJURIES

Though knee injuries occur commonly among older soccer players, several studies indicate that only about 1 out of every 1,000 children and young adolescents playing soccer suffers serious knee injuries. And only about 10 percent of serious soccer injuries among young players affect the knee. Sprains are the most common knee injury seen in children and adolescents, and these usually occur during attempts to steal the ball, called tackling. Ankle sprains occur about equally between tackling and running.

Adult soccer players have a high risk of meniscus damage; about one in two who start young and play into their adult years will suffer such an injury sometime during their career. Sometimes the injury results from a severe blow to the knee, but evidence suggests that far more often, meniscus problems result from deterioration of the cartilage caused by a series of tiny, seemingly harmless injuries that happen over years of play.

Strengthening the thigh muscles that support the knee provides soccer players, and other athletes as well, their best protection against injuring the joint. For those who suffer a knee injury, strengthening, the knee is a vital part of their rehabilitation, and, unfortunately, one that is too often ignored. A player who returns to the field with weakened thigh muscles courts reinjury.

MUSCLE CRAMPS AND STRAINS

Muscle cramps, sudden spasms usually due to an insufficient supply of oxygen, primarily strike the calf in soccer players. Cramping problems tend to increase as the game progresses, due to exertion, fatigue, and dehydration. Drinking plenty of water and fruit juices, which restore hydration and contain needed electrolytes, can help prevent muscle cramps. Soccer players, like all athletes, need to drink plenty of fluids to maintain hydration and to ward off heat disorders (see Chapter 6).

Muscle strains, which result from a sudden overstretching of a muscle, occur more often in the pre-season and early part of the season, before players get their bodies fully conditioned. Among soccer players, calf and thigh muscles most often suffer strains. The intense pain of a strain forces a player to a halt, and he or she must leave the game immediately—with no "playing through the pain" allowed. Strains call for RICE. Players can help prevent strains by keeping their bodies in top physical condition and by warming up and stretching their muscles before taking the field (see Chapter 2).

SKIN INJURIES

Bruises, cuts, and scrapes afflict everyone who competes in soccer. They go with, and often are a result of contact with, the turf.

A bruise (or contusion, to use the medical term) occurs when a blow damages blood vessels, causing a hemorrhage that ultimately manifests itself as a black-and-blue mark on the skin. Bruises can prove quite painful and can slow a player's speed for a few days. Sometimes a hemorrhage is so severe that a blood clot forms, and on occasion, a physician must surgically remove the clot. A contusion rather specific to soccer, called the "horse kiss" bruise, results from a blow by another player to the outside of the thigh.

Treating simple bruises calls for icing and compressing the injury immediately, then lightly exercising the injured muscle after 24 hours or so. This may take the form of walking a distance, walking up and down stairs, or climbing up on a chair and back down a number of times. If a bruise causes decreased muscle activity and increased pain for more than 24 hours, the player may need to consult a physician, especially for large thigh-muscle bruises.

Scrapes, or abrasions, usually occur when a player falls on a hard playing surface, and they often pick up dirt or other matter that contaminates the wound. Abrasions are best cleaned with clean, flowing water, then dried lightly with a lint-free towel or cloth, and treated with a disinfectant that contains no alcohol. If possible, the player should leave the wound exposed to the air to heal. If a bandage is applied, use a type that does not stick to the wound. If dirt, oil, or other matter remains embedded after cleaning, or if an infection develops, the player should seek medical care.

Cuts typically result from kicks, either from the edge of the shoe or from the cleats. Some cleat cuts go deep and may bleed profusely. Usually one can stop the bleeding by pinching the edges of the cut together for five to seven minutes. Cuts, too, should be cleaned, and treated as one would a severe scrape. Large cuts and those that continue bleeding may require stitches to close them and to limit scarring.

Finally, soccer players sometimes discover blood spreading around their toenails and blood beneath the nails, raising them up, causing pain that sometimes becomes excruciating. This results from repeatedly kicking the ball. A physician should examine this injury. Treatment often requires drilling several tiny holes in the nail to allow the blood to drain.

·BIBLIOGRAPHY·

Books

Garrick, James G., and Webb, David R. *Sports Injuries: Diagnosis and Management.* Philadelphia: W. B. Saunders Co., Harcourt Brace Jovanovich, Inc., 1990.

Meer, Jeff. *Drugs & Sports.* New York: Chelsea House, 1987.

Schneider, Richard C.; Kennedy, John C.; and Plant, Marcus L., eds. *Sports Injuries; Mechanisms, Prevention, and Treatment.* Baltimore: Williams and Wilkins, 1985.

Smith, Nathan J., ed. *Sports Medicine: Health Care for Young Athletes.* Evanston, IL: American Academy of Pediatrics, 1983.

Sullivan, J. Andy, and Grana, William A. *The Pediatric Athlete.* Park Ridge, IL: American Academy of Orthopaedic Surgeons, 1990.

Vinger, Paul F., and Hoerner, Earl F., eds. *Sports Injuries: The Unthwarted Epidemic.* 2d ed. Littleton, MA: PSG Publishing Co., 1986.

Weinstein, Allan M. *Asthma: The Complete Guide to Self-Management of Asthma and Allergies for Patients and Their Families.* New York: McGraw-Hill Book Co., 1987.

Young, Patrick. *Asthma and Allergies: An Optimistic Future.* Bethesda, MD: National Institute of Allergy and Infectious Diseases, 1980.

———. *Mental Disturbances.* New York: Chelsea House, 1988.

Articles

"Alcohol Use and Abuse: A Pediatric Concern." *Pediatrics,* March 1987, pp. 450–53.

Allman, Fred L., Jr.; Torg, Joseph S.; and Welsch, R. Peter. "Easing Elbow Overload Syndrome." *Patient Care,* April 15, 1987, pp. 94–101.

Andrews, James R. "Overuse Syndromes of the Lower Extremity." *Clinics in Sports Medicine,* March 1983, pp. 137–48.

Andrish, Jack T. "Knee Injuries in Gymnastics." *Clinics in Sports Medicine,* January 1985, pp. 111–21.

Appenzeller, Otto. "What Makes Us Run?" *New England Journal of Medicine*, Sept. 3, 1981, pp. 578–79.

Apple, David R., Jr. "Adolescent Runners." *Clinics in Sports Medicine*, October 1985, pp. 641–55.

———. "End Stage Running Problems." *Clinics in Sports Medicine*, October 1985, pp. 657–70.

Ariel, Gideon B. "Resistive Training." *Clinics in Sports Medicine*, March 1983, pp. 55–69.

Aronen, John Gary. "Problems of the Upper Extremity in Gymnasts." *Clinics in Sports Medicine*, January 1985, pp. 61–71.

Backous, Douglas D.; Friedl, Karl E.; Smith, Nathan J.; Parr, Thomas J.; and Carpine, William D., Jr. "Soccer Injuries and their Relation to Physical Maturity." *American Journal of Diseases in Children*, August 1988, pp. 839–42.

Baechle, Thomas R. "Women in Resistance Training." *Clinics in Sports Medicine*, October 1984, pp. 791–808.

Baker, Elizabeth, and Demers, Laurence. "Menstrual Status in Female Athletes: Correlation with Reproductive Hormones and Bone Density." *Obstetrics & Gynecology*, November 1988, pp. 683–87.

Balduini, Frederick C. "Abdominal and Groin Injuries in Tennis." *Clinics in Sports Medicine*, April 1988, pp. 349–57.

Ballor, Douglas L.; Katch, Victor L.; Becque, M. Daniel; and Marks, Charles R. "Resistance Weight Training during Caloric Restriction Enhances Lean Body Weight Maintenance." *American Journal of Clinical Nutrition*, 1988: 47, pp. 19–25.

Bar-Or, Oded. "Exercise in Prepubertal Girls: What Are the Limits?" *Contemporary Pediatrics*, January 1987, pp. 124–29.

Becker, Theodore J. "The Athletic Trainer in Swimming." *Clinics in Sports Medicine*, January 1986, pp. 9–24.

Berg, Kris. "Aerobic Function in Female Athletes." *Clinics in Sports Medicine*, October 1984, pp. 779–89.

Blair, Steven N.; Kohl, Harold W.; and Goodyear, Nancy N. "Rates and Risks for Running and Exercise Injuries: Studies in Three Populations." *Research Quarterly for Exercise and Sport*, 58, no. 3, pp. 221–28.

Bordelon, R. Luke. "Management of Disorders of the Forefoot and Toenails Associated with Running." *Clinics in Sports Medicine*, October 1985, pp. 717–24.

Brady, Joseph V. "A Biobehavioral Research Perspective on Alcohol Abuse and Alcoholism." *Public Health Reports*, November–December 1988, pp. 699–712.

Brady, Thomas A.; Cahill, Bernard R.; and Bodnar, Leslie M. "Weight Training–Related Injuries in the High School Athlete." *The American Journal of Sports Medicine*, 1982: 10, no. 1, pp. 1–5.

Brill, Judith E. "The Myth of the 'Drownproof' Child." *Contemporary Pediatrics*, June 1989, pp. 90–92.

Brown, Robert S. "Exercise and Mental Health in the Pediatric Population." *Clinics in Sports Medicine*, November 1982, pp. 515–27.

Bruno, Leonard A.; Gennarelli, Thomas A.; and Torg, Joseph S. "Management Guidelines for Head Injuries in Athletics." *Clinics in Sports Medicine*, January 1987, pp. 17–29.

Buckley, William E.; Yesalis, Charles E., III; Friedl, Karl E.; Anderson, William A.; Streit, Andrea L.; and Wright, James E. "Estimated Prevalence of Anabolic Steroid Use among Male High School Seniors." *Journal of the American Medical Association,* Dec. 16, 1988, pp. 3441–3445.

Bunch, Richard P.; Bednarski, Kathryn; Holland, D.; and Macinanti, Raymond. "Ankle Joint Support: A Comparison of Reusable Lace-on Braces With Taping and Wrapping." *The Physician and Sportsmedicine,* May 1985, pp. 59–62.

Cabrera, Jorge M., and McCue, Frank C., III. "Nonosseous Athletic Injuries of the Elbow, Forearm, and Hand." *Clinics in Sports Medicine,* October 1986, pp. 681–700.

Caine, Dennis J.; Cochrane, Barbara; Caine, Caroline; and Zemper, Eric. "An Epidemiologic Investigation of Injuries Affecting Young Competitive Female Gymnasts." *The American Journal of Sports Medicine,* November/December 1989, pp. 811–20.

Caine, Dennis J., and Lindner, Koenraad J. "Overuse Injuries of Growing Bones: The Young Female Gymnast at Risk?" *The Physician and Sportsmedicine,* December 1985, pp. 51–64.

Calabrese, Leonard H. "Nutritional and Medical Aspects of Gymnastics." *Clinics in Sports Medicine,* January 1985, pp. 23–30.

Cantu, Robert C. "Guidelines for Return to Contact Sports after a Cerebral Concussion." *The Physician and Sportsmedicine,* October 1986, pp. 75–83.

Cantwell, John D. "Cardiovascular Aspects of Running." *Clinics in Sports Medicine,* October 1985, pp. 627–40.

———. "Marfan's Syndrome: Detection and Management." *The Physician and Sportsmedicine,* July 1986, pp. 51–55.

Carson, William G., Jr. "Rehabilitation of the Throwing Shoulder." *Clinics in Sports Medicine,* October 1989, pp. 657–89.

Carter, Richard L. "Prevention of Springboard and Platform Diving Injuries." *Clinics in Sports Medicine,* January 1986, pp. 185–94.

Chambers, Richard B. "Orthopaedic Injuries in Athletes (Ages 6 to 17)." *The American Journal of Sports Medicine,* 1979: 7, no. 3, pp. 195–97.

Champaigne, Barbara N.; Gilliam, Thomas B.; Spencer, Martha L.; Lampman, Richard M., and Schork, M. Anthony. "Effects of a Physical Activity Program on Metabolic Control and Cardiovascular Fitness in Children with Insulin-dependent Diabetes Mellitus." *Diabetes Care,* January–February 1984, pp. 57–62.

Ciullo, Jerome V. "Swimmer's Shoulder." *Clinics in Sports Medicine,* January 1986, pp. 115–37.

Ciullo, Jerome V., and Jackson, Douglas W. "Pars Interarticularis Stress Reaction, Spondylolysis, and Spondylolisthesis in Gymnastics." *Clinics in Sports Medicine,* January 1985, pp. 95–110.

Clive, David M., and Stoff, Jeffrey S. "Renal Syndromes Associated with Nonsteroidal Antiinflammatory Drugs." *New England Journal of Medicine,* March 1, 1984, pp. 563–72.

Coady, Cathy, and Stanish, William D. "Emergencies in Sports: The Young Athlete." *Clinics in Sports Medicine,* July 1988, pp. 625–40.

Cohen, Jerald L.; Potosnak, Lisa; Frank, Oscar; and Baker, Herman.

"A Nutritional and Hematologic Assessment of Elite Ballet Dancers." *The Physician and Sportsmedicine*, May 1985, pp. 43–54.

Cook, Stephen D.; Kester, Marcus A.; Brunet, Michael E.; and Haddad, Ray J., Jr. "Biomechanics of Running Shoe Performance." *Clinics in Sports Medicine*, October 1985, pp. 619–26.

Cooper, Kenneth H.; Blair, Steven N.; and Gordon, Neil F. "Oxygen and Athletes." *Journal of the American Medical Association*, July 14, 1989, p. 264.

Corbin, Charles B. "Self-Confidence of Females in Sports and Physical Activity." *Clinics in Sports Medicine*, October 1984, pp. 895–908.

Costill, David L. "Water and Electrolyte Requirements during Exercise." *Clinics in Sports Medicine*, July 1984, pp. 639–48.

Counsilman, James E. "The Role of the Coach in Training for Swimming." *Clinics in Sports Medicine*, January 1986, pp. 3–7.

Cregler, Louis L., and Mark, Herbert. "Medical Complications of Cocaine Abuse." *New England Journal of Medicine*, Dec. 4, 1986, pp. 1495–1500.

Cox, Jay S. "Patellofemoral Problems in Runners." *Clinics in Sports Medicine*, October 1985, pp. 699–715.

Coyle, Edward F. "Ergogenic Aids." *Clinics in Sports Medicine*, July 1984, pp. 731–40.

D'Ambrosia, Robert D. "Orthotic Devices in Running Injuries." *Clinics in Sports Medicine*, October 1985, pp. 611–18.

Dardik, Irving I. "The Drug Problem: A Solution at Hand." *Clinics in Sports Medicine*, March 1983, pp. 101–3.

Dennison, Barbara A.; Straus, John H.; Mellits, E. David; and Charney, Evan. "Childhood Physical Fitness Tests: Predictor of Adult Physical Activity Levels?" *Pediatrics*, September 1988, pp. 324–30.

Deutsch, Ezra; Deutsch, Susan L.; and Douglas, Pamela. "Exercise Training for Competitive Tennis." *Clinics in Sports Medicine*, April 1988, pp. 417–27.

Dohm, G. Lynis. "Protein Nutrition for the Athlete." *Clinics in Sports Medicine*, July 1984, pp. 595–604.

Dominguez, Richard H. "Water Polo Injuries." *Clinics in Sports Medicine*, January 1986, pp. 169–83.

Donnelly, William H., and Indelicato, Peter A. "The Physician to a Swimming Team." *Clinics in Sports Medicine*, January 1986, pp. 25–32.

"Drug Abuse in Athletes: Anabolic Steroids and Human Growth Hormone." *Journal of the American Medical Association*, March 18, 1988, pp. 1703–5.

Duncan, John J., and Farr, James E. "Comparison of Diclofenac Sodium and Aspirin in the Treatment of Acute Sports Injuries." *The American Journal of Sports Medicine*, 1988: 16, no. 6, pp. 656–59.

DuRant, Robert H.; Linder, Charles W.; Sanders, Joe M.; Jay, Susan; Brantley, Gerry; and Bedgood, Ray. "Adolescent Females' Readiness to Participate in Sports." *Journal of Adolescent Health Care*, 1988: 9, pp. 310–14.

Dyment, Paul G. "Another Look at the Sports Preparticipation Examination of the Adolescent Athlete." *Journal of Adolescent Health Care*, November 1986 supplement, pp. 130S–32S.

————. "Drugs and the Adolescent Athlete. *Pediatric Annals,* August 1984, pp. 602–4.

Dyment, Paul G., et al. "Infant Exercise Programs." *Pediatrics*, November 1988, p. 800.

————. "Physical Fitness and the Schools." *Pediatrics*, September 1987, pp. 449–50.

Easterbrook, Michael. "Eye Protection in Racquet Sports." *Clinics in Sports Medicine,* April 1988, pp. 253–66.

Edlund, Larry D.; French, Ronald W.; Herbst, John J.; Ruttenberg, Herbert D.; Ruhling, Robert O.; and Adams, Ted D. "Effects of a Swimming Program on Children with Cystic Fibrosis." *American Journal of Diseases in Children,* January 1986, pp. 80–83.

Emans, S. Jean. "The Athletic Adolescent with Amenorrhea." *Pediatric Annals,* August 1984, pp. 605–9.

Estwanik, Joseph J., III; Bergfeld, John A.; Collins, H. Royer; and Hall, Richard. "Injuries in Interscholastic Wrestling." *The Physician and Sportsmedicine,* March 1980, pp. 111–21.

Faris, Gary J. "Psychologic Aspects of Athletic Rehabilitation." *Clinics in Sports Medicine,* July 1985, pp. 545–51.

Fielding, Jonathan E. "Smoking: Health Effects and Control." *New England Journal of Medicine,* Aug. 22, 1985, pp. 491–98 (part 1); Aug. 29, 1985, pp. 555–61 (part 2).

Fiore, Michael C.; Novotny, Thomas E.; Pierce, John P.; Hatziandreu, Evridiki J.; Patel, Kantilal M.; and Davis, Ronald M. "Trends in Cigarette Smoking in the United States." *Journal of the American Medical Association,* Jan. 6, 1989, pp. 49–55.

Fleck, Steven J., and Schutt, Robert C., Jr. "Types of Strength Training." *Orthopedic Clinics of North America,* April 1983, pp. 449–58.

Fowler, Peter J., and Regan, William D. "Swimming Injuries of the Knee, Foot, and Ankle, Elbow, and Back." *Clinics in Sports Medicine,* January 1986, pp. 139–48.

Francis, Lorna L.; Francis, Peter R.; and Welshons-Smith, Kim. "Aerobic Dance Injuries: A Survey of Instructors." *The Physician and Sportsmedicine,* February 1985, pp. 105–11.

Fritz, Robert L., and Perrin, David H. "Cold Exposure Injuries: Prevention and Treatment." *Clinics in Sports Medicine,* January 1989, pp. 111–28.

Galioto, Frank M., Jr. "Identification and Assessment of the Child for Sports Participation: A Cardiovascular Approach." *Clinics in Sports Medicine,* November 1982, pp. 383–96.

Ganim, Ronald J. "Gymnastics Safety for the Physician." *Clinics in Sports Medicine,* January 1985, pp. 123–33.

Garrick, James G. "Determinants of Return to Athletic Activity." *Orthopedic Clinics of North America,* April 1983, pp. 317–21.

————. "Pre-participation Sports Assessment." *Pediatrics*, November 1980, pp. 803–6.

Glick, James M. "The Doctor's Bag." *Orthopedic Clinics of North America,* April 1983, pp. 323–36.

Goldberg, Barry. "The Pediatrician and Athletic Injuries." *Pediatric Annals,* August 1984, pp. 596–600.

Goldberg, Barry; Rosenthal, Philip P.; Robertson, Leon S.; and Nicholas, James A. "Injuries in Youth Football." *Pediatrics,* February 1988, pp. 255–61.

Gose, John C., and Schweizer, Paul. "Iliotibial Band Tightness." *The Journal of Orthopaedic and Sports Physical Therapy,* April 1989, pp. 399–407.

Grandjean, Ann C. "Nutritional Concerns for the Woman Athlete." *Clinics in Sports Medicine,* October 1984, pp. 923–38.

———. "Nutrition for Swimmers." *Clinics in Sports Medicine,* January 1986, pp. 65–76.

Gregg, John R., and Torg, Elisabeth. "Upper Extremity Injuries in Adolescent Tennis Players." *Clinics in Sports Medicine,* April 1988, pp. 371–85.

Hageman, Charles E., and Lehman, Richard C. "Stretching, Strengthening, and Conditioning for the Competitive Tennis Player." *Clinics in Sports Medicine,* April 1988, pp. 211–28.

Hardaker, William T., Jr., and Erickson, Lars C. "Medical Considerations in Dance Training for Children." *American Family Physician,* May 1987, pp. 93–99.

Hardaker, William T., Jr.; Margello, Susan; and Goldner, J. Leonard. "Foot and Ankle Injuries in Theatrical Dancers." *Foot & Ankle,* October 1985, pp. 59–69.

Harvey, Jack. "The Preparticipation Examination of the Child Athlete." *Clinics in Sports Medicine,* November 1982, pp. 353–69.

Harvey, John S., Jr. "Nutritional Management of the Adolescent Athlete." *Clinics in Sports Medicine,* July 1984, pp. 671–78.

———. "Overuse Syndromes in Young Athletes." *Clinics in Sports Medicine,* November 1983, pp. 595–607.

Haskell, William L.; Montoye, Henry J.; and Orenstein, Diane. "Physical Activity and Exercise to Achieve Health-Related Physical Fitness Components." *Public Health Reports,* March–April 1985, pp. 202–12.

Hayden, Gregory F., and Miller, Lee T. "Swimmer's Itch, Breaststroker's Knee, and Other Watery Woes." *Contemporary Pediatrics,* May 1986, pp. 30–39.

Hecker, Arthur L. "Nutritional Conditioning for Athletic Competition." *Clinics in Sports Medicine,* July 1984, pp. 567–82.

Herring, Stanley A., and Nilson, Karen L. "Introduction to Overuse Injuries." *Clinics in Sports Medicine,* April 1987, pp. 225–39.

Hershman, Elliott B., and Mailly, Todd. "Stress Fractures." *Clinics in Sports Medicine,* January 1990, pp. 183–214.

Hill, James A. "Epidemiologic Perspective on Shoulder Injuries." *Clinics in Sports Medicine,* July 1983, pp. 241–45.

Hoffman, Martin D., and Lyman, Katherine A. "Medical Needs at High School Football Games in Milwaukee." *The Journal of Orthopaedic and Sports Physical Therapy,* November 1988, pp. 167–71.

Hofstetter, Angela; Schutz, Yves; Jequier, Eric; and Wahren, John. "Increased 24-Hour Energy Expenditure in Cigarette Smokers." *New England Journal of Medicine,* Jan. 9, 1986, pp. 79–82.

Horton, Edward S. "Role and Management of Exercise in Diabetes Mellitus." *Diabetes Care,* February 1988, pp. 201–11.

Howell, Damien. "Self-Help for the Athlete, Part 2: Treating Injuries." *American Pharmacy,* December 1986, pp. 35–44.

Hughes, Lauren Y., and Stetts, Deborah M. "A Comparison of Ankle Taping and a Semirigid Support." *The Physician and Sportsmedicine*, April 1983, pp. 99–103.

Hunter, Letha Y. "Braces and Taping." *Clinics in Sports Medicine*, July 1985, pp. 439–54.

———. "Women's Athletics: The Orthopedic Surgeon's Viewpoint." *Clinics in Sports Medicine*, October 1984, pp. 809–27.

Hunter, Stephen C., and Poole, Robert M. "The Chronically Inflamed Tendon." *Clinics in Sports Medicine*, April 1987, pp. 371–88.

Janda, David H.; Wojtys, Edward M.; Hankin, Fred M.; and Benedict, Milbry E. "Softball Sliding Injuries." *Journal of the American Medical Association*, March 25, 1988, pp. 1848–50.

Jobe, Frank W., and Bradley, James P. "The Diagnosis and Nonoperative Treatment of Shoulder Injuries in Athletes." *Clinics in Sports Medicine*, July 1989, pp. 419–38.

Jobe, Frank W., and Nuber, Gordon. "Throwing Injuries of the Elbow." *Clinics in Sports Medicine*, October 1986, pp. 621–36.

Jones, Donald C., and James, Stan L. "Overuse Injuries of the Lower Extremity." *Clinics in Sports Medicine*, April 1987, pp. 273–89.

Kandel, Denise B., and Logan, John A. "Patterns of Drug Use from Adolescence to Young Adulthood: I. Periods of Risk for Initiation, Continued Use, and Discontinuation." *American Journal of Public Health*, July 1984, pp. 660–66.

Kane, Mary Jo. "The Female Athletic Role as a Status Determinant within the Social Systems of High School Adolescents." *Adolescence*, Summer 1988, pp. 253–64.

Kaufman, David W.; Helmrich, Susan P.; Rosenberg, Lynn; Miettinen, Olli S.; and Shapiro, Sam. "Nicotine and Carbon Monoxide Content of Cigarette Smoke and the Risk of Myocardial Infarction in Young Men." *New England Journal of Medicine*, Feb. 24, 1983, pp. 409–13.

Kay, David B. "The Sprained Ankle: Current Therapy." *Foot & Ankle*, 1985: 6, no. 1, pp. 22–28.

Kibler, W. Ben; McQueen, Craig; and Uhl, Tim. "Fitness Evaluations and Fitness Findings in Competitive Junior Tennis Players." *Clinics in Sports Medicine*, pp. 403–16.

Kirkendall, Donald T. "The Applied Sport Science of Soccer." *The Physician and Sportsmedicine*, April 1985, pp. 53–59.

———. "Physiologic Aspects of Gymnastics." *Clinics in Sports Medicine*, January 1985, pp. 17–22.

Knortz, Karen A., and Reinhart, Randy S. "Women's Athletics: The Athletic Trainer's Viewpoint." *Clinics in Sports Medicine*, October 1984, pp. 851–68.

Kraus, Hans. "Unfit Kids: A Call to Action." *Contemporary Pediatrics*, April 1988, pp. 18–30.

Kulund, Daniel N., and Tottossy, Miklos. "Warm-Up, Strength, and Power." *Orthopedic Clinics of North America*, April 1983, pp. 427–48.

Leach, Robert E., and Miller, Jeffrey K. "Lateral and Medial Epicondylitis of the Elbow." *Clinics in Sports Medicine*, pp. 259–72.

Leach, Robert E.; Seavey, Mitchell S.; and Salter, Daniel K. "Results of Surgery in Athletes with Plantar Fasciitis." *Foot & Ankle*, December 1986, pp. 156–61.

Lehman, Richard C. "Shoulder Pain in the Competitive Tennis Player." *Clinics in Sports Medicine*, April 1988, pp. 309–27.

———. "Surface and Equipment Variables in Tennis Injuries." *Clinics in Sports Medicine*, April 1988, pp. 229–32.

Linder, Charles W.; DuRant, Robert H.; Seklecki, Roger M.; and Strong, William B. "Preparticipation Health Screening of Young Athletes: Results of 1268 Examinations." *The American Journal of Sports Medicine*, 1981: 9, no. 3, pp. 187–93.

Lloyd, Tom; Myers, Cathleen; Buchanan, James R.; and Demers, Laurence M. "Collegiate Women Athletes with Irregular Menses during Adolescence Have Decreased Bone Density." *Obstetrics & Gynecology*, October 1988, pp. 639–42.

Loosli, Alvin R.; Benson, Joan; Gillien, Donna M.; and Bourdet, Kathy. "Nutrition Habits and Knowledge in Competitive Adolescent Female Gymnasts." *The Physician and Sportsmedicine*, August 1986, pp. 118–29.

Lounsbury, Benjamin F. "Swimming Unprotected with Long-Shafted Middle Ear Ventilation Tubes." *Laryngoscope*, March 1985, pp. 340–43.

Lutter, Judy Mahle. "Health Concerns of Women Runners." *Clinics in Sports Medicine*, October 1985, pp. 671–84.

Lutter, Lowell D. "The Knee and Running." *Clinics in Sports Medicine*, October 1985, pp. 685–98.

Macdonald, Donald Ian. "How You Can Help Prevent Teenage Alcoholism." *Contemporary Pediatrics*, November 1986, pp. 50–72.

MacMahon, James R., and Gross, Ruth T. "Physical and Psychological Effects of Aerobic Exercise in Delinquent Adolescent Males." *American Journal of Diseases in Children*, December 1988, pp. 1361–66.

Maehlum, Sverre; Dahl, Erik; and Daljord, Odd A. "Frequency of Injuries in a Youth Soccer Tournament." *The Physician and Sportsmedicine*, July 1986, pp. 73–80.

Marcy, S. Michael. "Swimmer's Ear." *Contemporary Pediatrics*, May 1989, pp. 90–91.

———. "Swimmer's Ear: Keep It Clean." *Contemporary Pediatrics*, May 1986, pp. 20–28.

Marrero, David C.; Fremion, Amy S.; and Golden, Michael P. "Improving Compliance with Exercise in Adolescents with Insulin-Dependent Diabetes Mellitus: Results of a Self-Motivated Home Exercise Program." *Pediatrics*, April 1988, pp. 519–25.

Maylack, Fallon H. "Epidemiology of Tennis, Squash, and Racquetball Injuries." *Clinics in Sports Medicine*, April 1988, pp. 233–43.

McBryde, Angus M., Jr. "Stress Fractures in Runners." *Clinics in Sports Medicine*, October 1985, pp. 737–52.

McFadden E. R. "Exercise-induced Asthma: Recent Approaches." *Chest*, June 1988, pp. 1282–83.

McKeag, Douglas B. "Adolescents and Exercise." *Journal of Adolescent Health Care*, November 1986 supplement, pp. 121S–29S.

Micheli, Lyle J. "Back Injuries in Gymnastics." *Clinics in Sports Medicine*, January 1985, pp. 85–93.

————. "Overuse Injuries in Children's Sports: The Growth Factor." *Orthopedic Clinics of North America*, April 1983, pp. 337–60.

————. "The Traction Apophysitises." *Clinics in Sports Medicine*, April 1987, pp. 389–404.

Mofenson, Howard C.; Copeland, Patricia; and Carraccio, Thomas R. "Cocaine and Crack: The Latest Menace." *Contemporary Pediatrics*, October 1986, pp. 44–50.

Moore, Mike. "You Can't Play Yourself into Shape for Baseball These Days." *The Physician and Sportsmedicine*, April 1983, pp. 167–74.

Morgan, Randall C., and Crawford, Alvin H. "Surgical Management of Tarsal Coalition in Adolescent Athletes." *Foot & Ankle*, 1986: 7, no. 3, pp. 183–93.

Moynes, Diane Radovich. "Prevention of Injury to the Shoulder through Exercises and Therapy." *Clinics in Sports Medicine*, July 183, pp. 413–22.

Mueller, Frederick, and Blyth, Carl. "Epidemiology of Sports Injuries in Children." *Clinics in Sports Medicine*, November 1982, pp. 343–52.

Murphy, Robert J. "Heat Problems in the Tennis Player." *Clinics in Sports Medicine*, April 1988, pp. 429–34.

"National Children and Youth Fitness Study: Its Contribution to Our National Objectives." *Public Health Reports*, January–February 1985, pp. 1–3.

National Athletic Trainers' Association. Press release, June 12, 1989.

Nicholas, James A.; Rosenthal, Philip P.; and Gleim, Gilbert W. "A Historical Perspective of Injuries in Professional Football." *Journal of the American Medical Association*, Aug. 19, 1988, pp. 939–44.

Nickerson, Bruce G.; Bautista, Daisy B.; Namey, Maria A.; Richards, Warren; and Keens, Thomas G. "Distance Running Improves Fitness in Asthmatic Children without Pulmonary Complications or Changes in Exercise-Induced Bronchospasm." *Pediatrics*, February 1983, pp. 147–152.

Nielsen, Allan Buhl, and Yde, Johannes. "Epidemiology and Traumatology of Injuries in Soccer." *The American Journal of Sports Medicine*, 1989: 17, no. 6, pp. 803–7.

Nirschl, Robert P. "Soft-Tissue Injuries about the Elbow." *Clinics in Sports Medicine*, October 1986, pp. 637–52.

O'Donnell, Thomas F., Jr. "Management of Heat Stress Injuries in the Athlete." *Orthopedic Clinics of North America*, October 1980, pp. 841–55.

O'Neill, Daniel B., and Micheli, Lyle J. "Overuse Injuries in the Young Athlete." *Clinics in Sports Medicine*, July 1988, pp. 591–610.

Orenstein, David M. "Exercise Tolerance and Exercise Conditioning in Children with Chronic Lung Disease." *The Journal of Pediatrics*, June 1988, pp. 1043–47.

Orenstein, David M.; Reed, Marion E.; Grogan, Fred T.; and Crawford, Lloyd V. "Exercise Conditioning in Children with Asthma." *The Journal of Pediatrics*, April 1985, pp. 556–60.

Osterman, A. Lee; Moskow, Lonnie; and Low, David W. "Soft-Tissue Injuries of the Hand and Wrist in Racquet Sports." *Clinics in Sports Medicine*, April 1988, pp. 329–48.

"Participation/Injury Overview in High School Football 1986–1988." Fact sheet, National Athletic Trainers' Association.

Peltier, Leonard F. "The Lineage of Sports Medicine." *Clinical Orthopaedics and Related Research,* March 1987, pp. 4–12.

Pentel, Paul. "Toxicity of Over-the-Counter Stimulants." *Journal of the American Medical Association,* Oct. 12, 1984, pp. 1898–1903.

Pfeiffer, Ronald D., and Francis, Rulon S. "Effects of Strength Training on Muscle Development in Prepubescent, Pubescent, and Postpubescent Males." *The Physician and Sportsmedicine,* September 1986, pp. 134–43.

Pillemer, Francine G., and Micheli, Lyle J. "Psychological Considerations in Youth Sports." *Clinics in Sports Medicine,* July 1988, pp. 679–89.

Podoe, Dan Tunstall. "Prevention of Injury in Joggers and Runners." *The Practitioner,* Oct. 8, 1988, pp. 1109–12.

"Policy Statement: Anabolic Steroids and the Adolescent Athlete." *AAP News,* August 1988, p. 7.

Pope, Harrison G., Jr., and Katz, David L. "Affective and Psychotic Symptoms Associated with Anabolic Steroid Use." *American Journal of Psychiatry,* April 1988, pp. 487–90.

Porcello, Lorri A. "A Practical Guide to Fad Diets." *Clinics in Sports Medicine,* July 1984, pp. 723–29.

Priest, James D. "Elbow Injuries in Gymnastics." *Clinics in Sports Medicine,* January 1985, pp. 73–83.

Pritchett, James W. "A Claims-Made Study of Knee Injuries Due to Football in High School Athletes." *Journal of Pediatric Orthopaedics,* 1988: 8, no. 5, pp. 551–53.

Puffer, James C. "The Use of Drugs in Swimming." *Clinics in Sports Medicine,* January 1986, pp. 77–89.

Reppucci, N. Dickon. "Prevention and Ecology: Teen-Age Pregnancy, Child Sexual Abuse, and Organized Youth Sports." *American Journal of Community Psychology,* 1987: 15, no. 1, pp. 12–22.

Rians, Clark B.; Weltman, Arthur; Cahill, Bernard R.; Janney, Carol A.; Tippett, Steven R.; and Katch, Frank I. "Strength Training for Prepubescent Males: Is It Safe?" *The American Journal of Sports Medicine,* 1987: 15, no. 5, pp. 483–89.

Richardson, Allen B. "Overuse Syndromes in Baseball, Tennis, Gymnastics, and Swimming." *Clinics in Sports Medicine,* July 1983, pp. 379–90.

Richie, Douglas H. "Aerobic Dance Injuries: A Retrospective Study of Instructors and Participants." *The Physician and Sportsmedicine,* February 1985, pp. 130–38.

Robins, Lee N. "The Natural History of Adolescent Drug Use." *American Journal of Public Health,* July 1984, pp. 656–57.

Rooks, Daniel S., and Micheli, Lyle J. "Musculoskeletal Assessment and Training: The Young Athlete." *Clinics in Sports Medicine,* July 1988, pp. 641–77.

Rosenstein, Beryl J. "The Twin Perils of Heat Exhaustion and Heatstroke." *Contemporary Pediatrics.* May 1986, pp. 46–52.

Rovere, George D., and Nichols, Andrew W. "Frequency, Associated Factors, and Treatment of Breaststroker's Knee in Competitive Swimmers." *The American Journal of Sports Medicine,* 1985: 13, no. 2, pp. 99–104.

Rowland, Thomas W.; Swadba, Laurie A.; Biggs, Darlene E.; Burke, Edmund J.; and Reiter, Edward O. "Glycemic Control with Physical Training in Insulin-Dependent Diabetes Mellitus." *American Journal of Diseases in Children*, March 1985, pp. 307–10.

Rubinstein, Israel; Levison, Henry; Slutsky, Arthur S.; Hak, Hank; Wells, Janet; Zamel, Noe; and Rebuck, Anthony S. "Immediate and Delayed Bronchoconstriction after Exercise in Patients with Asthma." *New England Journal of Medicine*, Aug. 20, 1987, pp. 482–85.

Ruderman, Neil B., and Schneider, Stephen. "Exercise and the Insulin-Dependent Diabetic." *Hospital Practice*, May 30, 1986, pp. 41–51.

Ryan, John B.; Hopkinson, William J.; Wheeler, James H.; Arciero, Robert A.; and Swain, James H. "Office Management of the Acute Ankle Sprain." *Clinics in Sports Medicine*, July 1989, pp. 477–95.

Sady, Stanley P., and Freedson, Patty S. "Body Composition and Structural Comparisons of Female and Male Athletes." *Clinics in Sports Medicine*, October 1984, pp. 755–77.

Salem, Deeb N., and Isner, Jeffrey M. "Cardiac Screening for Athletes." *Orthopedic Clinics of North America*, October 1980, pp. 687–95.

Sammarco, G. James. "Diagnosis and Treatment in Dancers." *Clinical Orthopaedics and Related Research*, July/August 1984, pp. 176–87.

Sarnaik, Ashok P.; Vohra, Meena P.; Sturman, Stephen W.; and Belenky, Walter M. "Medical Problems of the Swimmer." *Clinics in Sports Medicine*, January 1986, pp. 47–64.

Schmidt, David R., and Henry, Jack H. "Stress Injuries of the Adolescent Extensor Mechanism." *Clinics in Sports Medicine*, April 1989, pp. 343–55.

Shangold, Mona M. "Athletic Amenorrhea." *Clinical Obstetrics and Gynecology*, September 1985, pp. 664–69.

———. "Gynecologic Concerns in the Woman Athlete." *Clinics in Sports Medicine*, October 1984, pp. 869–79.

Sharratt, Michael T. "Wrestling Profile." *Clinics in Sports Medicine*, January 1984, pp. 273–88.

Shields, Clarence L., Jr.; Beckwith, Vickie Zomar; and Kurland, Harvey L. "Comparison of Leg Strength Training Equipment." *The Physician and Sportsmedicine*, Feburary 1985, pp. 49–56.

Simon, Ellen R., and Hill, James A. "Rotator Cuff Injuries: An Update." *Journal of Orthopaedic and Sports Physical Therapy*, April 1989, pp. 394–98.

Smith, Nathan J. "Nutrition and the Athlete." *Orthopedic Clinics of North America*, April 1983, pp. 387–96.

———. "The Prevention of Heat Disorders in Sports." *American Journal of Diseases in Children*, August 1984, pp. 786–90.

———. "Weight Control in the Athlete." *Clinics in Sports Medicine*, July 1984, pp. 693–704.

Snook, George A. "A Review of Women's Collegiate Gymnastics." *Clinics in Sports Medicine*, January 1985, pp. 31–37.

Snyder, Robert B.; Lipscomb, A. Brant; and Johnston, Robert K. "The Relationship of Tarsal Coalitions to Ankle Sprains in Athletes." *The American Journal of Sports Medicine*, 1981: 9, no. 5, pp. 313–17.

Solomon, Ruth L., and Micheli, Lyle J. "Technique as a Consideration in Modern Dance Injuries." *The Physician and Sportsmedicine*, August 1986, pp. 83–89.

Squire, Deborah L. "Heat Illness." *The Pediatric Clinics of North America*, October 1990, pp. 1085–1109.

Stackpole, J. Ward. "The Team Physician." *Pediatric Annals*, August 1984, pp. 592–94.

Stanish, William. "Low Back Pain in Athletes: An Overuse Syndrome." *Clinics in Sports Medicine*, April 1987, pp. 321–44.

Stanish, William D.; Curwin, Sandra; and Rubinovich, Mitchell. "Tendinitis: The Analysis and Treatment for Running." *Clinics in Sports Medicine*, October 1985, pp. 593–609.

Stanitski, Carl L. "Environmental Problems of Runners." *Clinics in Sports Medicine*, October 1985, pp. 725–35.

Stark, Jack A., and Toulouse, Alan. "The Young Female Athlete: Psychological Considerations." *Clinics in Sports Medicine*, October 1984, pp. 909–21.

Steen, Suzanne Nelson, and McKinney, Shortie. "Nutrition Assessment of College Wrestlers." *The Physician and Sportsmedicine*, November 1986, pp. 100–16.

Steinbaugh, Maria. "Nutritional Needs for Female Athletes." *Clinics in Sports Medicine*, July 1984, pp. 649–70.

Stephenson, Sally H.; Jolly, John; and Harden, Patricia M. "Sports Psychology: How Can It Help the Adolescent Athlete?" *Seminars in Adolescent Medicine*, September 1987, pp. 205–13.

Stormont, Daniel M., and Peterson, Hamlet A. "The Relative Incidence of Tarsal Coalition." *Clinical Orthopaedics and Related Research*, December 1983, pp. 28–35.

Strauss, Richard H. "Anabolic Steroids." *Clinics in Sports Medicine*, July 1984, pp. 743–48.

Strauss, Richard H.; Lanese, Richard R.; and Leizman, Daniel J. "Illness and Absence among Wrestlers, Swimmers, and Gymnasts at a Large University." *The American Journal of Sports Medicine*, 1988: 16, no. 6, pp. 653–55.

Strong, William B., and Wilmore, Jack H. "Unfit Kids: An Office-Based Approach to Physical Fitness." *Contemporary Pediatrics*, April 1988, pp. 33–48.

Sullivan, Dennis; Warren, Russell F.; Pavlov, Helene; and Kelman, Gary. "Stress Fractures in 51 Runners." *Clinical Orthopaedics and Related Research*, July/August 1984, pp. 188–92.

"Summary of Findings from National Children and Youth Fitness Study II." *Journal of Physical Education, Recreation, and Dance*, November–December 1987, pp. 50–96.

Tally, Jean. "Reward for Increasing Football Helmet Safety? Legal Hassles." *The Physician and Sportsmedicine*, February 1985, pp. 161–68.

Tarnopolsky, Mark A.; MacDougall, J. Duncan; and Atkinson, Stephanie A. "Influences of Protein Intake and Training Status on Nitrogen Balance and Lean Body Mass." *Journal of Applied Physiology*, January 1988, pp. 187–93.

Teeter, Ruskin, "Scientific Origins of Adolescent Sport." *Adolescence*, Summer 1987, pp. 253–57.

Teitz, Carol C.; Hermanson, Bonnie K.; Kronmal, Richard A.; and Diehr, Paula H. "Evaluation of the Use of Braces to Prevent Injury to the Knee in Collegiate Football Players." *The Journal of Bone and Joint Surgery,* January 1987, pp. 2–9.

Tibone, James E. "Shoulder Problems in Adolescents." *Clinics in Sports Medicine,* July 1983, pp. 423–27.

Torg, Joseph S.; Pavlov, Helene; and Torg, Elisabeth. "Overuse Injuries in Sport: The Foot." *Clinics in Sports Medicine,* April 1987, pp. 291–311.

Turco, Vincent J. "Injuries to the Ankle and Foot in Athletics." *Orthopedic Clinics of North America,* July 1977, pp. 669–82.

Tysvaer, Alf T., and Storli, Odd-Vebjørn. "Soccer Injuries to the Brain." *The American Journal of Sports Medicine,* 1989: 17, no. 4, pp. 573–78.

"Use of Crack and Other Illicit Drugs Has Declined Significantly Among Young Americans." Press release, University of Michigan News and Information Services, Jan. 23, 1991.

Vizsolyi, Peter; Taunton, Jack; Robertson, Gordon; Filsinger, Lynda; Shannon, Harry S.; Whittingham, Diane; and Gleave, Martin. "Breaststroker's Knee: An Analysis of Epidemiological and Biomechanical Factors." *The American Journal of Sports Medicine,* 1987: 15, no. 1, pp. 63–71.

Wagner, Jon C. "Substance-Abuse Policies and Guidelines in Amateur and Professional Athletics." *American Journal of Hospital Pharmacy,* February 1987, pp. 305–10.

Waitley, Denis E.; May, Jerry R.; and Martens, Rainer. "Sports Psychology and the Elite Athlete." *Clinics in Sports Medicine,* March 1983, pp. 87–99.

Webb, David R. "Strength Training in Children and Adolescents." *The Pediatric Clinics of North America,* October 1990, pp. 1187–1210.

Webber, Anthony. "Acute Soft-Tissue Injuries in the Young Athlete." *Clinics in Sports Medicine,* July 1988, pp. 611–24.

Weight, Lindsay M.; Myburgh, Kathryn H.; and Noakes, Timothy D. "Vitamin and Mineral Supplementation: Effect on the Running Performance of Trained Athletes." *American Journal of Clinical Nutrition,* 1988: 47, pp. 192–95.

Weight, Lindsay M.; Noakes, Timothy D.; Labadarios, Dimitri; Graves, John; Jacobs, Peter; and Berman, Peter A. "Vitamin and Mineral Status of Trained Athletes Including the Effects of Supplementation." *American Journal of Clinical Nutrition,* 1988: 47, pp. 186–91.

"Weight Training and Weight Lifting: Information for the Pediatrician." American Academy of Pediatrics policy statement, July 1982.

Weiker, Garron G. "Evaluation and Treatment of Common Spine and Trunk Problems." *Clinics in Sports Medicine,* July 1989, pp. 399–417.

———. "Injuries in Club Gymnastics." *The Physician and Sportsmedicine,* April 1985, pp. 63–66.

———. "Introduction and History of Gymnastics." *Clinics in Sports Medicine,* January 1985, pp. 3–5.

Weinberg, Sarah K. "Medical Aspects of Synchronized Swimming." *Clinics in Sports Medicine,* January 1986, pp. 159–67.

Williams, Melvin H. "Vitamin and Mineral Supplements to Athletes: Do They Help?" *Clinics in Sports Medicine,* July 1984, pp. 623–37.

Wilson, Holly. "Coping with Shin Splints." *The Physician and Sportsmedicine*, November 1973, pp. 68–69.

Wilson, Jean D. "Androgen Abuse by Athletes." *Endocrine Reviews*, 1988: 9, no. 2, pp. 181–99.

Winter, F. David; Snell, Peter G.; and Stray-Gundersen, James. "Effects of 100% Oxygen on Performance of Professional Soccer Players." *Journal of the American Medical Association*, July 14, 1989, pp. 227–29.

Wood, Elizabeth R; Wilson, Claire D.; and Masland, Robert P., Jr. "Weight Control Methods in High School Wrestlers." *Journal of Adolescent Health Care*, September 1988, pp. 394–97.

Yarnell, Philip R., and Lynch, Steve. "The 'Ding': Amnestic States in Football Trauma." *Neurology*, February 1973, pp. 196–97.

Yocum, Lewis A. "The Diagnosis and Nonoperative Treatment of Elbow Problems in the Athlete." *Clinics in Sports Medicine*, July 1989, pp. 439–51.

Young, Patrick. "Exercise Can Be Safe for Many Asthma Victims." *Staten Island (N.Y.) Advance*, Oct. 10, 1987, p. B1.

Zach M.; Oberwaldner, B.; and Hausler, F. "Cystic Fibrosis: Physical Exercise versus Chest Physiotherapy." *Archives of Disease in Children*, 1982: 57, pp. 587–89.

Zach, Maximillian S.; Purrer, Barbara; and Oberwaldner, Beatrice. "Effects of Swimming on Forced Expiration and Sputum Clearance in Cystic Fibrosis." *The Lancet*, Nov. 28, 1981, pp. 1201–3.

·INDEX·

(Page numbers in *italics* refer to illustrations.)

·ABOUT THE AUTHORS·

Alan R. Figelman, M.D., is a board-certified pediatrician with a specialty in adolescent medicine and a specific interest in child and adolescent sports medicine. He has 18 years' experience treating children and adolescents and currently serves as director of pediatrics at the Regional Institute for Children and Adolescents (RICA) in Rockville, Maryland; clinical assistant professor of pediatrics at Georgetown University School of Medicine; and as a pediatrician in private practice. He formerly served as chief of the ambulatory pediatrics service and chief of adolescent medicine at Walter Reed Army Medical Center in Washington, D.C.

As head of ambulatory pediatrics at Walter Reed, Dr. Figelman supervised a clinic for the dependents of Army personnel that has 60,000 contacts with children and adolescents a year. Nearly one-sixth of these are sports- or exercise-related, either for injuries or for preparticipation physical examinations, which total around 4,500 a year. In his new position at RICA, Dr. Figelman continues to treat patients daily, particularly adolescents. His training of medical students at Georgetown includes specific instructions in treating sports injuries to children and adolescents.

Patrick Young is editor of *Science News*, a 227,000-circulation weekly newsmagazine covering the biological, physical, behavioral, and space sciences. He formerly served as chief science and medical correspondent for the Newhouse News Service in Washington, D.C., where he also authored a weekly personal health column, "Better Health."

Mr. Young's previous books include *Asthma and Allergies: An Optimistic Future*, published by the National Institutes of Health in 1980; and four books for young adults: *Schizophrenia* (1988), *Mental Disturbances* (1988), and *Drugs and Pregnancy* (1987) for Chelsea House; and *Drifting Continents, Shifting Seas: An Introduction to Plate Tectonics* (1976) for Franklin Watts. His magazine articles have appeared in *Smithsonian, Family Circle, Good Housekeeping, Reader's Digest, Psychology Today, Harper's, Vogue, Parade, Better Homes and Gardens, Science Digest*, and *Mosaic*.

Among Mr. Young's nearly two dozen national writing awards are the William Harvey Award for Journalistic Achievement in Writing on Hypertension, the Howard W. Blakeslee Award from the American Heart Association, the Russell L. Cecil Writing Award of the Arthritis Foundation, the American Chemical Society's James T. Grady Award for Interpreting Chemistry to the Public, and the American Institute of Physics Science Writing Award in Physics and Astronomy.